AF378195

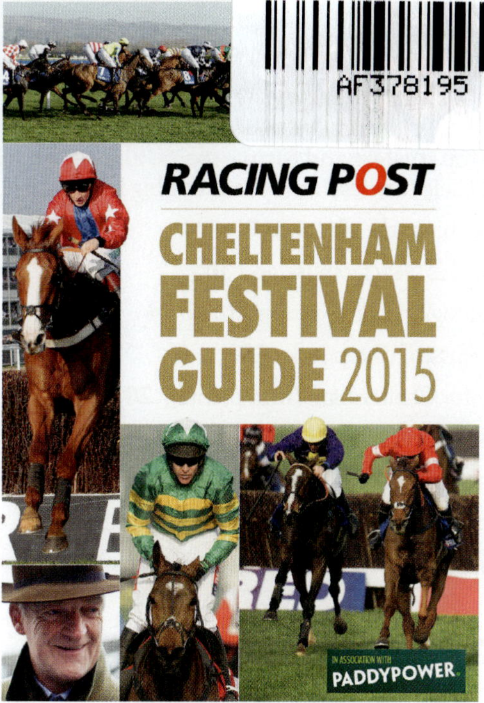

RACING POST

CHELTENHAM FESTIVAL GUIDE 2015

Edited by Nick Pulford

Foreword by Edward Whitaker

Contributors

Richard Birch
Marcus Buckland
Dave Edwards
Ronan Groome
David Jennings
Paul Kealy
Andrew King
Richard Lowther
Rodney Masters
Kevin Morley
Tony O'Hehir

Dave Orton
Tom Pennington
Sam Price
Dave Randall
Graeme Rodway
Colin Russell
Craig Thake
Sam Walker
Johnny Ward
Nick Watts

Designed by David Dew
Cover artwork by Jay Vincent
Inside artwork by David Cramphorn, Nigel Jones and Stefan Searle

Published in 2015 by Racing Post Books, Raceform Ltd, 27 Kingfisher Court, Hambridge Road, Newbury, RG14 5SJ
Copyright © Racing Post 2015

All rights reserved. No part of this publication may be reproduced, stored in a retrieval system, or transmitted in any form or by any means, electronic, mechanical, photocopying, recording, or otherwise, without the prior written permission of the publishers. A catalogue record for this book is available from the British Library.

ISBN 978-1-909471-84-9

Printed by Polestar Stones

Racing Post iPad app

The journey to Cheltenham goes fast so don't hang about. Start your 30-day free trial now and receive the next 30 newspapers delivered straight to your iPad.

'Cheltenham gives you everything'

THE first festival I covered for the Racing Post was in 1988, when I was 22, and I've done every one since. I was even there to take pictures of the empty racecourse when the festival was cancelled in 2001 because of foot and mouth. I've been lucky enough to photograph many great horses – Desert Orchid, Istabraq, Best Mate, Kauto Star, Denman, Sprinter Sacre – and the festival is always one of the highlights of my year.

In the early days I was shooting black and white film but now it's all digital and I send pictures after every race – everyone wants instant images. It's physically demanding going from the course to the winner's enclosure to the press room, the gear weighs about 15kg and you're covering a lot of ground, and I'm always shattered by the end of the week.

I'll start work two days before the festival when I'm down on the gallops on the Sunday and the Monday. With the sun coming up, you can get the most amazing pictures. I really enjoy the Sunday because it's the start of the week and you can get up close and personal with some of the great Irish horses, like Hurricane Fly.

On racedays I arrive about 9.30am to get everything set up. I send test pictures to make sure everything is working and then I go out with a couple of cameras to take pictures of people coming through the gates, the steam train arriving at the racecourse station, bookies setting up their pitches, the Guinness village. There's always a great buzz of anticipation.

For the races I'll be on the winning line or at the last fence or flight of hurdles. You have to anticipate what might happen, where the story is. It's not always just about the winner, like when Big Buck's was beaten in last year's World Hurdle. I have to take an opinion on where to be and what to focus on.

I try to create a portfolio of pictures, with different angles and different emotions. When a jockey wins you can see in their eyes what it means to win a race at the festival and you want to capture that.

It's a great challenge and I love the whole week. What's great about Cheltenham is that it gives you everything and it's very accessible. Everything comes together perfectly.

Edward Whitaker
Racing Photographer of the Year

Views from the specialists

The Racing Post's team of experts reveal their festival fancies and the major bookmakers discuss the big issues in our Q & A

Head for Windsor Park

Richard Birch makes Dermot Weld's classy novice hurdler his best bet of the week

After Windsor Park had won with contemptuous ease on the Flat at Galway last October, his rider Robbie McNamara said: "Forgotten Rules [113-rated on the Flat] might be the [Ascot] Gold Cup horse for next year, but if I was for guessing I would say Windsor Park's a similar type of horse. He'll stay galloping all day and he's classy."

I remember ringing that quote in red ink in the following day's Racing Post and I have followed Windsor Park's career closely ever since with a wager in the Neptune Investment Management Novices' Hurdle at the forefront of my mind.

Windsor Park was equally impressive when he made his hurdling debut at Christmas, slamming the confidently ridden Royal Caviar by two and a half lengths in a Leopardstown maiden hurdle, and he will have learned plenty from his two subsequent starts in Graded company.

Dermot Weld's six-year-old remains unexposed at staying trips over hurdles and the step up to 2m5f at Cheltenham on the likely good ground that suits him so well seems sure to conjure a career-best performance. He boasts unlimited potential and, at around 12-1, rates my best bet of the four days.

Apache Stronghold, another highly progressive Irish raider, holds standout claims in the JLT Novices' Chase for Noel Meade. Although put firmly in his place by Don Poli in the Grade 1 Topaz Novice Chase at Leopardstown over Christmas, there was no disgrace in going down by three lengths to what is potentially the next Willie Mullins superstar.

The likeable seven-year-old travelled strongly before being outstayed by Don Poli towards the finish of that 3m contest on testing ground and he looked much better suited by a shorter trip – at this stage of his career at least – when he took the Grade 1 Flogas Novice Chase (better known as the Dr PJ Moriarty) over 2m5f at Leopardstown in February.

Apache Stronghold appears tailor-made for the JLT, especially with the prospect of less stamina-sapping ground at Cheltenham, and makes plenty of punting appeal at around 7-1.

One of the races I am most looking forward to at the festival is the RSA Chase, even though the only winner of it I can ever recall backing is the mighty Denman, who stormed up the hill in 2007 to send favourite backers into orbit.

I have loved Kings Palace since the day he made his debut in a Plumpton bumper under AP McCoy in December 2012 and sauntered 18 lengths clear up the home straight to win in a canter. Was he really available at 5-2 that afternoon? My betting records confirm he most certainly was.

The son of King's Theatre has taken particularly well to fences and already boasts two wins over them at Cheltenham, but he has yet to be taken on for the lead since switching from hurdles and it is unrealistic to expect him to enjoy an easy time of it in an RSA.

Southfield Theatre impressed at Exeter, is held in high regard by both Paul Nicholls and Sam Twiston-Davies, and holds strong each-way

Tipster forum

Will Silviniaco Conti finally win the Gold Cup?

Graeme Rodway He recorded a career-best performance when landing the King George and is the best three-miler around, but I couldn't back him for a Gold Cup until he has proved he can win at the track.

Richard Birch He clearly has the best form but would have won the race by now if he was destined to. In a far from vintage Gold Cup it wouldn't take much improvement from Holywell or Many Clouds to beat him. I favour Holywell, who comes alive at the festival.

Nick Watts He's the one who has really put his hand up this season and, with the cheekpieces to help, there's no reason why he can't win. Holywell is the biggest danger as he loves the spring, loves Cheltenham and the blinkers will be on.

Johnny Ward He looks really solid and quite hard to oppose. He basically seems a better horse this season and the rest are much of a muchness.

David Jennings He's a worthy favourite and there isn't enough evidence to say definitively he doesn't like Cheltenham. But there are plenty of bigger-priced alternatives – the most appealing is Boston Bob.

Paul Kealy Having backed him for the last couple of years I hope so. If you look at the form of this season's King George, which he won easily, he has far more in hand over his rivals than some much shorter-priced horses in other races. The question mark is Cheltenham and last year's wayward performance after the last, but he had genuine excuses for that.

MEMBERS' CLUB

Your Cheltenham Services

We've got the best tipping, analysis, statistics, ratings and special offers around – ensuring you arrive at Cheltenham ready.

Join the best service around from just 40p a day.

racingpost.com/membersclub

Don Poli can repel all-comers in a strong renewal of the RSA

claims of outrunning odds of 12-1, but both are likely to be playing for place money at best if **Don Poli**, who can be backed at 4-1, is the horse I think he is.

The Mullins team for Cheltenham is simply awesome and Don Poli rates as one of his best chances of the week. Unbeaten in two starts over fences, he already boasts festival-winning form, having landed the Martin Pipe Conditional Jockeys' Handicap Hurdle last March, and appears to have improved enormously since.

Having trumpeted **The New One** for the Stan James Champion Hurdle in the past two years, it would be foolish to desert him now even though hot favourite Faugheen looks a machine.

I am sure The New One, who should enjoy his ideal ground conditions on the big day, will be available to back at around 7-2 on the morning of the race when all the firms are at their most competitive, so the intention is to back him each-way.

On overall form Silviniaco Conti should land the Betfred Cheltenham Gold Cup, but his lack of success at the course is a huge concern and I have the feeling he is destined not to win it.

The one I like is the Jonjo O'Neill-trained **Holywell**, who has enjoyed success at the last two festivals (over hurdles and fences) and was awesome in the Mildmay Novices' Chase at Aintree last April, powering ten lengths clear of Don Cossack and looking every inch a potential Gold Cup winner. Don't forget he was ante-post favourite for the Gold Cup at the beginning of the season before a couple of defeats saw his odds lengthen to 14-1.

Nobody is more adept at getting his big guns to fire at the festival than O'Neill and Holywell will arrive fresh after a light campaign. While February's Kelso win didn't really prove anything in terms of form, it looked the perfect prep for the big day, when his high cruising speed and acceleration from the final fence will be hard to resist.

FOLLOW
CHELTENHAM

FOR ALL THE UPDATES, PRICES & RESULTS
DIRECT TO YOUR PHONE

SELECT 'CHELTENHAM' IN THE FAVOURITES SCREEN...

...GET THE NEWS YOU WANT, ON THE GO!

DOWNLOAD THE APP NOW
SEARCH PP MESSENGER IN THE APP STORE

NEW PADDY POWER CUSTOMERS ONLY

BET £10, GET A FREE £20 BET
WHEN YOU REGISTER ON THE APP NOW!

PADDYPOWER.

CALL 0800 904 7933

WHEN THE  STOPS STOP

gambleaware.co.uk 18+

Free bet available to new Paddy Power customers only. One free bet per customer & max £20. Prices displayed are for demonstration purposes only. T&C's apply.

Tipster forum

Is Faugheen the one in the Champion Hurdle?

David Jennings He most certainly is. You can point to the fact that he hasn't had a bout with a heavyweight fighter like Hurricane Fly or Jezki but he looks the most exciting hurdler we've seen for some time and he jumps better at speed.

Graeme Rodway He hasn't beaten a top-class two-miler yet but is eight from eight without being stretched and looks something special. It's between him and The New One and I've been disappointed with The New One.

Johnny Ward It's still hard to say how good Faugheen is and his price seems cramped enough but he'll probably take the beating and is admirably uncomplicated.

Paul Kealy Part of me thinks he could be a superstar, but the cynic has to question what he has really done. None of the horses he has beaten would be less than 50-1 for the Champion Hurdle. I'll probably back The New One, who was unlucky in last year's race, but not with any real confidence.

Richard Birch Faugheen looks sensational but needs to take his game to another level against The New One, Jezki and Hurricane Fly. I cannot see The New One finishing out of the first three, so back him each-way at around 7-2 on the day.

Nick Watts It's The New One for me. He should have won last year and, while he wasn't impressive at Haydock last time, he was when winning the International before that. No horse in training gets up the hill as well as he does.

Nephew offers relative value

David Jennings looks to Neil Mulholland's stable for the best bet on day one

Day one is dangerous this year, treacherous in fact. If all goes to script, first up is Douvan, then Un De Sceaux, followed by Faugheen, Annie Power and perhaps Don Poli. All trained in Ireland. All trained by Willie Mullins. All unbeaten this season when they have stayed on their feet. All potential superstars. There is nothing that can make a price shorten quite like potential. Potential, it seems, is far more important than proven ability.

Amid all the hullabaloo, the best bet on day one may be **The Druids Nephew** at 12-1 in the Ultima Business Solutions Handicap Chase. Neil Mulholland may be pinning his hopes of a first festival success on The Young Master but he could get off the mark earlier than expected as this eight-year-old looks well treated on a mark of 146.

It is worth looking back at how well The Druids Nephew was travelling on the home turn in the 3m3½f handicap chase on Paddy Power day in November. He was unable to pass the dour stayer Sam Winner but was 25 lengths clear of third-placed Saint Are (a winner at Catterick recently).

Sam Winner is rated 15lb higher now and is Gold Cup-bound, whereas The Druids Nephew has gone up only 5lb. Mulholland protected his chase mark by giving him his final pre-festival run in the Cleeve Hurdle, where he was far from disgraced behind Saphir Du Rheu.

From a punting perspective, Wednesday is far more attractive. No favourite shorter than 11-4 in the ante-post betting, most of the market leaders looking vulnerable and a Champion Chase that looks ripe for an upset.

Alvisio Ville was all the rage for the Neptune Investment Management Novices' Hurdle prior to his disappointing effort in the Deloitte at Leopardstown in February, but it was the runner-up in that Grade 1 who caught the eye.

Simply Ned: value in Champion Chase

Windsor Park is not the finished article but he is getting there and to wind up so close to Nichols Canyon was a remarkable effort. The winner never missed a beat and was quick and accurate at his hurdles from the front, whereas Windsor Park looked a fish out of water for the opening mile.

He wasn't great over the second hurdle, guessed at the third and was being niggled along by Davy Russell, who looked anything but happy. Once Dermot Weld's runner realised he was in a Grade 1 run at a proper pace, however, he gradually began to work his way through the field and was doing his best work in the closing stages.

The step up to 2m5f on a quicker surface should see Windsor Park come into his own. His Deloitte experience will stand him in good stead and the hurly-burly of the Neptune will not be such a shock to the system now. His bumper form was as good as it gets and 12-1 looks too big.

If you could be sure **Don Poli** was going for the RSA rather than the National Hunt Chase, 4-1 would be a more than fair price. The Topaz Novice Chase at Christmas looked a top-notch renewal and he scored by three lengths from Apache Stronghold, with Lots Of Memories 11 lengths behind in third and some decent sorts further back. He is a natural at his fences, would love nothing better than a battle and will appreciate the better ground.

Sprinter Sacre and Sire De Grugy appear to have regressed considerably since their Champion Chase wins and **Simply Ned** is the value option against them.

Although the ground was softer than ideal and he walloped the last fence, Nicky Richards' gelding still managed to finish ahead of Dodging Bullets in the Shloer Chase. He did nothing to put me off in the Paddy Power Dial-A-Bet Chase at Leopardstown when chasing home Twinlight and Hidden Cyclone and there should be loads of improvement to come on better ground. How Hidden Cyclone can be half his price is a mystery, while Champagne Fever looks a shocking price given that he has yet to run over two miles this season.

Gordon Elliott has a live chance in the Fred Winter with Hostile Fire, but the one I like, really like, is **Mick Jazz** from the Harry Fry yard at 16-1. The ease with which he travelled to the second-last in both his races at Newbury stamps him as a better juvenile than his mark of 130 implies and he wasn't brushed aside too easily by the 144-rated Top Notch last time, albeit in receipt of 10lb. The faster pace should help him settle better and Noel Fehily will be playing his hand late.

With Un De Sceaux being aimed at the Racing Post Arkle, Vautour is likely to switch to the JLT Novices' Chase on Thursday, which looks far more competitive. He could

What do you fancy for the World Hurdle?

Richard Birch Saphir Du Rheu already boasts eyecatching form against the likes of Reve De Sivola and Whisper on testing ground and he can take another step forward on the better going Paul Nicholls is adamant he needs.

Paul Kealy The doubts about More Of That throw this wide open and it wouldn't be a major surprise if Annie Power was rerouted as she'd be a worthy favourite if she lined up. However, I think Zarkandar is a better horse than last year and is a cracking each-way bet whatever the make-up.

David Jennings Zarkandar looks to have rock-solid credentials, given that he's been trained for the race this time and Paul Nicholls and Sam Twiston-Davies would have learned a lot from his Long Walk display. He needs to be played late over three miles.

Graeme Rodway The fact we haven't seen More Of That since November is a big negative. Saphir Du Rheu comes into this in top form and is the obvious alternative.

Nick Watts I fancied Zarkandar before the news about More Of That's broken blood vessel and fancy him even more now. He looked really good in the Long Walk for 99 per cent of the race and whoever rides him will surely hold on to him for longer.

Johnny Ward I fancy Monksland to run a big race. His jumping was electric at Gowran and, while he has to prove he is the horse he was, he has plenty of class and stays well. He could be overpriced.

struggle to cope with **Apache Stronghold**, who gained revenge on Valseur Lido at Leopardstown in the Grade 1 Flogas despite a mixed round of jumping.

Apache Stronghold has bundles of ability as he almost came down at the seventh, hit the ninth and was carried widest of all coming out of the back straight. For him to knuckle down and beat the tough Valseur Lido after all that suggests he is the best horse Noel Meade has right now, even better than Road To Riches, so the 7-1 should be snapped up.

A point shorter at 6-1 is **Zarkandar** for the World Hurdle and he has been my banker of the week for some time. I managed to pinch some 14-1 a while back and couldn't be happier with my position. I would be surprised if Sam Twiston-Davies rode Saphir Du Rheu, even though the bookmakers seem to think otherwise.

Zarkandar ran in the race last year as an afterthought but still put up a decent show with an honourable fourth to a fit and healthy More Of That. This time it seems Paul Nicholls has trained him for this one day and, with a more patient ride than he was given in the Long Walk Hurdle, he looks good enough to win a substandard renewal.

Don Cossack has done little wrong this term and might well take full advantage of Dynaste's defection from the Ryanair Chase. His price looks right at around 4-1 and it is hard to see him being any shorter on the day.

One who could shorten for the Ryanair is **Ballynagour**, so now is the time to take the 33-1. He won the Byrne Group Plate in a hack canter last year off a mark of 140, once again showing he is best fresh. He has not run since he failed to see out the Hennessy trip behind Many Clouds, having been still on the bridle leaving the back straight for the final time. When he's good, he's very good and he could be worth chancing.

There seems to have been an overreaction to the tame effort by **No More Heroes** behind Outlander at Leopardstown last time, given that he was reported to have scoped dirty afterwards. He was 5-1 favourite for the Albert Bartlett before that and is 10-1 now. His defeat of Shaneshill at Navan looks a strong piece of form and he is the most likely winner if he can reproduce that.

The Gold Cup picture is either muddier than a rugby field in December or crystal clear. You either fancy Silviniaco Conti or you don't. From an Irish perspective, Road To Riches and Carlingford Lough, the last two winners of the Galway Plate, have done little wrong this season but neither has screamed that they are a Gold Cup winner.

Boston Bob *(right)* has not been fully wound up yet this season and I'm happy to take some 25-1 in the hope that he returns to the sort of form that saw him land Grade 1s at Aintree and Punchestown at the end of last season.

FOLLOW ANY
HORSE OR JOCKEY

FOR ALL THE UPDATES, PRICES & RESULTS
DIRECT TO YOUR PHONE

JUST SELECT ANY HORSE OR JOCKEY IN THE FAVOURITES SCREEN...

...GET THE NEWS YOU WANT, ON THE GO!

DOWNLOAD THE NEW APP NOW
SEARCH PP MESSENGER IN THE APP STORE

NEW PADDY POWER CUSTOMERS ONLY
BET £10, GET A FREE £20 BET
WHEN YOU REGISTER ON THE APP NOW!

PADDYPOWER.
CALL 0800 904 7933

WHEN THE **FUN** STOPS STOP

gambleaware.co.uk    18+

Free bet available to new Paddy Power customers only. One free bet per customer & max £20. Prices displayed are for demonstration purposes only. T&C's apply.

March 2014
The 2015 festival may be 12 months away but The New One is the first addition to the portfolio, the week after finishing third in the Champion Hurdle. The price of 6-1 doesn't have a huge amount of mileage in it, but it would have been shorter if he'd won at Cheltenham, as I believe he was unlucky not to do.

November
The Gold Cup picture has looked a mess ever since the end of last season's race. In an attempt to simplify matters, Holywell goes into the portfolio at 14-1. He is a dual festival winner, at his best in the spring and will have the blinkers on that seem to spark improvement every time he wears them. His reappearance at Carlisle wasn't without promise – third to Many Clouds over an inadequate trip.

22 The New One wins at Haydock in a manner that doesn't impress everyone, while Irish raider Faugheen puts away sub-standard opposition easily at Ascot. Bookies are much more impressed by him than The New One.

23 Milsean – in the portfolio for the Albert Bartlett already – wins a 2m maiden hurdle at Navan, although none too impressively.

27 Days after I put him up for the RSA Chase at 16-1, Southfield Theatre is beaten at Newbury by Carraig Mor at odds of 4-11. It's far from ideal and results in a hefty price drift, but the ground was far too soft for him and all is not lost for Cheltenham.

December
6 Holywell has a disaster at Aintree (going nowhere when unseating) but it later becomes clear Jonjo O'Neill was at the start of a winless December, with all of his string under a cloud.

Any Currency will do
Nick Watts identifies his main fancies and runs through his ante-post portfolio

There are never any soft races at Cheltenham but this year's Glenfarclas Cross Country Chase has a distinctly winnable feel and the one to back is Martin Keighley's **Any Currency**.

This year there will be no Balthazar King, who is heading straight to the Grand National, and sadly there will be no Big Shu following his demise at Cheltenham in December. Their absences should leave the way clear for Any Currency to step up on last year's short-head defeat.

He is a 12-year-old now, but age is no handicap in this race and for some reason he seems to have found improvement at this late stage of his career. He gave Balthazar King an almighty fright in last year's race and on his latest start over the cross-country course he thrashed Quantitativeeasing by 12 lengths.

He heads the market, deservedly so, and with form figures of 932241 on the

Cross Country ace Any Currency with trainer Martin Keighley

cross-country course at Cheltenham he is about as safe an each-way investment as you could get.

More unproven at Cheltenham is **Don Cossack**, who fell in last season's RSA Chase but still has a fine chance in the Ryanair Chase.

All his wins this season have come right-handed but that is not his fault – it is just that the programme book in Ireland for two-and-a-half-mile chasers is dominated by Down Royal, Punchestown and Thurles. Previous wins at Navan and Naas show he can go left-handed and he looks such an improved horse this season that he is hard to oppose.

A feature of his recent displays has been his strength from the final fence. At Punchestown in December he was challenged on all sides at the last, yet went away to beat Boston Bob by four and a half lengths. Then last time out in the Kinloch Brae he had just about mastered Champagne Fever at the last when that rival fell, leaving him to come home alone.

Gigginstown House Stud, which owns Don Cossack, will probably take the National Hunt Chase too – but with which horse? Don Poli was installed as ante-post favourite but surely ought to be going for the RSA Chase. If he does line up in the three-miler, Wounded Warrior and **Thunder And Roses** are useful back-up for Gigginstown and the latter is fancied to give Sandra Hughes an emotional success, just four months after taking the reins from her late father Dessie.

Thunder And Roses looks like the type who will thrive over extreme distances and his form in novice chases has been good. He was second behind Apache Stronghold at Down Royal in October and won easily at Fairyhouse with a tough staying performance.

He was only third in his final prep at Navan, but that was on yielding to soft and good ground may help him. With Hughes having stated the National Hunt Chase is the target, odds of 20-1 are more than reasonable, particularly if Don Poli is diverted to the RSA.

Ante-post diary

7 Don Cossack wins the John Durkan and, despite not looking at his best, there is something impressive about the way he strides clear after the line. He goes into the portfolio at 10-1 for the Ryanair.

13 That's more like it from The New One. He dispatches Vaniteux easily in the International, jumping well too. He is now down to 5-2 in places and the 6-1 is looking a good deal.

20 Zarkandar, who went in the portfolio a few weeks ago at 14-1 for the World Hurdle, idles in front in the Long Walk and allows Reve De Sivola to fight back. It's a frustrating reverse, but in hindsight Sam Twiston-Davies should have waited longer and I'm not discouraged.

26 Oscar Barton impresses in the hunter chase at Down Royal and is snapped up at 7-1.

January

15 A big day at Thurles with two portfolio horses running. Don Cossack furthers his claims for the Ryanair by winning the Kinloch Brae and is cut to 5-1 generally, half the price he was put up at. Unfortunately Milsean loses at 1-4 in a 2m6f novice hurdle. He isn't an Albert Bartlett contender on that and I'm on the lookout for a replacement.

17 Heart-in-mouth stuff at Haydock as The New One makes hard work of an apparently easy task. Taking the positives, he still managed to win despite almost everything going wrong and he was giving 8lb to a decent horse in Bertimont. It will be different at Cheltenham.

24 Having attended Trials Day at Cheltenham, I'm impressed with the performance in defeat of Dan Skelton's Value At Risk and he is backed for the Albert Bartlett at 12-1. He just loses out to Ordo Ab Chao and looks like he wants 3m.

February

4 Bad news for Dynaste fans as he is ruled out of a repeat bid in the Ryanair due to injury. However, it's not such bad news for supporters of Don Cossack, who is cut to 7-2 in most places. The 10-1 is looking good value.

6 Now it's the turn of the portfolio to be hit by injury, with Oscar Barton out for the season.

8 Southfield Theatre boosts his RSA claims with a fluent performance at Exeter over an inadequate trip. He's now into 12-1.

8 In the increasing belief that Don Poli will contest the RSA, Thunder And Roses goes into the portfolio for the NH Chase. His novice chase form this season is good and he should love an extreme trip. At 20-1, he's a decent each-way bet.

12 Although his jumping doesn't wholly convince, Holywell wins his Gold Cup prep at Kelso and is now 10-1 in most places.

15 Thunder And Roses finishes third in a Grade 2 at Navan. Disappointing, but there's still hope of better on good ground.

Watts' festival portfolio

The New One 6-1
(Champion Hurdle)

Southfield Theatre 16-1
(RSA Chase)

Zarkandar 14-1
(World Hurdle)

Don Cossack 10-1
(Ryanair Chase)

Holywell 14-1 *(Gold Cup)*

Milsean 20-1
(Albert Bartlett)

Oscar Barton 7-1
(Foxhunter)

Value At Risk 12-1
(Albert Bartlett)

Thunder And Roses 20-1
(NH Chase)

An eyecatcher for the handicaps is the Nicky Henderson-trained, JP McManus-owned **Cup Final**. It is not certain where he will go, as he is prominent in the market for both the Pertemps Final (3m) and the Martin Pipe conditionals' event (2m4½f), but he appears better suited by the longer race.

His pedigree points that way – his dam is four-time Grade 1-winning staying hurdler Asian Maze – and he has improved as he has been stepped up in trip. Third behind Morito Du Berlais on his reappearance at Cheltenham over 2m5f, he improved to win a Pertemps qualifier at Sandown next time over a furlong further.

There should be more to come when he steps up to three miles and he appeals for the Pertemps more than stablemate Dawalan, who rather showed his hand recently when scooting up at Musselburgh.

Another McManus-owned handicap fancy is **Eastlake**, who has a quote of 16-1 for the Grand Annual.

He ran in the race last season and finished a fair sixth behind Savello off a mark of 147. This season, in keeping with many of Jonjo O'Neill's string, he did nothing in the early part of the campaign. However, at Ascot last time out he was much more like his old self, travelling strongly until his effort petered out in the home straight and he had to settle for third behind Rebel Rebellion over an extended 2m5f that may have been a shade too far for him.

He now gets to race off a 2lb lower mark than he did for last season's festival and will be of interest whether he goes for the Grand Annual again or the Stable Plate – particularly if AP McCoy rides, as he has won on him seven times already.

Eastlake: capable of a handicap win off a lower mark than last year

LIGHTNING QUICK BETTING
NEIGH BOTHER

WITH PADDY POWER MESSENGER

EASILY FIND THE BET YOU WANT...

...**PLACE IT, QUICK** AS A FLASH

DOWNLOAD THE APP NOW
SEARCH PP MESSENGER IN THE APP STORE

NEW PADDY POWER CUSTOMERS ONLY
BET £10, GET A FREE £20 BET
WHEN YOU REGISTER ON THE APP NOW!

PADDYPOWER.
CALL 0800 904 7933

gambleaware.co.uk   18+

Free bet available to new Paddy Power customers only. One free bet per customer & max £20. Prices displayed are for demonstration purposes only. T&C's apply.

Graeme Rodway Un De Sceaux is the most exciting novice to run at the festival since Sprinter Sacre and should win the Arkle, although Josses Hill has the talent to give him a race. That one has looked an erratic jumper of fences but is sure to have done plenty of work on the schooling grounds and a clean round would make him a player against Un De Sceaux.

Richard Birch Sam Twiston-Davies was adamant after Southfield Theatre's Newbury defeat in November that it should be erased from memory owing to the exceptionally tacky ground. He looked the real deal when scoring at Wincanton, Chepstow and Exeter and rates the RSA Chase value.

Nick Watts Un De Sceaux is a standout in the Arkle – he deserved all the superlatives going for his performance at Leopardstown last time. Vautour at his best would take a lot of beating in the JLT, while on good ground Southfield Theatre (*below*) has a lively chance in the RSA Chase.

Nicholls holds pair of aces

Graeme Rodway fancies the champion trainer to strike with Dodging Bullets and Ptit Zig

Dodging Bullets comes into the Cheltenham Festival in the form of his life and can confirm himself the best in the two-mile division this season by landing the Betway Queen Mother Champion Chase.

Paul Nicholls' gelding did not deliver at the highest level last season but anyone who dismissed him as falling short of the top class has had to think again. Although he was beaten on his reappearance over the Champion Chase course and distance in November, that defeat came in a race run at a muddling gallop on ground softer than ideal and Nicholls has admitted Dodging Bullets was short of fitness.

Dodging Bullets has put that below-par run firmly behind him in two subsequent starts, recording consecutive career-high RPRs. He jumped and travelled well en route to a comfortable victory in the Tingle Creek at Sandown in December and made short work of a useful field that included Sprinter Sacre in the Clarence House Chase at Ascot the following month.

Those Grade 1 successes represent a considerable step up from his Grade 2-winning form as both a novice hurdler and a novice chaser. Last season his chase wins at that level came over course and distance in November and at Kempton in December, before he was a neck behind Module on unsuitably heavy going in another Grade 2 at Newbury in February.

He was unable to reproduce that level of form when fifth in the Arkle last year and disappointed at Aintree next time, but those uninspiring efforts in Grade 1 company came at the end of a long season and it is probably best to put a line through them.

Sprinter Sacre was returning from a year off the track when he was beaten by Dodging Bullets in January and the former champion looked a shadow of the unbeatable performer he once was. Dodging Bullets was well on top at the finish and should confirm the form.

Last year's winner Sire De Grugy, who unseated on his belated reappearance at Newbury, is another whose best form is probably behind him after a long layoff. Mr Mole, winner of the Newbury race, is rapidly progressive and could prove the biggest danger to his stablemate Dodging Bullets.

The JLT Novices' Chase is shaping up to be one of the races of the week and the Willie Mullins-trained Vautour looks likely to be a warm order. However, he was disappointing at Leopardstown over Christmas and beat little over 2m3f at that course last time. His best form is over shorter and he may find **Ptit Zig** too strong over 2m4f in the JLT.

Paul Nicholls' gelding is unbeaten in completed starts over fences this season and gave the smart Josses Hill 4lb and a nine-length beating when bolting up in a 2m3f Grade 2 at Ascot in December.

He went off at even-money for the Grade 2 Dipper Novices' Chase over the JLT course and distance the following month and slammed Champagne West, who was previously unbeaten over fences, by six lengths. The front two recorded impressive sectionals in the closing stages and pulled 19 lengths clear of the remainder. They included Ned Stark, who has since franked the form by landing the Grade 2 Towton Novices' Chase at Wetherby.

Ptit Zig fell when favourite to beat some battle-hardened chasers in the Ascot Chase last time but jumped well up to that point and is preferred to Apache Stronghold and Valseur Lido back in novice company.

Alan King's two likely runners in the JCB Triumph Hurdle offer some value. They are headed by **Pain Au Chocolat**, who was second to Seamour in a hot juvenile contest at Market Rasen in December and has made good progress since. He broke his maiden over hurdles against his elders in a 2m novice event at Plumpton in January and built on that when running away with a juvenile hurdle at Sandown by nine lengths later that month. He is going the right way and there is more to come.

Karezak, King's other likely representative, should not be discounted. This battle-hardened performer has been competing well against the best juveniles in Britain on ground softer than ideal and could improve with better going.

The Novices' Handicap Chase became a 0-140 in 2011 and has been won by a horse carrying more than 11st 3lb every year since. It should pay to stick with those towards the head of the weights and the 134-rated **Thomas Crapper** fits the bill.

Robin Dickin's eight-year-old has an impressive record at Cheltenham (two wins, one second and two thirds from seven starts) and was beaten only by the top-class Don Poli when runner-up off a hurdle mark of 134 in the Martin Pipe at last year's festival.

He is still a maiden after five starts over fences, but his first three runs came over an inadequate 2m and he did well to mix it with some smart types over the distance, recording figures of 322.

Thomas Crapper ran to a similar level when second behind Irish Saint over 2m5½f at Ascot in December and was far from disgraced when fourth in a hot 2m4½f contest at Kempton last time. He appears to have been trained with the Cheltenham race in mind and can be expected to improve back at his favourite course and distance.

Thomas Crapper: good Cheltenham form and likely to be well weighted in novice handicap chase

On track for success

Dave Randall sifts through the course form in search of strong contenders

Fourteen of the 27 winners at last year's festival had either won or reached the frame at the course previously, which emphasises that vital punting clues can be found in the Cheltenham records.

Of course, trainers are just as keen as punters to find out whether a particular horse acts round Cheltenham and that means many runners will have been given the opportunity to prove themselves before the festival. Previous good runs in the white-hot competition of the festival are particularly significant – seven of last year's winners (of the ten to have run there) had finished in the first four at an earlier festival.

Those figures look even better when considering that most Irish runners will not have competed at Cheltenham before – so how can they be spotted? A good place to look with the Irish runners is Navan, which is a Grade 1 track with similar characteristics as Cheltenham, being left-handed and undulating.

Eight of the 12 Irish-trained winners at last year's festival had competed in the past at Navan, with two winning and another four placed. That means 19 of last year's 27 winners had placed form at Cheltenham or Navan, and here is a selection of those who might follow suit this year.

SPRINTER SACRE (Cheltenham form 3111) Nicky Henderson's troubled superstar is going to be on the lips of many festival-goers in the run-up to his bid to regain the Champion Chase crown and is likely to split opinion like no other horse this year.

He is a superb jumper who travels really well through his races and has electric speed on his favoured good ground, which enabled him to rack up ten wins in a row over fences before his dominance was interrupted by a heart problem. He was particularly impressive at Cheltenham, where he put in his best display as a novice chaser when winning the 2012 Arkle and recorded the first of his two 190 Racing Post Ratings in the 2013 Champion Chase.

He ran to an RPR of 171 and a Topspeed figure of 156 on his return to the track at Ascot in January, where he showed his natural alacrity over the fences before ring-rustiness took its toll and he was beaten three lengths by Tingle Creek hero Dodging Bullets.

Those were strong figures on unfavourable ground after an absence of more than a year and at the age of nine Sprinter Sacre can build on that return back at Cheltenham. The 11-4 non-runner no bet appeals.

IRISH CAVALIER (Cheltenham form 3) The Rebecca Curtis-trained novice chaser has been an exciting jumping prospect ever since winning a Worcester bumper virtually on the bridle on good ground in May 2013 and, although every run since then has been with soft or heavy in the going description, he has continued to progress.

Having won three novice hurdles last season, he was switched to chasing this term and appears to be on a good handicap mark of 137

after recording form figures of 323 at 2m3f-2m5f. The most eyecatching run came on his first try round Cheltenham on Trials Day in January when he finished on the front foot up the hill and recorded his best RPR of 143.

Curtis has always maintained the best of him will be seen on better ground and, with conditions more likely to be in his favour at the festival, he is strongly fancied to go well in the Novices' Handicap Chase on the opening day. It is worth noting that Curtis's three previous festival winners all had at least one good Cheltenham run on their record prior to their success.

BUYWISE (Cheltenham form 515) His Cheltenham figures might not look that good at first glance, but bear in mind that the fifth places were in the Novices' Handicap Chase at last year's festival and this season's Paddy Power Gold Cup.

In between, the Evan Williams-trained eight-year-old produced his best RPR of 151 in winning a Grade 2 handicap chase over 2m5f at Cheltenham in April 2014. That is one of four wins in seven starts over fences up to 2m7½f on ground ranging from good (for his Cheltenham success) to heavy.

He recorded an RPR of 151 again in the Paddy Power Gold Cup in November, even though that was over an inadequate 2m4½f on soft.

He goes well fresh and there is surely more to come from him over three miles on better ground from a workable mark of 146 in the Ultima Business Solutions Handicap Chase on the opening day.

BLAKLION (Cheltenham form 21) Nigel Twiston-Davies's six-year-old has compiled remarkably consistent form figures (11112132) under rules since winning an Irish maiden point-to-point in January 2014.

Two of those runs have been at Cheltenham and on his second visit in December he proved staying was his game when running out an 11-length winner of a Grade 2 contest over three miles on good to soft ground. He achieved a peak RPR of 147 on that occasion and has since run well twice in defeat. The shorter trip looked against him

Irish Cavalier (right): on a good mark of 137 and fancied to go well in the Novices' Handicap Chase

Tipster forum

What do you fancy for the novice hurdles?

Paul Kealy The confidence behind Douvan for the Supreme suggests he is not overrated, but does he really deserve to be 2-1 and less for beating a 136-rated three-miler by less than four lengths, especially when you consider the third was beaten 20 lengths next time? When Vautour won last year he went off at 7-2 after beating a 150-rated rival in the Grade 1 Deloitte. He's not for me and I was quite taken by Jollyallan even in defeat at Sandown. I get the impression Kilcrea Vale is top class and have backed him for the Neptune, while No More Heroes still has me buzzing for the Albert Bartlett. He scoped badly after his recent defeat but Gordon Elliott will have him right on the day.

Vital statistics
The festival by numbers

Eight of the last ten Arkle winners had won at Cheltenham or been placed at the festival before. Three had finished 124 in the previous year's Neptune

13

Of the last 14 Plate winners went off at double-figure odds, including Ballynagour (below) last year

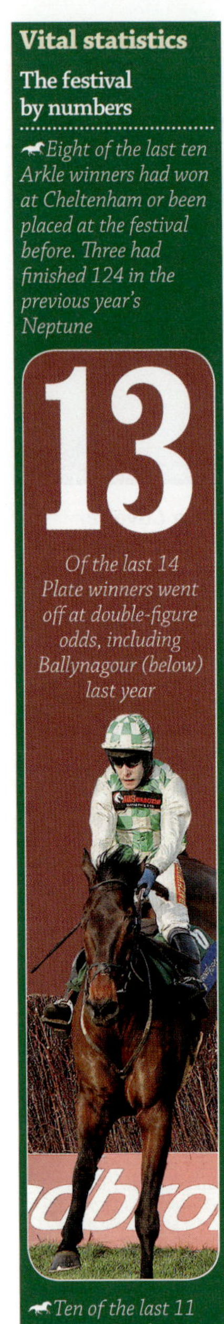

Ten of the last 11 Pertemps Final winners started at double-figure odds

in the Grade 1 Challow Hurdle at Newbury and he was collared in the closing stages on his blindside in Grade 2 company over 3m½f at Doncaster in January.

He makes each-way appeal at around 14-1 for the Albert Bartlett Novices' Hurdle on the Friday of the festival.

ORDO AB CHAO (Cheltenham form 1) Alan King's improving novice hurdler has won four of his six starts under rules and his most notable performance came on Cheltenham's Trials Day when he scored a neat success in the Grade 2 Neptune trial, which has proved a significant pointer in the past.

There should be more to come from him on the good/good to soft surface usually prevalent in March as he is not short of speed and at 20-1 he is fair each-way value for the Neptune Novices' Hurdle.

THE NEW ONE (Cheltenham form 16121131) Most of the main players for the Champion Hurdle and Gold Cup already have significant Cheltenham form in their locker, with The New One particularly blessed in this department.

He is a virtual bet-to-nothing each-way non-runner no bet at 3-1 in the Champion Hurdle and a Placepot banker on the opening day. He was unlucky not to win last year and may well be able to track and beat last year's Neptune winner Faugheen, whose inconsistent jumping will be tested in the best company.

MANY CLOUDS (Cheltenham form 9BD1) Oliver Sherwood's Hennessy winner is the best jumper of a fence in training but is surely ground dependent. He put up a stellar show over a furlong shorter than the Gold Cup trip on soft going on Trials Day, remaining unbeaten in three starts this season, and if rain arrives on the Friday he will be interesting each-way.

SMAD PLACE (Cheltenham form 03322) Alan King's grey has yet to win on the course but has performed well there (on RPR his two best hurdle runs and two best chase figures have been achieved at Cheltenham). Last year's RSA Chase runner-up was second again on his latest visit, behind Many Clouds in January, but is less ground dependent than the winner and on offer at 25-1 each-way for the Gold Cup.

EDEYMI and REGAL ENCORE This pair have significant festival form and have shown their potential in recent weeks in qualifiers for the Pertemps Final, a Listed 3m handicap hurdle on day three.

Edeymi (Cheltenham form 2B) is trained by Tony Martin, a specialist at getting one ready for a race of this type, and makes significant appeal at 14-1 each-way the first four in the Pertemps. The seven-year-old achieved a peak RPR of 139 when staying on well up the hill to finish a close runner-up behind Une Artiste in the 2012 Fred Winter Juvenile Handicap Hurdle. On his latest start, a second run back from an absence, he was close to that level (RPR 137) as he caught the eyes of everyone watching with a never-nearer fourth behind Dawalan over 3m½f at Musselburgh at the beginning of February.

Anthony Honeyball's **Regal Encore** (Cheltenham form 20) has been something of a slow-burner since finishing seven-lengths second

Ordo Ab Chao (right) wins the Neptune trial at Cheltenham

behind Briar Hill in the 2013 Champion Bumper, but a belated step up in trip really suited him when he won a Class 2 2m7½f handicap hurdle at Exeter in early February. That left him vying for Pertemps favouritism at 10-1 and he also appeals each-way, especially with Tony McCoy likely to take the ride for owner JP McManus at his last Cheltenham Festival.

NAVAN FORM This can be a good guide with Irish runners, especially those yet to compete at Cheltenham, and several catch the eye.

Willie Mullins won with a trio of Cheltenham debutants at last year's festival and it may be significant that all three had a good run at Navan to their credit (Vautour and Faugheen had won and Don Poli had been a close second).

One to note this year is Champion Bumper hope **Bordini**, who recorded an RPR of 132 with a decisive victory at Navan in December, while would-be layers of Arkle favourite **Un De Sceaux** may be encouraged by his lack of Cheltenham experience but should remember he won a novice hurdle at Navan in January 2014 by a distance, achieving an RPR of 161.

Noel Meade's **Apache Stronghold** also has strong hurdles form at Navan in the book and should not be fazed by the course in either the JLT Novices' Chase or RSA Chase.

The Irish challenge for the Albert Bartlett Novices' Hurdle is typically strong and Gordon Elliott's **No More Heroes** looked the right type when winning the Grade 2 Navan Novice Hurdle in December over two and a half miles on yielding to soft. He finished strongly and a step up to three miles on better ground should suit the son of Presenting.

From the same yard, **Don Cossack** is unbeaten in four starts at 2m4f-2m7f over fences this season on contrasting ground, including the Grade 1 John Durkan Memorial at Punchestown in December. He fell six out when still moving well in last year's RSA and, having won a Grade 2 bumper and his maiden hurdle at Navan, the uphill climb at Cheltenham is unlikely to find him out.

The Gold Cup trip is not necessarily beyond him but the preferred option appears to be the Ryanair Chase and he looks hard to beat.

Every junction of the festival covered Come join the debate

RACING POST
Your Cheltenham guide

Festival Q & A
The major bookmakers discuss the leading contenders and the betting markets

Will Silviniaco Conti finally win the Gold Cup?

Bet365 *Pat Cooney* The cheekpieces he's worn in his last two wins seem to have made a big difference, but I can't get away from the fact he was beaten in the Gold Cup last season and this year's race looks even harder. The each-way value at current prices is the unexposed Djakadam. I expect Ruby Walsh to ride him and he's sure to go off at single figures on the day in that case.

Betfair *Brian Kearney* He's nought from three at Cheltenham and it's questionable if he has improved. I can see him being in front after the last again and wobbling up the hill. Win or lose, at 3-1 he's poor value. Holywell loves Cheltenham and stays well, while Carlingford Lough is also a strong stayer and will be bang there if he jumps round.

Betfred *Matt Hulmes* I can't recall too many horses winning their first Gold Cup at the third attempt, so although on this season's form Silviniaco is the one to beat, there are too many question marks to be taking 3-1. I would rather side with the proven festival form of Lord Windermere and Holywell at much bigger prices.

Betway *Alan Alger* I'd have liked to see him go to Cheltenham outside

Djakadam: set to shorten if chosen by Ruby Walsh

of the festival and get his head in front there, although the figure '4' from last year's race doesn't tell the full story of how close he was. He's a worthy favourite but isn't any value. I wouldn't rule out The Giant Bolster running another big race at a big price.

BoyleSports *Alan Reilly* I'm ignoring last year's race as I feel if it were run five times you'd get five different results. So on that basis, yes he can win a Gold Cup, and whatever beats him will probably win. I was very taken with Many Clouds both last time and in the Hennessy. He'll be difficult to pass in what is always a slog. I feel Smad Place will run well at a big price.

Coral *Andrew Lobo* He does seem to have improved this season and will no doubt go off favourite, but it looks a competitive race and there are plenty with chances. At a big price Smad Place could reach the frame given his excellent festival record.

Ladbrokes *Calum Boyd* I don't subscribe to the notion that he's improved this season and in a similar-quality renewal to last year I expect him to run a similar race. Many Clouds is the obvious alternative and, on a form line through the consistent Houblon Des Obeaux, Coneygree has a serious chance if he runs.

Paddy Power *Brendan Duke* I suspect he'll be this year's Sire De Grugy – hard to lay based on the bogus assumption that he doesn't like Cheltenham. I could easily see him being 5-1 in the morning, in which case he'd rate a good bet. I see the other contenders as much of a muchness.

Sporting Index *John O'Connell* His finishing effort last year is a slight concern and there are now a few improving sorts in the reckoning. Djakadam impressed me in the Thyestes and looks overpriced with Ruby Walsh very likely to ride him. Lord Windermere is coming nicely to the boil and a dry week would be a big plus.

William Hill *Jamie McBride* He's clearly the one to beat on what we've seen this season but he has yet to win at Cheltenham and I suspect bookmakers will want to lay him on the day. At a big price Boston Bob is possibly worth one more chance after shaping better than the bare result in the Irish Hennessy.

The Coral Cup has been won by only one outright favourite (plus one joint-favourite) in its 21-year history

11

Of the last 12 defending title-holders who ran in the Champion Chase were beaten. Sire De Grugy (below) puts his title on the line this year

Ruby Walsh hasn't had a chase winner at the festival since he scored on Kauto Star in the 2009 Gold Cup

Essential info

A quick guide to festival betting

In the shops Most betting shops open earlier during the festival, usually at 8.30-9am

Free bets Many bookmakers offer free bets for new customers during the festival, but remember to check the terms and conditions. For a great range of free bets, go to racingpost.com

Compare the odds Find the best odds on your selections from a range of bookmakers by using the odds comparison table at racingpost.com

Early prices Be quick if you want to take an advertised price on the morning of the race – most firms hold their prices for a maximum of 15 minutes when their shops open and some offer no guarantee

Each-way Bookmakers often extend their place terms during the festival. In the big handicaps, it can pay to look for firms offering a quarter the odds for the first five places, or paying out on six places. The standard each-way terms are a quarter the odds for the first four places

Best odds Several firms offer 'best odds guaranteed', which means they will match the SP if you have taken an early price and your selection wins at bigger odds

Non-runner no bet Most bookmakers offer this concession from early March – some earlier on the bigger races. In this case, your stake is returned if your selection doesn't run

Specials A vast range of special bets is available at the festival, including perennial favourites such as top trainer, top jockey and the number of Irish winners

Is Faugheen the one in the Champion Hurdle?

Bet365 He's the most likely winner in a race where only a handful have a genuine chance. My only doubt is that he has made some jumping errors but apart from that his form, particularly on good ground, is high class and he's versatile from a tactical viewpoint. I'd rather lay The New One than Faugheen at current prices.

Betfair At 5-4 he has to be a lay. If he jumps like he did in the Neptune he'll be found out over two miles and he has made small mistakes on both starts this campaign. I can't have The New One either. He looks like he's ready for a step up in trip and has never jumped well enough for this level at two miles. Jezki looks the most solid each-way alternative.

Betfred Faugheen's hurdling has improved and I believe he's something special. He seems uncomplicated and would be happy to front-run in a small field. Although The New One appeared unlucky last year, I think he lost the race being outpaced down the hill and I'd be surprised if he won this time.

Betway Faugheen has to be that short, but if we're theoretically looking for a doubt we could maybe point to the possibility of a slower, tactical race because the field size is cutting up. Maybe that wouldn't suit him, but the rest certainly have it all to do. I like Jezki, who looks solid.

BoyleSports I think he's the real deal and I haven't been as excited about a hurdler since Istabraq. The only real danger is The New One, who would have beaten Jezki last year with a trouble-free run. I know Jezki will improve on better ground but the best he can hope for is a place.

Coral Faugheen looks a rock-solid favourite. We know he handles the track and stays further, which always helps. This will be his stiffest task to date but most of his opponents have shown their hand, whereas he has yet to hit his limit.

Ladbrokes He looks awesome and we still don't know how good he is. The Champion Hurdle is always run at a relentless pace, which will put pressure on the sometimes unreliable jumping of The New One. Jezki is tailor-made for this test and could chase Faugheen home.

Paddy Power Since last year's wrecking-ball performance Faugheen's jumping has got progressively better, and with the likelihood that Ruby Walsh can dictate his own pace he'll prove hard to pass. The New One is the obvious danger and looks a knocking each-way bet.

Sporting Index He looks the real deal and I'd be shocked if he was turned over. I have a nagging doubt whether The New One has the speed to eclipse the favourite and Jezki may be the one to follow him home.

William Hill Faugheen looks very hard to beat. He can jump sloppily at times, but it doesn't seem to stop him. The New One has looked laboured, albeit on heavy ground, and Jezki had everything go his way last year.

How do you see the Champion Chase?

Bet365 Dodging Bullets has fewer question marks about him than any of his rivals and is the safe selection. We know how much the betting public adore Sprinter Sacre, but from a bookmaking view we wouldn't mind taking him on. Hidden Cyclone makes some each-way appeal as good ground on a left-handed track is what he needs.

Betfair It's very messy. Sprinter Sacre should be able to improve 3lb on Dodging Bullets – he jumped much better as the race unfolded at Ascot and I expect some improvement. I would rather be a backer than a layer at 3-1 but it's close. I can see Mr Mole hunting around picking up the pieces.

Betfred Champagne Fever can enhance his festival record. Sprinter Sacre is hard to fancy after his well-documented issues – any bookmaker worth his salt will be out to get him – and Sire De Grugy has many questions to answer. At a big price I can see Simply Ned staying on and grabbing some place money if they go too fast.

Betway This is the toughest to call because we need to see which horses line up on the day – more so than in any other race. Hidden Cyclone has similar figures and recent form to 2006 winner Newmill, and I like him at the prices.

BoyleSports I couldn't help being disappointed with Sprinter Sacre's return; he went from full to empty very quickly. Sire De Grugy also has a number of unanswered questions, but from a bookmakers' perspective it opens the race up. Hidden Cyclone probably jumped better than ever when winning the Tied Cottage and has always run well at Cheltenham.

Coral Sprinter Sacre has a chance but the market suggested he was pretty fit last time and he still ran 20lb below his best. Connections of other runners won't be afraid to take him on.

Ladbrokes A fascinating puzzle. Sprinter Sacre lacked his trademark zest last time but I preferred that to Sire De Grugy's comeback, when his usually solid jumping was missing. Dodging Bullets has put it all together this season.

Paddy Power Sprinter Sacre should be taken on. I'll plump for Dodging Bullets, who's had a fine season, and Special Tiara might run well at a price. He was undone by his stablemate last year and might find it easier on the front end this time.

Sporting Index The comeback runs of the last two winners posed more questions than answers and there will be no shortage of layers on the day. It looks as though Dodging Bullets has really turned the corner and he now looks the most solid of the leading contenders. A patiently ridden Simply Ned could hit the frame.

William Hill Sprinter Sacre will probably never reach the same heights he did previously, but he may need to improve only 3lb to reverse the Ascot form with Dodging Bullets and I wouldn't be as quick to write him off as some. Mr Mole continues to surprise and could run a big race.

What do you fancy for the World Hurdle?

Bet365 Annie Power non-runner no bet looks the safest option but of the definite contenders Zarkandar is narrowly the best in an open race. I like Un Temps Pour Tout at a double-figure price as he's still improving.

Betfair In the likely absence of More Of That I'd be keen on Annie Power if they were tempted to run her, or alternatively Lieutenant

Essential info
Longer distances, smaller fields

Punters might like to take note of changes to race distances and field sizes for a number of races at the festival.

🐎 The changes to the three-mile handicap chase starts on both the Old course and the New course, to improve the starts and used at previous meetings this season, will also apply at the festival.

🐎 The Ultima Business Solutions Handicap Chase (race three on Tuesday) will be run over a distance of 3m1f (previously 3m½f).

🐎 The Fulke Walwyn Kim Muir Handicap Chase (race six on Thursday) will be run over a distance of 3m2f (previously 3m1½f).

🐎 In addition, the Brown Advisory & Merriebelle Stable Plate (race five on Thursday) will revert to 2m5f, having been reduced to 2m4f last year.

🐎 Following a review with the BHA, the maximum field sizes for the following hurdle races have been reduced to improve bypassing arrangements:

Supreme Novices'
22 runners (from 24)

Neptune Novices'
22 runners (from 24)

Coral Cup
26 runners (from 28)

Fred Winter
22 runners (from 24)

Triumph
22 runners (from 24)

County
26 runners (from 28)

🐎 A couple of allowances have changed for the Martin Pipe Conditional Jockeys' Handicap Hurdle. In the past jockeys riding for their own stable received a 3lb allowance and riders without a winner had a 7lb allowance, but these have now been removed.

Vital statistics

The festival by numbers

20-1 has been the SP of both Nicky Henderson winners of the Grand Annual (Greenhope in 2006 and Bellvano in 2012) since the race was renamed in honour of his father Johnny in 2005. Be wary of shorter-priced Henderson runners – he has had three beaten favourites in the past seven years

13

Of the last 15 RSA Chase winners have been aged seven, including O'Faolain's Boy (below), who was successful in the race last year

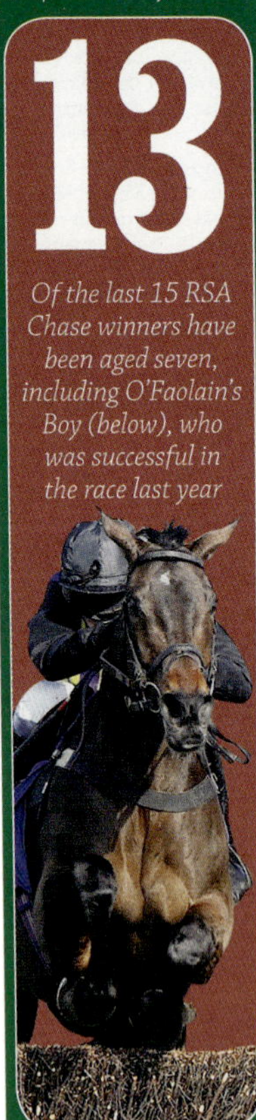

Colonel at 10-1 as he's still young and progressive. I respect Zarkandar and Saphir Du Rheu, but I'll be happy to take on both of them.

Betfred Paul Nicholls holds the key and the one I like best is Zarkandar. He has a decent festival record and, having proved he stays three miles at Ascot, I can see him being patiently ridden before pouncing late. His stablemate Saphir Du Rheu is an obvious danger.

Betway I like the look of solid Rock On Ruby to take another championship race at the festival.

BoyleSports The setback to More of That is most unfortunate but it has opened up the race. The biggest cheer of the week would undoubtedly go to the Sandra Hughes-trained Lieutenant Colonel if he won. He's an out-and-out stayer who will find more going up the hill and must have a major chance.

Coral Saphir Du Rheu impressed with his attitude last time and should come on for the run, while Rock On Ruby loves it round Cheltenham and could improve for the trip. Obviously if Annie Power were to run she'd have a big chance.

Ladbrokes Rock On Ruby, if getting his ground, would be a strong fancy, while Blue Fashion is an interesting outsider judged on last season's Haydock second to More Of That. Annie Power's fitness and target doubts make her hard to recommend at present.

Paddy Power My each-way shout is Un Temps Pour Tout, who finished the Cleeve off well despite being plenty keen early. He could turn the form around with Saphir Du Rheu and Reve De Sivola.

Sporting Index I would love to see Rock On Ruby win and he may well do. He shapes now as though the trip could be within his compass. If the breathing operation has worked Cole Harden could hit the frame at a big price.

William Hill Zarkandar holds outstanding claims in what looks a weak renewal. He can improve on last year's fourth place with a more positive ride now he has proved his stamina. Cole Harden is possibly a touch overpriced if his recent wind op has had the desired effect.

What do you fancy for the novice hurdles?

Bet365 L'Ami Serge looks the real deal and I expect him to be a lot closer in the Supreme market with Douvan on the day. Windsor Park looks the type to appreciate a step up in trip and appeals for the Neptune. Black Hercules seems a worthy favourite for the Albert Bartlett on form but we've not seen him since early December, which is a concern. The Triumph is all about Peace And Co, but his chances may have been overrated. Remember, he's had only three races and all were on soft ground.

Betfair I was impressed with Nichols Canyon at Leopardstown. He has a good blend of speed and stamina and I'd have something on him in the Supreme if he lined up. Douvan's Punchestown form has taken several knocks and he has to be a lay. In the Albert Bartlett I strongly fancy No More Heroes. You can put a line through his last run as he scoped terribly and jumped worse. Less exposed among the Mullins battalions are Avant Tout, who is worth a speculative bet at a big price if he lines up in the Albert Bartlett or the Neptune, and Dicosimo, who could be best of the Irish in the Triumph.

Betfred Douvan has done nothing wrong but is skinny at 2-1 for the Supreme, while L'Ami Serge has been doing all his winning on soft ground, and I'll take a punt on Silver Concorde to follow up last year's Bumper win at a generous 33-1. Nothing stands out in the Neptune from a form perspective, but there has been interesting money for Nicky Henderson's Kilcrea Vale. The front three in the Albert Bartlett betting are vulnerable and Thomas Brown rates a decent each-way play. He looked to be all about stamina when winning at Cheltenham on New Year's Day.

Betway You have to respect the favourites, especially Douvan, but equally as bookmakers you must take on the short ones. I was impressed with Qewy at Newbury and this Listed Flat winner deserves plenty of respect wherever he lines up. Tea For Two could go well at a price in the Albert Bartlett or the Neptune. The Henderson duo of Top Notch and Peace And Co could be the ones to follow in the Triumph.

BoyleSports It's hard to get away from Douvan and the manner in which he's won his two starts in Ireland. Nichols Canyon was most impressive at Leopardstown and the Neptune is not looking a great race, while I'm hoping Hargam can put it up to his stablemate Peace And Co and win the Triumph.

Coral If Jollyallan can learn from his Sandown defeat he could be the value in the Supreme. For the Neptune I was impressed by Outlander's recent win and Kilcrea Vale, despite having only one start under rules, was mightily impressive at Market Rasen. Thomas Brown looks a fair bet in the Albert Bartlett.

Ladbrokes Douvan looks special and Willie Mullins has said he's ahead of where Vautour was at the same time last year, which is high praise. Kilcrea Vale looked smart on his debut and has been well backed for the Neptune. I fancy No More Heroes to bounce back in the Albert Bartlett and in the Triumph we've been impressed with Peace And Co all season.

Paddy Power I like Nichols Canyon for the Supreme. His toughness and stamina might see him home. In the Neptune I still have a sneaking regard for Shaneshill. His jumping will need to improve but better ground will help and he has festival form. The Albert Bartlett looks tailor-made for Black Hercules. In the Triumph I can see the more streetwise Hargam getting the better of his stablemate Peace And Co.

Sporting Index Douvan looks a class act in the Supreme and Nichols Canyon put down a strong marker for the Neptune at Leopardstown, especially as I have reservations about the form of the Challow Hurdle won by Parlour Games. Thomas Brown looks as though the step up to three miles will be perfect for him in the Albert Bartlett. Everybody is expecting Nicky Henderson to win the Triumph and he probably will, although I prefer Hargam of his big guns.

William Hill Douvan and Peace And Co have both impressed me greatly and I wouldn't be in a hurry to oppose either. The Neptune and Albert Bartlett are lacking standout candidates.

Which novice chasers stand out?

Bet365 Un De Sceaux is 'bar a fall' in the Arkle. Valseur Lido was having his first run since November when just beaten at Leopardstown last time, so he can improve again and looks a contender for the JLT. I've always been a fan of Don Poli, even more so this season, so he'll do for me in the RSA.

Betfair Un De Sceaux looks a class apart in the Arkle, although I'd be happy to take him on with something each-way as he's had only two completed starts and can be quite buzzy. Vautour will be hard to beat in the JLT but the RSA is wide open and Wounded Warrior looked the part when stepped up to three miles on his latest run. If he runs in this over the National Hunt Chase he could be worth a bet. I'm a big fan of The Young Master and he's a fair price at 10-1.

Betfred If Un De Sceaux stays on his feet nothing will get near him in the Arkle. The JLT is the likely target for Vautour and he looks rock solid. He could be a serious Betfred Gold Cup contender next year. Gigginstown's Don Poli and Valseur Lido won't take each other on in the RSA, so I'll be backing whoever turns up on the day.

Betway Ptit Zig looks a decent inclusion in the JLT for any each-way multiples. I like the way Three Kingdoms has been finishing his races this season and I'm sure that style will suit the run-in at Cheltenham. He's a decent each-way shout wherever they decide to place him. Coneygree will be head and shoulders above the opposition if he goes for the RSA. The weight of money suggests Don Poli will be Willie Mullins' choice in the RSA and you'd have to swerve being a layer there.

BoyleSports The Arkle is all about the favourite. If he were mine Coneygree would go for the RSA. The Gold Cup might well be open but that doesn't mean it will take less winning and for a novice it's a big ask. Vautour is a worthy favourite in the JLT if he's allowed to take his chance.

Coral The JLT looks a cracker with a strong Irish contingent but if I had to plump for one at this stage it would be Ptit Zig, whose form has gone to a new level over fences. The RSA also looks interesting. Coneygree and Kings Palace both seem at their best when dominating, which could count against them, so I'd look to get both beaten. If Don Poli runs I'd be keen but otherwise Southfield Theatre, who stays and has course form, can place if not win. Un De Sceaux is the obvious one in the Arkle, as much for the lack of credible opponents as for him being a superstar.

Ladbrokes Un De Sceaux is impossible to oppose in the Arkle. Vautour is the slightly forgotten horse of the festival after his defeat but he was better last time and sets a high standard in the JLT. The form of Don Poli's last win is working out well and, with Coneygree possibly diverting to the Gold Cup and Kings Palace not impressing last time, he should take all the beating in the RSA.

Paddy Power Un De Sceaux is the most exciting jumps horse in training. As soon as we get the pronunciation right and he bolts up in the Arkle we'll start writing poetry about him. Vautour looked a natural at Navan. It hasn't quite gone to plan since but I'll stick with

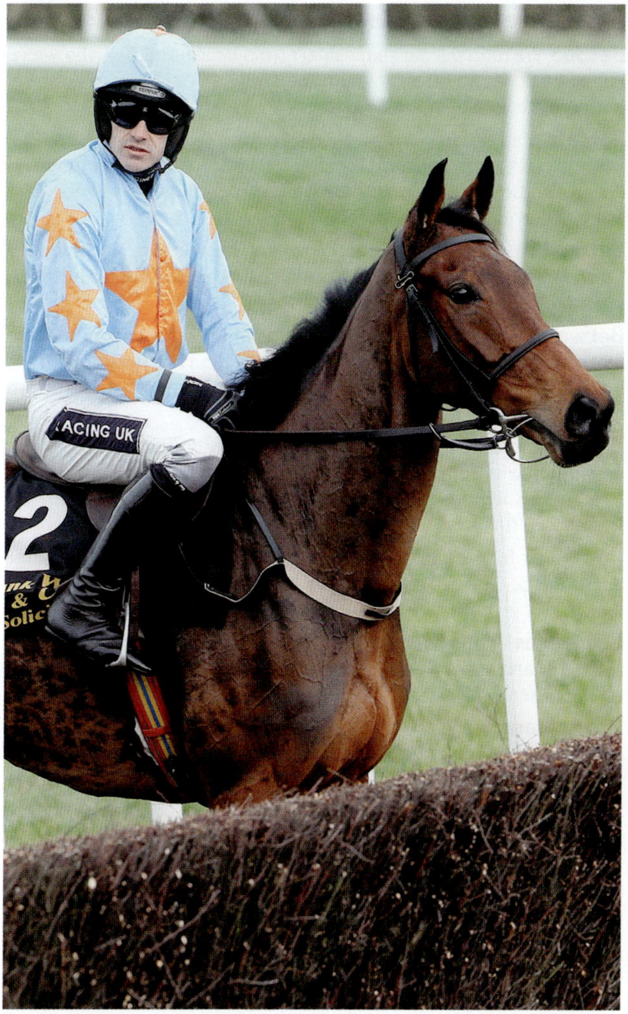

Un De Sceaux: "The most exciting jumps horse in training"

him in a deep JLT. Don Poli will win the RSA assuming sanity prevails and he runs in it.

Sporting Index Un De Sceaux looks a class apart in the Arkle but the other races are more difficult. At least we know Apache Stronghold is set to go for the JLT and his win in the Flogas was impressive. As for the RSA, with a nagging doubt about Kings Palace should he be taken on for the lead and Coneygree very likely to go for the Gold Cup, The Young Master could be the way to go.

William Hill It will be disappointing if Un De Sceaux doesn't dominate the Arkle. Ptit Zig and Don Poli have solid chances in the JLT and RSA.

BET WITH YOUR HEAD

The Racing Post App. It's not just a betting app, it's a knowing what to bet on app.

Get the most important information, tips and predictions to help you make a swift and savvy bet on the racing from Cheltenham.

Available on the App Store

Available at racingpost.com

m.racingpost.com

Please gamble responsibly. 18+
www.gambleaware.co.uk

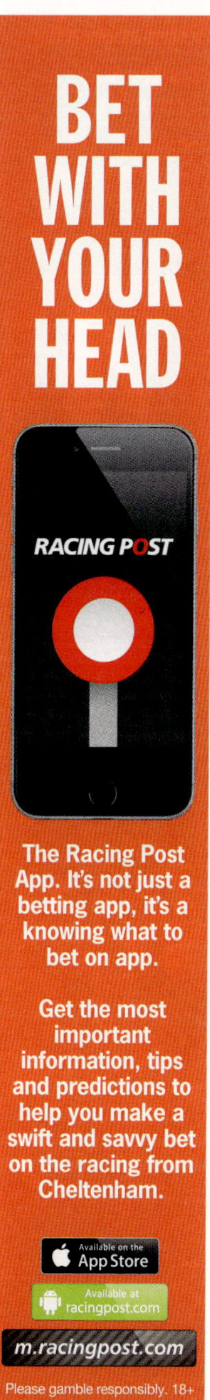

Vital statistics

The festival by numbers

🐎 *Eight of the nine Champion Bumper runners that started 3-1 or less have been beaten*

4

Of the last six RSA Chase winners have been Irish-trained and all of that quartet had prepped in what is now the Flogas Novice Chase, which was won by Apache Stronghold (below) this season

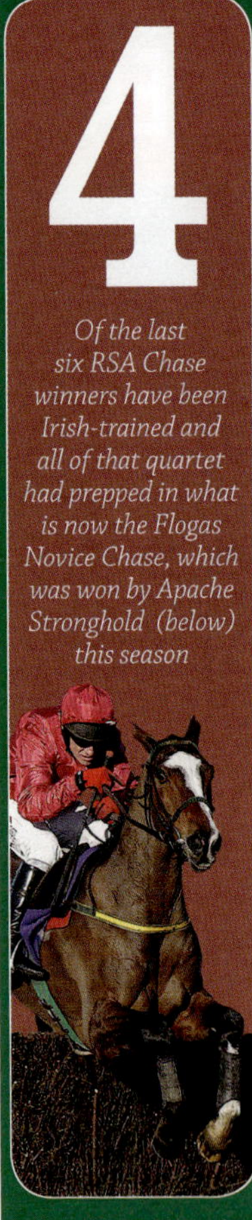

🐎 *Six of David Pipe's ten festival winners wore headgear*

🐎 *Seven of the ten winners of the Fred Winter have been fillies*

What are the biggest losers in your book?

Bet365 We're in decent shape apart from Peace And Co, who we've laid at 25-1 and all rates down for the Triumph. Carlingford Lough is our main headache in the Gold Cup. We've laid him at 33-1 and 25-1.

Betfair Many Clouds in the Gold Cup, Un De Sceaux in the Arkle, Saphir Du Rheu in the World Hurdle, Tell Us More in the Neptune and Peace And Co in the Triumph. Un De Sceaux is the one we need beat as he's been in every ante-post multiple.

Betfred We set out our stall at the start of the season to lay Silviniaco Conti for the Gold Cup and The New One for the Champion Hurdle. A win for either of those would be costly.

Betway We've been very competitive in our Betway Champion Chase market, so a few of the principals there will take a fair chunk out of the book. Obviously Un De Sceaux, Annie Power, Faugheen and Douvan will all cause palpitations in the trading room.

BoyleSports Douvan, Peace And Co and Silviniaco Conti. Every betting shop in Ireland will have multiples starting with Douvan and five Mullins winners, or even four, on day one will be a disaster for Irish-based firms.

Coral Our biggest losers are Douvan in the Supreme and Sprinter Sacre in the Queen Mother. If both win, the ante-post figures will look pretty grim.

Ladbrokes Un Temps Pour Tout in the Ladbrokes World Hurdle, Ptit Zig in the JLT and Lord Windermere in the Gold Cup are the worst. Despite trying to keep Peace And Co onside in the Triumph he'd cost plenty.

Paddy Power The top three are Sprinter Sacre, The New One and Silviniaco Conti, but I wouldn't say we're overly concerned about any of them. What is really giving us the willies is the Mullins run-ups on day one.

Sporting Index As a spread company we have no ante-post liabilities but come the week we'll be cheering against the Mullins/Walsh hotpots.

William Hill Faugheen, Sprinter Sacre, Kings Palace and Peace And Co are currently the worst results but none of them have gotten away from us and all are manageable amounts.

Who are the ones to watch from Ireland?

Bet365 The National Hunt Chase over four miles looks ideal for Noel Meade's Wounded Warrior. He's talented but his best form has been on soft, so I'll wait until the day before backing him.

Betfair No More Heroes, Don Cossack and I can't get away from Jezki each-way. Douvan is the most overrated on bare form. The Irish bankers will surely be Un De Sceaux and Annie Power if everything is okay with her. Tuesday has the potential to be a blowout or a bonanza for the punters.

Betfred Bellshill catches the eye at a price in the Bumper following positive recent comments in the press and Champagne Fever is a decent each-way play in the Champion Chase given the uncertainty surrounding the market leaders. Gordon Elliott has a decent record at the festival and his upwardly mobile Don Cossack will take some beating in his owner's sponsored race. There's little doubt that the Un De Sceaux/Faugheen double will be the Irish banker of the meeting.

Betway I like Hidden Cyclone. From a personal point of view, as a follower of speed figures I sometimes get caught out opposing 'machines' from Ireland that have won on the bridle in an egg-and-spoon race but still have the ability to win at Cheltenham as they like.

BoyleSports Ryanair favourite Don Cossack is one we'll be looking to lay. Interestingly we've been non-runner no bet for a few weeks now and Irish customers aren't exactly knocking the door down for him. Annie Power has to be the banker of the week.

Coral Faugheen looks the Irish banker. Don Poli also looks a solid favourite wherever he goes, but Douvan may have found his price for the Supreme and I'm sure bookmakers will be looking to lay him on the day. Pylonthepressure was an impressive winner at Naas and will be a definite player in the Bumper. Away from the Willie Mullins yard, Apache Stronghold and Martello Tower look credible runners in their respective novice races.

Ladbrokes Faugheen is their banker on a first day that could turn into the Willie Mullins show. Outside of his yard, Road To Riches in the Gold Cup and Lieutenant Colonel in the World Hurdle will both be popular as the best of the Irish in those races but we're happy to lay them both.

Paddy Power Unfortunately I see Willie Mullins having a beano and I suppose Annie Power is the banker. Salsify put up an encouraging comeback at Leopardstown and he looks a fair price for the Foxhunter.

Sporting Index A banker, Irish or otherwise, is Annie Power in the Mares' Hurdle. I'm looking to forward to seeing Sort It Out in the County Hurdle if connections go there after his easy win at Leopardstown.

William Hill Willie Mullins has ridiculous strength in depth and could easily win the top trainer award with his runners on Tuesday alone. One of his in danger of being slightly overhyped is Vautour, as not many of the principals from last year's Supreme have gone forward this season. Away from the Mullins battalions, Vigil's festival experience will be an advantage in the Bumper and Waxies Dargle would be on my shortlist for the County Hurdle if entered.

Give us a value bet for the festival

Bet365 Windsor Park in the Neptune or even the Albert Bartlett. A step up in trip and better ground will see further improvement.

Betfair Wounded Warrior in the RSA if he gets a run. He's overpriced and looks an out-and-out three-miler. Alternatively, Buywise in the Plate.

Betfred Hostile Fire should go well in the Fred Winter for the same owner-trainer combination that won the race in 2013.

Betway A value each-way yankee on Hidden Cyclone, Qewy, Three Kingdoms and Tea For Two.

BoyleSports He doesn't approach the race in the same form as

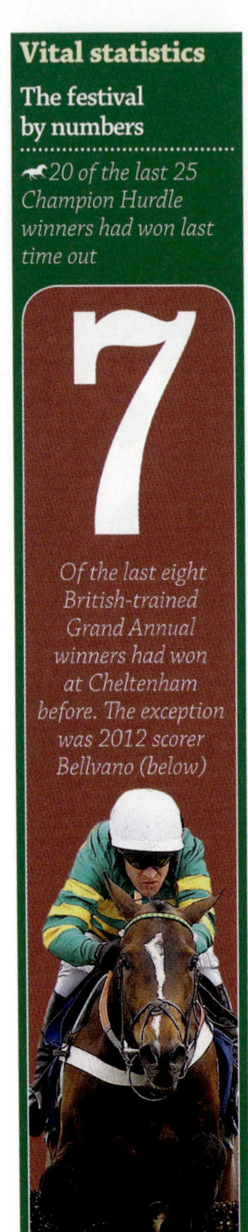

two years ago but Cue Card has a major chance in the Ryanair if he's anywhere near his best. Around 7-1 represents good value.

Coral Thomas Brown in the Albert Bartlett. Trained by the excellent Harry Fry, he has progressed really well throughout the season. His defeats of Otago Trail, Vago Collonges and Robinsfirth have been franked and his defeat at Newbury can be easily excused. The step up in trip looks sure to suit.

Ladbrokes There's value to be had in the National Hunt Chase, with a few of those at the head of the market likely to take their chance in the RSA instead. Wounded Warrior looked like a marathon trip would suit last time and should go well.

Paddy Power Nichols Canyon rates a good each-way play in the Supreme. It strikes me as the ideal race for him and I can't see much to trouble him outside of the top two in the betting.

Sporting Index Assuming the handicapper hasn't weighted him out of the Novices' Handicap Chase following his Plumpton success, Traffic Fluide will take some beating. If he's absent, Thomas Crapper is interesting back at his favourite track.

William Hill Boston Bob has been expensive to follow this season but shaped with promise in the Irish Hennessy and has a decent record at Cheltenham in March. He can go well at a big price in an open-looking Gold Cup.

What's your best bet of the festival?

Bet365 I'd like to see Activial move up in trip and have a crack at the Coral Cup after his excellent run at Newbury, but even if he remains over two miles I'll be with him in the County Hurdle.

Betfair Don Cossack. The Ryanair is made for him and this year's renewal is very winnable. I have a soft spot for Johns Spirit, who didn't get home in the King George. I'll be on the reverse forecast.

Betfred No prize for originality, but Faugheen looks the real deal in the Champion Hurdle. At a bigger price, Any Currency has a great record over the cross-country fences.

Betway Tea For Two in whichever novice hurdle he goes for.

BoyleSports It has to be Many Clouds in the Gold Cup. He's the most progressive in the race and his course form with the unfortunate Dynaste puts him right up there.

Coral Don Poli looks one to be on wherever he runs.

Ladbrokes No More Heroes has doubled in price for the Albert Bartlett after his defeat last time but there were genuine excuses that day and his previous win over Shaneshill was impressive. In an open race he should go well.

Paddy Power Don Poli in whichever race he runs in.

Sporting Index Annie Power is on a totally different level to her rivals in the Mares' Hurdle.

William Hill In a race where it's hard to get excited about too many, Zarkandar holds a solid chance in the World Hurdle.

Conti v the improvers

Racing Post Ratings expert **Sam Walker** weighs up the proven form and potential

GOLD CUP Lord Windermere won a weak renewal of this race last year – his RPR of 170 was the lowest winning mark for 20 years – and it remains an open division.

Silviniaco Conti tops the ratings after posting RPRs of 178 for wins in the Betfair Chase and King George, hitting a level that matches the ten-year average for Gold Cup winners. If he can run to his mark he will take all the beating.

He has been beaten in the Gold Cup twice before but had excuses then (fell when in contention, stomach ulcers) and the recent addition of cheekpieces seems to have really sharpened him up.

There is a 6lb gap back to leading Irish challenger Road To Riches (172), who posted Grade 1 wins at Down Royal and Leopardstown. The second-season chaser beat a top-notch field in the Lexus and has gone from strength to strength this term. If he can improve again he will not be far away.

Carlingford Lough (169) is another interesting runner from Ireland, having stayed on strongly with another smart second-season chaser, Foxrock (168), to land the Irish Hennessy Gold Cup on his latest start.

Leading 3m novice Coneygree (169) is also in the RSA but if he takes the Gold Cup route he warrants respect. He impressed with his relentless front-running display against seasoned campaigners in the Denman Chase on just his third chase start and that level looks unlikely to be his limit.

Other potential improvers include Holywell (170), who hacked up at Kelso last time, and Many Clouds (169).

CHAMPION HURDLE Faugheen (169) is clear favourite, having made a seamless transition from exceptional novice to high-class second-season hurdler, and the word is there could be more to come.

Certainly his profile suggests that could be the case, as he has improved his RPR with each run and went up another 7lb when he was eased down to win the Christmas Hurdle at Kempton by eight lengths on just his second start of the campaign.

The ten-year average winning RPR for the Champion Hurdle stands at 170, so Faugheen is not that far off, although the average has crept up recently and a slightly higher figure may be required this year.

The last two winners of the race, Hurricane Fly and Jezki, both hit 173 and with that pair in opposition, along with top-notch The New One, Faugheen will probably have to hit a similar standard to win.

The New One (173) could prove the biggest danger to the favourite. He was hampered when Our Conor fell in last year's Champion and still managed to get within three lengths of the winner in third. Factoring in the ground lost, he earned the same RPR (173) as the winner.

He has not hit that standard against lesser opposition this season, although it is hard to be too downbeat about a four-from-four record.

Gold Cup

This year's top rated	RPR
Silviniaco Conti	178
Road To Riches	172
Ma Filleule*	171
Lord Windermere	170
On His Own	170
The Giant Bolster	170
Holywell	170
Coneygree	169
Carlingford Lough	169
Houblon Des Obeaux	169
Many Clouds	169

Includes 7lb mares' allowance

How the past ten winners rated

Year	Winner	Win RPR	Pre-race RPR
2014	Lord Windermere	170	157
2013	Bobs Worth	181	174
2012	Synchronised	173	171
2011	Long Run	181	181
2010	Imperial Commander	182	177
2009	Kauto Star	185	184
2008	Denman	184	183
2007	Kauto Star	175	184
2006	War Of Attrition	173	167
2005	Kicking King	177	177

10yr winning average RPR: 178

Champion Hurdle

This year's top rated	RPR
Jezki	173
The New One	173
Annie Power*	171
Hurricane Fly	170
Faugheen	169
Arctic Fire	165
Diakali	165
Purple Bay	160
Zamdy Man	159
Irving	157

Includes 7lb mares' allowance

How the past ten winners rated

Year	Winner	Win RPR	Pre-race RPR
2014	Jezki	173	167
2013	Hurricane Fly	173	173
2012	Rock On Ruby	171	166
2011	Hurricane Fly	171	169
2010	Binocular	172	172
2009	Punjabi	165	164
2008	Katchit	165	162
2007	Sublimity	167	148
2006	Brave Inca	171	170
2005	Hardy Eustace	168	170

10yr winning average RPR: 170

How the past ten winners rated

Year	Winner	Win RPR	Pre-race RPR
2014	Sire De Grugy	173	174
2013	Sprinter Sacre	190	178
2012	Finian's Rainbow	175	167
2011	Sizing Europe	176	166
2010	Big Zeb	172	171
2009	Master Minded	169	186
2008	Master Minded	186	168
2007	Voy Por Ustedes	167	167
2006	Newmill	172	155
2005	Moscow Flyer	182	181

10yr winning average RPR: 176

Includes 7lb mares' allowance

How the past ten winners rated

Year	Winner	Win RPR	Pre-race RPR
2014	More Of That	172	161
2013	Solwhit	166	165
2012	Big Buck's	170	175
2011	Big Buck's	162	176
2010	Big Buck's	174	176
2009	Big Buck's	176	166
2008	Inglis Drever	174	170
2007	Inglis Drever	169	167
2006	My Way De Solzen	166	159
2005	Inglis Drever	167	165

10yr winning average RPR: 170

He earned RPRs ranging from 157 to 164 for those wins, so he will have to improve, but he may do just that back at Cheltenham.

Jezki (173) and Hurricane Fly (170) have had their own private battle in small-field Grade 1s in Ireland this season and the evergreen Hurricane Fly has been winning.

The old boy has lost only once since 2009 in Ireland, but the stronger pace at the festival requires a different style of racing and last year he could finish only fourth in the Champion Hurdle.

At the age of 11 a third Champion win against this strong field seems unlikely but a place could well be on the cards.

Jezki can be excused all three recent defeats on account of the steady pace. He also made a mistake at the final flight in the Irish Champion last time, which saw him lose significant ground. In last season's Champion Hurdle off a stronger pace he defeated Hurricane Fly and he can be expected to post a season's best rating at Cheltenham.

CHAMPION CHASE This race hangs on how much ability the 2013 winner Sprinter Sacre retains. At his best he was a 190 performer, but a lot has happened since then (heart irregularity, year off) and he seems unlikely ever to reach those dizzying heights again.

He did nothing wrong on his comeback run behind Dodging Bullets, where he jumped and travelled well before failing to pick up in the straight and posting an RPR of 171. With that under his belt he could easily get closer to the typical race-winning standard of 176. If Sprinter Sacre fails to improve, however, this race could really open up.

Sire De Grugy won the race with an RPR of 173 last year, but he arrived in roaring form and does not look so appealing this time. He made a couple of mistakes and looked held when unseating Jamie Moore at Newbury on his return from a long absence, which left his current level of form in doubt.

The best runner on this season's form is Dodging Bullets (174), who has improved throughout the campaign and took the scalp of Sprinter Sacre in January. The problem with him is that he has failed to make the frame in three starts at the festival.

The 'now' horse could be Mr Mole (171). Of course he is vulnerable if one of the big guns manages to fire and it is worrying that he was slow to jump off when the tapes went up at Newbury last time, but it is hard to fault what he achieved in hacking up that day. He is a fast jumper and things might just fall right for him.

WORLD HURDLE This race could produce an upset. Last year's winner More Of That (172) sets the standard on RPRs, but after suffering a 25-length defeat on his only start this season, and later a broken blood vessel at home, there is no guarantee he will get there at his best, if at all.

With RPR second-best Annie Power (171) also having been on the sidelines (and more likely heading to the Mares' Hurdle) it could pay to look beyond the top of the market.

Ten-year-old veterans Reve De Sivola (165) and Rock On Ruby (165) are still banging out big performances, but they are both operating just below the standard required to win a typical World Hurdle and improvement looks unlikely given their advancing years.

It could be a race for each-way players and Whisper (159), who won the Coral Cup last year and followed up with a Grade 1 win at Aintree, looks interesting as a potential improver. He has not run over hurdles this season, but his figures have risen gradually throughout his career and a personal-best could be on the cards.

Saphir Du Rheu (162) beat Whisper the last time they met (February 2014) and he looked strong when winning the Cleeve Hurdle in January. He is still just a six-year-old and there could be more to come.

Ireland's leading hope is Lieutenant Colonel (159), who is two from two over hurdles this season, with both wins coming at Grade 1 level. He has not been asked to go a sustained gallop yet this season and there is every chance of further improvement when he is.

RYANAIR CHASE The complexion of this race changed in early February when two of the leading players, Dynaste and Al Ferof, were ruled out. Don Cossack (169) currently tops the market and it is easy to see why, as he has not put a foot wrong this season, winning four from four at distances from 2m4f to 2m7f.

The average winning mark for the Ryanair over the last five years stands at just over 170, which leaves Don Cossack a bit more to find and there is a niggling concern that all his wins this season have been in small fields.

The one to take him on could be Champagne Fever (167), who would have finished very close to Don Cossack but for a final-fence fall at Thurles in January and this time the rematch is at his favourite course.

Champagne Fever landed the Champion Bumper in 2012, the Supreme Novices' Hurdle in 2013 and finished a close second in the Arkle last year. At twice the price of Don Cossack, he has to be worth a second look.

The in-form Balder Succes (169) is entitled to make the frame judged on his Grade 1 win at Ascot last time.

Ryanair Chase	
This year's top rated	RPR
Menorah	174
Ma Filleule*	171
Wishfull Thinking	170
Balder Succes	169
Carlingford Lough	169
Don Cossack	169
Champagne Fever	167
Cue Card	167
Twinlight	166
Module	166
Wonderful Charm	166
Eduard	166
Uxizandre	166

Includes 7lb mares' allowance

10yr winning average RPR: 167

Don Cossack: in good form this season but still has a bit to find on Racing Post Ratings

Arkle Chase

This year's top rated	RPR
Un De Sceaux	171
Ptit Zig	165
Vibrato Valtat	164
God's Own	160
Gitane Du Berlais*	160
Gilgamboa	156
Three Kingdoms	155
Apache Stronghold	155
Dunraven Storm	153
Top Gamble	153
Josses Hill	153
Vautour	153
Melodic Rendezvous	153

Includes 7lb mares' allowance

10yr winning average RPR: 165

RSA Chase

This year's top rated	RPR
Coneygree	169
Ptit Zig	165
Gitane Du Berlais*	162
Valseur Lido	158
Irish Saint	157
If In Doubt	157
Kings Palace	156
Apache Stronghold	155
The Young Master	155
Southfield Theatre	154
Don Poli	154

Includes 9lb age/ mares' allowance

10yr winning average RPR: 161

NOVICE CHASES Un De Sceaux stands out like a giraffe in the Arkle Chase. With a peak RPR of 171 he is set to become the joint highest-rated novice chaser, alongside Sprinter Sacre, to run at the festival. He demolished a small but select field in a Grade 1 at Leopardstown and if he reproduces that class in the pressure cooker at Cheltenham he will win.

Vibrato Valtat (164) ranks clear second best for the Arkle. He has been progressing throughout the season and looked a class act when sauntering to victory in the Grade 2 Kingmaker in February.

There is every chance of more to come but quite simply he may be up against a monster. He is of interest in the betting without the favourite market, or as number two in the forecast.

The three-mile novice chase division has another standout in the form of Coneygree (169), who is also engaged in the Gold Cup. If he lines up for the RSA he should win, as he is already rated higher than any of the last ten winners. If he goes to the Gold Cup, the RSA could really open up.

A lot of the leading players may yet divert to the JLT Novices' Chase, but Kings Palace (156) and The Young Master (155) are likely to take in the longer race and could set the standard without Coneygree.

Ptit Zig (165) looks the pick in the JLT. Although he fell at Ascot last time, his earlier form has worked out well. His peak RPR already ranks him up with past winners of the race.

The biggest danger could be Gitane Du Berlais (153), who ranks as the leading Irish challenger for the staying novice chases once you factor in her age and sex allowances.

Don Poli (154) is favourite for the RSA Chase, but his price is a

Gitane Du Berlais (beating Irish Saint at Sandown): leading Irish challenger for the staying novice chases once her age and sex allowances are factored in

reflection of Willie Mullins' record at the meeting rather than his own achievements. Equally interesting Irish challengers in the longer races include Apache Stronghold (155) and Valseur Lido (158), who finished first and second in a Grade 1 at Leopardstown in February.

NOVICE HURDLES Willie Mullins will be hoping Douvan (149) can get his bandwagon rolling in the Supreme Novices' Hurdle, but the five-year-old's short price seems more to do with his potential and connections than what he has achieved on the track.

The form of his two wins in Ireland, including a Grade 2 victory over Alpha Des Obeaux (139), is sound enough, but based purely on those runs he should not be 2-1 or less.

L'Ami Serge (152) tops the ratings for the Supreme after impressive wins at Newbury, Ascot and Sandown. He has already achieved an RPR close to the ten-year winning average of 154 and there is still room for improvement from Nicky Henderson's five-year-old.

At bigger odds Seedling (144) could be of interest. He has won all three starts this season and his Cheltenham success over Some Plan in December has worked out well.

In the Neptune and Albert Barlett it is always difficult to pin down which horses will be going for which races. Winners of those races generally require an RPR of at least 153.

Nichols Canyon (150) leads the ever-powerful Mullins raiding party in the staying novice races. He ran out a convincing winner of a strong renewal of the Deloitte Hurdle at Leopardstown, which has been won in recent years by Champagne Fever and Vautour en route to Cheltenham success.

Supreme Novices'

This year's top rated	RPR
L'Ami Serge	152
Jollyallan	151
Nichols Canyon	150
Douvan	149
Shaneshill	148
Morning Run*	148
Parlour Games	148
Windsor Park	147
Sempre Medici	146
Tell Us More	145

*Includes 7lb mares' allowance

10yr winning average RPR: 154

Neptune Novices'

This year's top rated	RPR
L'Ami Serge	152
Nichols Canyon	150
No More Heroes	150
Vyta Du Roc	148
Shaneshill	148
Morning Run*	148
Parlour Games	148
Windsor Park	147
Sempre Medici	146
Caracci Apache	146
Tea For Two**	146

*Includes 7lb mares' allowance
**Rider unable to claim 7lb allowance

10yr winning average RPR: 154

Tea For Two (right): highest-rated staying novice hurdler but rider Lizzie Kelly is unable to claim 7lb in a Grade 1 race

Triumph Hurdle	
This year's top rated	**RPR**
Peace And Co	145
Fiscal Focus	144
Kalkir	144
Bristol De Mai	144
Petite Parisienne*	143
Hargam	142
Bivouac	138
Karezak	137
Top Notch	137
Dicosimo	136
Includes 7lb mares' allowance	
10yr winning average RPR: 151	

Nichols Canyon had a rating of 113+ over staying trips on the Flat and has won all three of his completed starts over hurdles, so there is obvious room for further improvement.

Windsor Park (147) was held up and stayed on for an encouraging second in the Deloitte. He could run into the frame in one of the Cheltenham contests at a slightly bigger price.

No More Heroes (150) is another of the leading Irish challengers and has shaped as if he will improve for a strong pace over 3m, making him an obvious candidate for the Albert Bartlett. You can ignore his defeat at Leopardstown in January, as he scoped dirty afterwards. He beat leading Neptune hope Shaneshill (148) on his previous start, which puts him near the top of the Irish pecking order.

British hopes in the longer novice races are headed by proven Grade 1 winner Parlour Games (148) and Nicky Henderson's less exposed Kilcrea Vale (144), who romped in at Market Rasen on his hurdling bow.

The highest-rated staying novice in Britain and Ireland is Tea For Two (153), but he will be at a 7lb disadvantage as in Grade 1 company his regular rider, Lizzie Kelly, will not be able to utilise the 7lb allowance she has been claiming all year, effectively putting him on 146.

Peace And Co (145) sets a good standard in the Triumph Hurdle, where his chief dangers could be the Mullins pair Petite Parisienne (143) and Kalkir (144), who finished first and second in the Spring Juvenile Hurdle at Leopardstown.

Dicosimo (136) is a bit of an unknown quantity from the Mullins camp but impressed on his Irish debut at Gowran in January.

The Special One

Dave Edwards (Topspeed) says The New One can topple Faugheen in the Champion Hurdle

CHAMPION HURDLE Nine Champion Hurdle winners in the past decade went to post with a pre-race Topspeed rating in excess of 150, but hot favourite Faugheen fails that time test with a best of 141 and has to be opposed.

Supporters will point to his unblemished record in seven runs over hurdles, including victory in the Neptune Novices' Hurdle at last year's festival. Neptune winners have a fine record in the following year's Champion and it has to be said that the ease of Faugheen's successes means he has not been pushed to fast times.

Assuming there is no hanging about, his jumping will come under more scrutiny in the Champion and he could be vulnerable. Alternatively, of course, he could be waiting for a strongly run race to show his true class, but the evidence of the clock at this stage makes him a short-priced favourite to take on.

Last year's winner Jezki has been beaten three times by evergreen Hurricane Fly this term but he got it right on the day last year and his two best speed figures have been earned on the first day of the festival.

The New One was a workmanlike winner at Haydock in January but changes to the course make time evaluation of that effort impractical. He was two seconds quicker than the smart novice Aso over course and distance on the same day, but given the relative merits of the pair that was to be expected.

Last year The New One lost both ground and momentum when Our Conor came to grief and, although TurfTrax data revealed he covered the climb to the line from the last faster than any other hurdler that day, he came up short. Overall he boasts an excellent Cheltenham record and is strongly fancied.

GOLD CUP Last year's race was a messy affair and it does not look a great deal clearer this time, with question marks over each of the main protagonists.

Eight winners in the past ten years had a pre-race Topspeed best above 150, with six of them 160-plus. In the race itself 170-plus was recorded by three winners and another four had a figure in excess of 150. Last year's winner Lord Windermere had low figures both before and in the race, reflecting the below-par standard of the 2014 edition.

Silviniaco Conti has won the Betfair Chase and King George decisively this season but Cheltenham has not been a happy hunting ground for him. He fell three out when in contention two years ago and last year he wandered around on the run-in and faded into fourth.

Apparently gastric ulcers contributed to that defeat and now the problem has been resolved he looks a class act but the Gold Cup trip, particularly if the race is run at a strong gallop, may find him out again.

The Giant Bolster has finished second, fourth and third in the last three renewals and clearly the race brings out the best in him.

Champion Hurdle

Topspeed figures	Career best	Season best
Hurricane Fly	161	142
Jezki	160	142
The New One	156	128
Annie Power*	146	76
Irving	143	143
Vaniteux	142	132
Garde La Victoire	142	142
Faugheen	141	141
Arctic Fire	140	140
Purple Bay	140	140

*Includes 7lb mares' allowance

How the past ten winners rated

Year	Winner	Win TS	Pre-race TS
2014	Jezki	160	151
2013	Hurricane Fly	135	161
2012	Rock On Ruby	167	160
2011	Hurricane Fly	149	153
2010	Binocular	163	158
2009	Punjabi	155	160
2008	Katchit	157	157
2007	Sublimity	145	139
2006	Brave Inca	173	151
2005	Hardy Eustace	152	155

Gold Cup

Topspeed figures	Career best	Season best
Bobs Worth	164	8
The Giant Bolster	162	96
Ma Filleule*	159	125
First Lieutenant	157	138
Silviniaco Conti	157	148
Coneygree	152	152
Houblon Des Obeaux	149	149
Road To Riches	149	149
Champagne Fever	149	142

*Includes 7lb mares' allowance

How the past ten winners rated

Year	Winner	Win TS	Pre-race TS
2014	Lord Windermere	144	123
2013	Bobs Worth	144	164
2012	Synchronised	164	151
2011	Long Run	157	163
2010	Imperial Commander	180	173
2009	Kauto Star	172	176
2008	Denman	178	157
2007	Kauto Star	144	168
2006	War Of Attrition	153	133
2005	Kicking King	158	160

Dodging Bullets: heads this season's Topspeed ratings in Champion Chase

Champion Chase

Topspeed figures	Career best	Season best
Sizing Europe	166	137
Sprinter Sacre	165	156
Somersby	165	142
Dodging Bullets	159	159
Finian's Rainbow	159	-
Sire De Grugy	158	-
Hidden Cyclone	157	144
Balder Succes	153	153
Special Tiara	150	150
Twinlight	150	150

How the past ten winners rated

Year	Winner	Win TS	Pre-race TS
2014	Sire De Grugy	152	158
2013	Sprinter Sacre	153	165
2012	Finian's Rainbow	159	154
2011	Sizing Europe	146	166
2010	Big Zeb	168	159
2009	Master Minded	161	185
2008	Master Minded	185	143
2007	Voy Por Ustedes	159	160
2006	Newmill	163	155
2005	Moscow Flyer	145	177

Exciting novice Coneygree threw his hat into the ring with a clear-cut Newbury success against seasoned campaigners. After a season of pedestrian races his exhilarating front-running display was a breath of fresh air and his time, only six seconds slower than the 3m benchmark on officially soft ground, was remarkable. His presence would add a new dimension to the race as he will ensure there is no hanging about.

Irish raider Road To Riches looks progressive but a Topspeed best of 149 leaves him with a bit to find and it will be interesting to see how he fares on his first trip to Cheltenham, having won a slowly run Lexus at Leopardstown in December.

Despite the trials and tribulations Bobs Worth could be a value wager, although it needs a leap of faith to take the plunge.

Prior to last season's lacklustre effort the 2013 Gold Cup winner boasted an unblemished Cheltenham record and festival form tends to be worth its weight in gold. He finished last of eight in the Lexus but the ground was against him and he was beaten only just over a dozen lengths in a muddling contest.

CHAMPION CHASE Nine winners in the past decade had a pre-race rating of at least 154 and plenty of this year's principals have reached that mark, but this revolves around Sprinter Sacre – if the real one turns up, the rest may as well stay at home. Admittedly it's a big 'if' but his scintillating festival successes in the 2012 Arkle and the 2013 Champion Chase left an indelible impression and his Topspeed figures of 165 and 153 were excellent given the decisive nature of those victories.

When he returned from his lengthy absence at Ascot in January, there was plenty to like about his effort in the circumstances. On ground softer than ideal, his rivals made it a real test – as Sprinter Sacre's Topspeed rating of 156 confirms – and unsurprisingly he tired in the closing stages behind Dodging Bullets. Some were unconvinced but time-wise there were far more positives than negatives.

Sire De Grugy won six from seven last season and his timeline mirrored his progressive profile, but he is another who has had problems.

The fly in the ointment could be Dodging Bullets, who has been a revelation this season. Last year's Arkle fourth has had his breathing issues resolved and the assistance of a tongue tie has seen him make giant strides. He recorded a personal best when defeating Sprinter Sacre but overall on the clock he still has a bit to find. Everything was in his favour at Ascot but it could be a different ball game at Cheltenham.

WORLD HURDLE Although this race is run over three miles and billed as a test of stamina, the speed ratings are invariably well below what might be expected in a championship race. When Solwhit, best known for his efforts around two miles, won the race two years ago it was 'run' at a crawl and his finishing speed proved decisive.

If this year's renewal is moderately paced it could favour Rock On Ruby, who has yet to run over three miles. Admittedly his Topspeed of 167 was earned when he won the 2012 Champion Hurdle but he gave The New One a fright over 2m4f at Aintree in April and has won twice over half a furlong further at Cheltenham this term, albeit in moderately paced events.

Back in 2011 Rock On Ruby beat all bar First Lieutenant in the Neptune (2m5f) and is a stronger, more mature performer now. Testing ground would be a worry but if the race unfolds at its customary modest pace and only warms up on the second circuit he could stalk the opposition before pouncing on the climb to the line. If he is successful he would be the first Champion Hurdle winner to add the World Hurdle since 1959.

Paul Nicholls' pair Zarkandar and Saphir Du Rheu, the Cleeve Hurdle winner, look the pick of the rest.

RYANAIR CHASE The final line-up is difficult to predict but 2013 winner Cue Card can only go for this race as he does not have another festival entry. Although he has been below par this season, his overall Cheltenham timeline makes good reading and he could bounce back. Balder Succes *(below left)*, a wide-margin Kempton winner in January and successful at Ascot a month later, merits respect. Effective at the minimum trip, he has won all four chase starts over 2m3½f-plus.

World Hurdle

Topspeed figures	Career best	Season best
Rock On Ruby	167	141
Zarkandar	159	106
Reve De Sivola	152	150
Zaidpour	152	84
Saphir Du Rheu	147	147
Annie Power*	146	83
Jetson	141	119
Un Temps Pour Tout	141	141
Beat That	138	-
More Of That	135	119

Includes 7lb mares' allowance

How the past ten winners rated

Year	Winner	Win TS	Pre-race TS
2014	More Of That	135	118
2013	Solwhit	31	167
2012	Big Buck's	161	154
2011	Big Buck's	119	147
2010	Big Buck's	139	147
2009	Big Buck's	131	147
2008	Inglis Drever	175	162
2007	Inglis Drever	141	162
2006	My Way De Solzen	145	122
2005	Inglis Drever	148	162

Ryanair Chase

Topspeed figures	Career best	Season best
Ma Filleule*	159	125
Hidden Cyclone	157	144
First Lieutenant	157	142
Cue Card	156	144
Rajdhani Express	154	110
Balder Succes	153	153
Hunt Ball	153	-
Twinlight	150	150
Eduard	149	149

Includes 7lb mares' allowance

L'Ami Serge: better figures than Supreme favourite Douvan

ARKLE CHASE A Topspeed figure around 150 is the usual requirement and, with five entrants separated by just a point, this may be more open than the betting suggests. Hot favourite Un De Sceaux is among that quintet but supporting odds-on chasers in such a high-quality contest is not for the fainthearted. The old adage "never be afraid of one horse" springs to mind and Three Kingdoms is a viable alternative. John Ferguson's six-year-old has not done much wrong, with three wins from four chase runs, and has proved he can jump clinically at speed.

RSA CHASE Coneygree looks head and shoulders above the rest if he lines up here rather than in the Gold Cup. Unlike many of his rivals, jumping fluently at a fierce pace will not faze him and his forcing tactics could unsettle those who have been mollycoddled in slow, small-field races. Interesting at a big price is Carole's Destrier, who gained valuable experience when fourth on Cheltenham's Trials Day in January and emerged the 'best' horse in the race at the weights. He has since won at Ascot.

SUPREME NOVICES' HURDLE Market leader Douvan is conspicuous by his absence from the upper end of the Topspeed ratings, as a figure of just 106 tells its own tale. He has had plenty of hype but his three wins have been in single-figure fields and the festival opener may prove a shock to the system, with the last ten winners having needed to produce at least 140 on the day. Best of the home team may be L'Ami Serge, who earned decent figures when completing a hat-trick at Sandown in January.

NEPTUNE NOVICES' HURDLE A pre-race rating of 142 for Tea For Two is more than enough to fulfil the normal time requirements for the race and he sets a formidable standard despite defeat at Ascot last time. Nick Williams' six-year-old clocked a standout time and exploited a favourable handicap mark when routing his Kempton rivals in January and, while this will be tougher, he had tons left in the locker. Soft ground brings out the best in him.

Bred for success

Tom Pennington of the Racing Post bloodstock team picks out big-race pedigree pointers

CHAMPION HURDLE Tuesday's main event looks set to be the race of the week, as it has been for the past couple of years. Faugheen, last year's Neptune winner, is a short price but looks banker material. He is one of three festival winners for his late sire Germany, the others being Captain Cee Bee (Supreme Novices' Hurdle) and Tiger Cry (Grand Annual Chase), who were both at their best over two miles.

The New One is the main danger and will be trying to bolster his sire King's Theatre's strong festival record. The late son of Sadler's Wells had two winners last year – Balthazar King (Cross Country) and Fingal Bay (Pertemps Final). Jezki (by stamina influence Milan) may need a step up in trip as he gets older and could be done for speed.

Advice Faugheen win

CHAMPION CHASE With the most recent winners Sprinter Sacre and Sire De Grugy still to prove themselves after injury setbacks, Wednesday's feature race looks more open than usual.

The Frankie Dettori-bred Dodging Bullets looks vastly improved this season but his sire Dubawi is yet to have a festival winner, albeit from only a handful of runners.

Champagne Fever, a dual festival winner, and Hidden Cyclone look good value. Both are sons of Stowaway and they went close at last year's meeting, with Champagne Fever losing out by a head in the Arkle Chase and Hidden Cyclone finishing second in the Ryanair Chase.

The drop in trip should suit both, as Stowaway's offspring do not appear devoid of speed.

Advice Champagne Fever win, Hidden Cyclone each-way

GOLD CUP Silviniaco Conti is the form horse in this year's race, following impressive wins in the Betfair Chase and King George VI Chase. However, he didn't appear to get up the hill last year and his sire Dom Alco has sired only one festival winner (Al Ferof in the Supreme Novices' Hurdle over two miles).

It could be worth siding with the Willie Mullins-trained pair Djakadam and Boston Bob. Djakadam put a poor effort in the Hennessy behind him with an impressive victory in the Thyestes Chase. His sire Saint Des Saints had a festival winner last year with Salut Flo (Stable Plate) and is a proven source of three-mile chasers, the list headed by dual Grade 1 winner Quito De La Roque and 2013 RSA Chase runner-up Lyreen Legend.

Boston Bob is a son of the late Bob Back, who has a fine festival record with a winners-to-runners ratio of nine per cent. His recent winners include 2013 Gold Cup winner Bobs Worth and the same year's National Hunt Chase scorer Back In Focus, who both excelled for the test of stamina that Cheltenham provides.

Advice Boston Bob and Djakadam each-way

Sire watch

Oscar progeny excel on good ground

It would have been worth siding with Coolmore stalwart Oscar at last year's festival as he provided two winners – Lord Windermere (Gold Cup) and O'Faolains Boy (RSA Chase).

Oscar gets runners who perform at both ends of the distance spectrum and there is no doubt his offspring improve for the better ground at Cheltenham in March. It is worth considering all his runners if good appears in the going description and a standout is **Rock On Ruby** (World Hurdle).

Runners by Poliglote had been knocking on the door at Cheltenham in recent years, with Spirit Son and Far West both finishing second in Grade 1 races, and the sire broke his festival duck last year with Martin Pipe Handicap Hurdle winner **Don Poli**, who looks tailor-made for the RSA Chase. The French sire is also responsible for Nicky Henderson's smart juvenile **Top Notch**, who could go one better than Far West in the Triumph Hurdle.

Progeny by Milan are worth following at the festival, especially over longer trips, and **Apache Stronghold** (JLT Novices' Chase) and **Beat That** (*below*, World Hurdle) could outrun their prices.

Inside the stables

Willie Mullins and Paul Nicholls discuss their main hopes, plus an in-depth look at the challengers from Ireland and the major British training centres

Hot favourites

Willie Mullins has a host of market leaders and here he discusses his main contenders

Annie Power Mares' Hurdle She had a setback which has kept her off the track this season. We're happy with her progress and very hopeful she'll make the festival. She was a good second in the World Hurdle last year – it was the only time she's been beaten – and we're keeping our options open, but the Mares' Hurdle is a Grade 1 this year and that race has been the plan all along. It would be great if she could follow on from Quevega's historic achievement in winning the race six times.

Black Hercules Albert Bartlett It looks the obvious race for him as he appears to be a real staying type. He won a couple of bumpers last season and has done everything right over hurdles, winning both his starts including a three-mile Grade 3 at Cork in December.

Boston Bob Gold Cup He came good last spring when he won a Grade 1 at Aintree before following up in the Punchestown Gold Cup. He was disappointing in the Hennessy at Leopardstown last time but he'll take his chance in the Gold Cup and will appreciate better ground if he gets it. He's better than his recent runs suggest.

Champagne Fever Champion/Ryanair Chase His festival record is very good and he was only just touched off in the Arkle a year ago. He appeared not to stay in the King George but was none the worse for his last-fence fall at Thurles in January when he was vying for the lead with the much-improved Don Cossack. He had a nice confidence-builder at Gowran and we'll decide nearer the time which race to go for.

Dicosimo Triumph He won over hurdles in France before we got him and, although he fluffed a few hurdles on his debut for us at Gowran Park in January, he made all and won well, going away at the finish. He'll have learned from the experience and should represent us well.

Djakadam Gold Cup We thought at the start of the season that he might become a Gold Cup contender and his performance in the Thyestes Chase in January, when he defied a big weight and won by eight lengths, confirmed that impression. He needs to improve and hopefully he will, as he's had only the two runs this season. He's only six, though, and it's possible he might be more of a Gold Cup horse next year.

Don Poli RSA/National Hunt Chase He won the Martin Pipe over hurdles at the festival last year and has taken very well to fences. He jumps well and stays very well. He won a Grade 1 over three miles at Leopardstown in December and we have the RSA Chase as an option, but I've had the four-miler in mind for him all along.

Douvan Supreme He's won both his races for us and does everything, at home and on the track, very easily. They tried to get him off the bridle in a Grade 2 at Punchestown in January but he toyed with them. He jumps and travels so well and I don't think ground conditions matter

30 day FREE trial

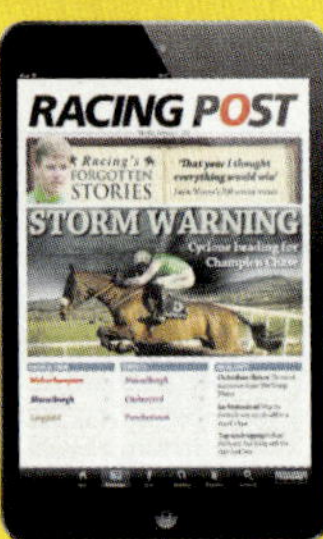

Racing Post iPad app

The journey to Cheltenham goes fast so don't hang about. Start your 30-day free trial now and receive the next 30 newspapers delivered straight to your iPad.

Available on the App Store

RACING POST
Your Cheltenham guide

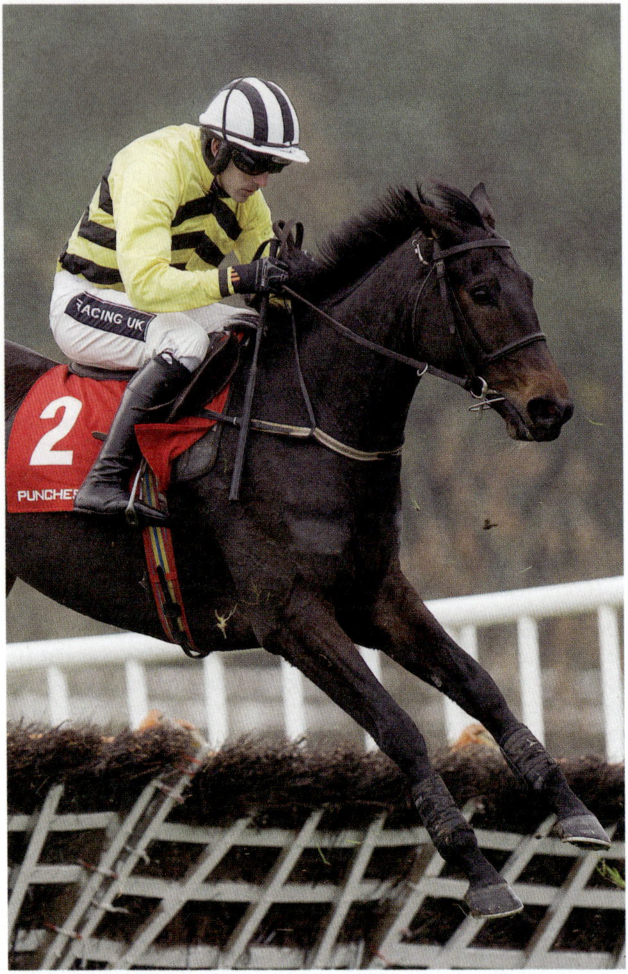

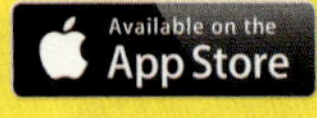

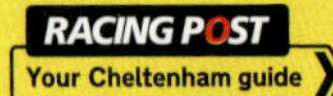

Glens Melody: should go well in the Mares' Hurdle again

to him. He's exciting. Vautour won the same Punchestown race last year and went on to win the Supreme.

Faugheen Champion Hurdle A year ago when he won the Neptune at the festival we weren't anticipating Faugheen being a Champion Hurdle contender, never mind a short-priced favourite for the race. But he's been a revelation this season and will carry an unbeaten record into the race. It'll be his biggest test to date as he hasn't taken on Hurricane Fly, Jezki and The New One before, so it's going to tell us a lot and whether he's the real deal.

Glens Melody Mares' Hurdle She ran a cracking race in the race last year when running Quevega to three-quarters of a length and came back

RESULTS
DIRECT TO YOUR PHONE
WITH PADDY POWER MESSENGER

RESULTS THAT YOU WANT TO SEE...

...AND WINNING BET ALERTS

DOWNLOAD THE APP NOW
SEARCH PP MESSENGER IN THE APP STORE

NEW PADDY POWER CUSTOMERS ONLY

BET £10, GET A FREE £20 BET
WHEN YOU REGISTER ON THE APP NOW!

PADDYPOWER.

CALL 0800 904 7933

gambleaware.co.uk   18+

Free bet available to new Paddy Power customers only. One free bet per customer & max £20. Prices displayed are for demonstration purposes only. T&C's apply.

Vital statistics

The festival by numbers

The last four top-rated runners in the National Hunt Chase have finished 1112 for an £11.25 profit to a £1 level stake

9

Of the last 14 Supreme winners have been Irish-trained, including last year's winner Vautour (below)

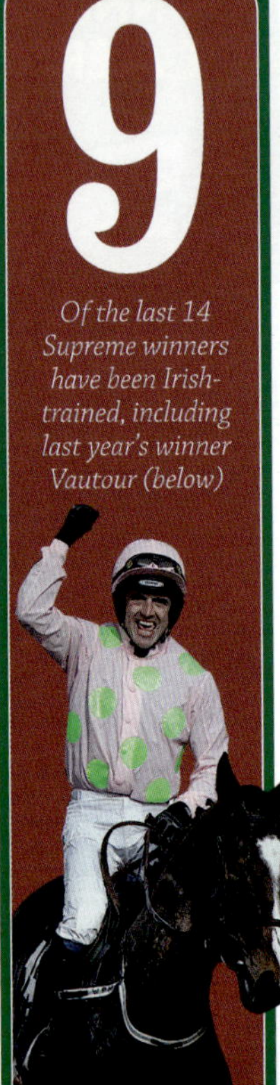

Willie Mullins has had 15 favourites in Grade 1 races at the past five festivals, with four winning (for a level-stake loss)

Nichols Canyon: longer trip in Neptune should suit him

to form on her most recent start when winning well at Warwick. She deserves another tilt at the race and hopefully she'll run in the money.

Hurricane Fly Champion Hurdle What more can be said about him? He's our hero and, while the stats might be against him at the age of 11, he hasn't shown any sign, at home or on the track, that he's in decline. It would be fantastic if he could win the title for the third time and nobody can question his right to have another crack at the race.

Kalkir Triumph He's tough and consistent and has been placed at Grade 2 and Grade 1 level since winning a Grade 3 at Fairyhouse by eight lengths. He jumps well and stays well and you'd imagine the track will suit him, so he'll go there with a fighting chance.

McKinley Albert Bartlett He's done well this season, winning four times and landing a Grade 1 over two and a half miles at Naas. He didn't run to his best in the Deloitte Hurdle last time and the trip might have been on the short side for him. He's in all three novice hurdles and I'm not sure which he'll run in, but he seems to stay well.

Nichols Canyon Neptune He's won a couple of Grade 1s and was probably unlucky not to have won another one at Leopardstown in December when he blundered and unseated early on. He did it the hard way when winning the Deloitte Hurdle last time, making the running.

Free bet available to new Paddy Power customers only. One free bet per customer & max £20. Prices displayed are for demonstration purposes only. T&C's apply.

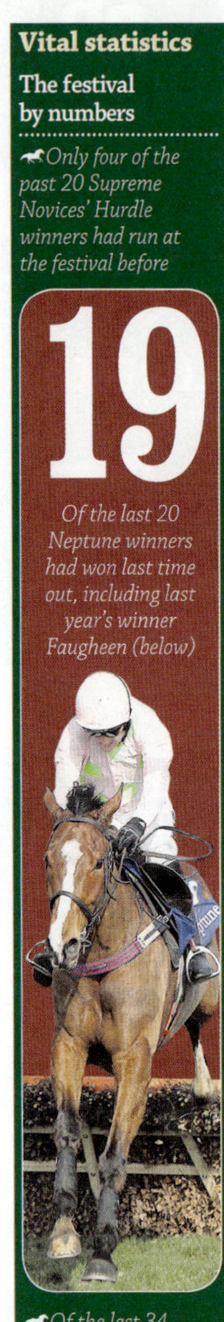

He'll be going up in distance but his performance in the Deloitte and the fact he was a smart stayer on the Flat suggest the longer trip won't be an issue.

On His Own Gold Cup He was unlucky to be touched off in the race last year and we were delighted with his run in the Lexus Chase at Christmas when he finished a good second. However, we were disappointed with him in the Hennessy where he dropped away after making most of the running. He'll take his chance but will need to come back to last year's form.

Outlander Neptune We had high hopes for him after he won three bumpers two seasons ago but he was off the track for a long time and it was really only when he won a Grade 2 at Leopardstown in January that we saw him display the sort of ability we knew he had. He has other options but the Neptune looks the most obvious target.

Petite Parisienne Triumph She was a bit unlucky on her hurdling debut at Punchestown when the winner got first run on her but the decision to go straight for a Grade 1 at Leopardstown paid off well. She won nicely and earned her Triumph ticket. The fillies' allowance will be a big help again.

Hurricane Fly: no sign of decline, at home or on the track, as he tries to regain the Champion Hurdle for a second time

Un De Sceaux Arkle He's a really exciting, fast novice who races from the front and bowls along at a really good tempo. His performance when winning the Irish version of the Arkle at Leopardstown was hugely impressive. He jumped really well and found plenty when asked to go away from two very useful rivals. Better ground shouldn't be a problem and he'll be going there with a serious chance.

Valseur Lido RSA/JLT Novices' Chase He was impressive in the Grade 1 Drinmore Chase at Fairyhouse in November when he won by eight lengths but he lost out by half a length to the Drinmore runner-up, Apache Stronghold, when they met again in the Flogas Chase at Leopardstown. It's possible he might have needed the run following his break, although the winner clearly improved a good bit. He's a good horse and should represent us well.

Vautour JLT He was very good in the Supreme Novices' last year but with the exception of his chasing debut win at Navan he hasn't really impressed this season. He wasn't right and made a bad mistake when he disappointed at Leopardstown in December and his jumping wasn't perfect when he won an uncompetitive race there last time. We still think he's seriously good and we're expecting a lot better to come.

Vital statistics
The festival
by numbers

Dorans Pride in 1995 was the last winning favourite in the World Hurdle who had not landed the race before

1

Winning favourite out of 16 for Paul Nicholls at the past five festivals, apart from Big Buck's (below)

Only two Triumph Hurdle winners have followed up in the Champion Hurdle the following year (Persian War in 1968 and Katchit in 2008)

Nicholls facts

🐎 Manor Farm Stables, Ditcheat, Somerset

🐎 British champion trainer 2005-06, 2006-07, 2007-08, 2008-09, 2009-10, 2010-11, 2011-12, 2013-14

🐎 Festival winners: 34 (19 in chases, 15 over hurdles)

🐎 Top festival trainer six times (1999, 2004, 2006, 2007, 2008, 2009)

🐎 Last five festivals (earliest first): 2/3/2/1/1

🐎 Has had at least one winner at each of the past 12 festivals

🐎 Fourteen of his first 17 festival wins came in chases (up to 2007) but 12 of the last 17 have been over hurdles (since 2008)

🐎 Has not had a chase winner since Kauto Star's second Gold Cup in 2009 and has returned a level-stakes loss on all chase runners at the festival for ten years in a row

🐎 His best handicap races are the County Hurdle (four winners) and the Grand Annual Chase (two winners) – both at around two miles

Bullets to fire

Paul Nicholls discusses his leading contenders including Dodging Bullets and Silviniaco Conti

Calipto County Hurdle He ran very well when fourth in the Betfair Hurdle at Newbury recently and should be suited by the way this race is likely to pan out. They'll go a million miles an hour and you need a horse who stays and has a bit of speed.

Caid Du Berlais Stable Plate He seems to run better fresh and wants good ground. The New course, which they use for the first time on the Thursday of the meeting, will suit him well.

Ceasar Milan Novices' Handicap Chase He finished third at Kempton behind Third Intention, who is very good on his day. Hopefully the race will be run to suit him as he does not have to make the running like he did when beating Whisper at Exeter.

Calipto (left): Betfair Hurdle fourth should be suited by the fast pace of the County

Dodging Bullets Champion Chase He's much improved since being sent over fences as he won the Tingle Creek and then beat Sprinter Sacre at Ascot. On the face of that run he deserves to be favourite for the race and should go very close.

Hinterland Champion Chase He was travelling really well in the race upsides Sire De Grugy last year only to be nearly knocked over four out and unshipping Noel Fehily. He needs to be fresh and so we haven't run him since Christmas.

Just A Par Kim Muir Will Biddick will ride and he should run a tidy race at a decent price as Cheltenham suits him well.

Keltus Novices' Handicap Chase We've left him since he was second at Newbury on Hennessy Gold Cup day in November as he seems best fresh and wants decent ground, which has been in short supply for most of the winter.

Mr Mole Champion Chase He has won his last four races – although he is a bit of a character, most of the good horses are. He has almost copied

Vital statistics

The festival by numbers

Non-claiming amateurs have been successful in the Kim Muir Chase eight times in the last ten runnings

77

The current losing sequence of Paul Nicholls-trained chasers at the festival, since the 2009 Gold Cup won by Kauto Star (below)

Just four Neptune winners were sent off bigger than 17-2 in the past 24 years

Just four of the last 18 to start 3-1 or shorter in the Supreme have been successful

Vital statistics

The festival by numbers

Paul Nicholls has had a winner, two runners-up, a third and a fourth from ten runners in the Fred Winter in the past five years

10

Of the last 11 County Hurdle winners were first- or second-season hurdlers, including last year's winner Lac Fontana (below)

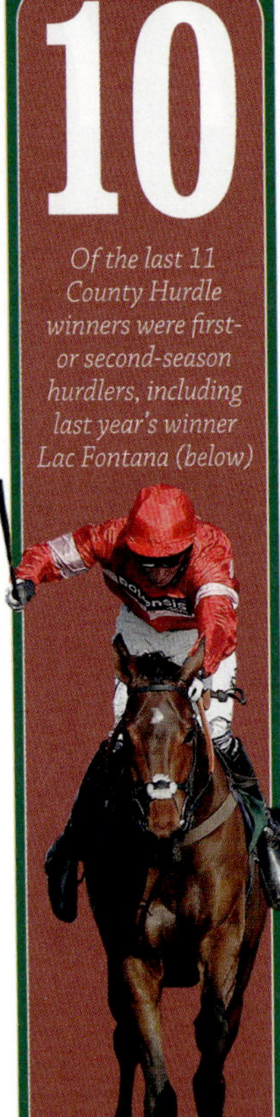

Novices have won four of the last 11 runnings of the Ultima Business Solutions Handicap Chase

Silviniaco Conti winning the King George: more confident in his races since having treatment for gastric ulcers

the route Master Minded took before winning the race and should not be far away where it matters.

Ptit Zig JLT He won his first four chases this term and looks like being the best of the British contenders, so he fully deserves to be second favourite to Vautour. I particularly liked the way he beat Champagne West at Cheltenham. He seems none the worse for his rather novicey fall in the Ascot Chase and the plan is still to go to Cheltenham.

Sam Winner Gold Cup The long and the short of it is he looks a better horse this season and wants better ground, which hopefully he will get on Gold Cup day. He was a good third in the Lexus Chase, which now looks very solid form, and he's one of a number of horses in the line-up who have a really decent chance of making the frame.

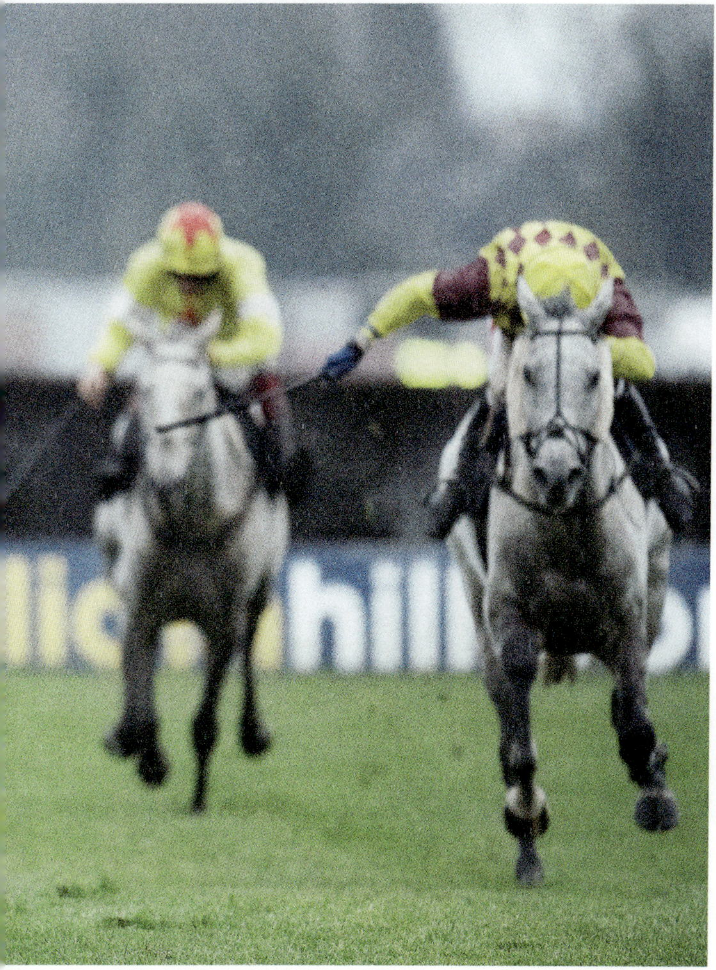

San Benedeto Triumph He might run but we're just as likely to keep him for next season. It must be the first time in about 20 years that we haven't got a number of juveniles to run in the race but it pans out like that sometimes.

Saphir Du Rheu World Hurdle He's improving fast and comes into the race on really good terms with himself. We switched him back to hurdles as his try over fences ended up being patchy. It looks like we might have made the right move as he beat Reve De Sivola at the course at the trials meeting. He has a leading chance.

Silviniaco Conti Gold Cup He jumped the last like the winner 12 months ago but then hung to his left before straightening up to be beaten less than two lengths. He made amends at Aintree when showing how tough

LIVE
CHELTENHAM FESTIVAL
BLOG
racingpost.com
POLLS
VIDEO
NEWS
Stay up to date and follow the Festival action with our top bloggers Tom Kerr and David Jennings.
racingpost.com
Available on mobile, tablet and web.
RACING POST
Your Cheltenham guide

Vital statistics

The festival by numbers

Twelve of the last 14 winners of the Ultima Handicap Chase had finished in the first three last time out (eight had won)

18

Of the last 24 Grand Annual winners had made the first four on their previous start. The 2013 winner Alderwood (below) had finished second on his previous start

Only three RSA Chase winners in the past 23 years have gone to post with fewer than three chase starts

he is by beating Dynaste. We found he might have been suffering from gastric ulcers and since we had that treated he seems more confident in his races. It's third time lucky for him in the Gold Cup, I hope.

Sire Collonges Cross Country He needs to be fresh and wants better ground to be seen at his best. He seems to enjoy the merry-go-round of these races and has an each-way chance.

Solar Impulse Grand Annual He's creeping up the weights and I'll have a good look at the race nearer the time before deciding if he goes for this race or waits until Aintree.

Southfield Theatre RSA This race has been the aim since he was beaten a nostril by Fingal Bay in the Pertemps Hurdle Final last March and I've been very pleased with the way he has taken to fences. The race he won at Exeter last time was on the sharp side for him and he had to bowl along in front, which did not really suit.

Southfield Theatre: RSA Chase has been the aim since last year's near miss in the Pertemps Final

Vibrato Valtat Arkle We knew he was talented but he'd not been finishing his races over hurdles, so we gave him a breathing operation over the summer. He's now typical of a horse who can breathe properly and is very progressive, as he showed when winning so well at Warwick.

Vivaldi Collonges NH Chase We've always had this race in mind for him as he comes from a real staying family. He goes into the race with the same sort of profile as Topsham Bay, who won the race in 1990, and I was heavily involved with that horse in my time with David Barons.

Wonderful Charm Ryanair He didn't stay in the King George. He's a lively outsider here as he needs to be fresh and wants good ground.

Zarkandar World Hurdle He has Grade 1-winning form in the book and we know he stays, so we can ride how we want to. He has purposely been given plenty of time between his races as he's better going into races fresh. He has to be in the mix as he goes on any ground.

Banking on Mullins

Johnny Ward says the Irish challenge is mainly – though not exclusively – about the champion's team

Not so long ago Cheltenham Festival winners came at a trickle for Willie Mullins, a steady enough stream but nothing spectacular. This year there might be a torrent for his Closutton yard, now undoubtedly the strongest in Britain and Ireland.

Mullins was responsible for seven of the ante-post favourites in the first nine races of the festival as the prep races drew to a close in mid-February – a remarkable position considering the powerful battalions massed against him on the other side of the Irish Sea. Having taken a stranglehold on Irish racing in the past decade, he might be on the verge of doing the same at the biggest festival in jump racing.

The Irish challenge is not all about Mullins, but most followers will be looking to him for their bankers of the meeting. The fortunes of the Irish travelling party are now inextricably bound up with how the Mullins team fares.

GOLD CUP Ireland had a one-two last March with Lord Windermere and On His Own, although once again neither of them is that strongly fancied this year even though it looks a fairly open renewal. Apart from that pair, Ireland has realistic chances with Road To Riches, Djakadam, Carlingford Lough and Foxrock.

Road To Riches' Lexus form can be questioned, certainly as On His Own finished runner-up after continually jumping right. However, Road To Riches won readily, could progress again for the new trip and will be a fresh horse come Gold Cup day.

Djakadam follows the route taken by On His Own last year: Gold Cup after carrying top weight to Thyestes victory. Through the fog at Gowran, Djakadam seemed to do pretty much everything right and that performance was a revelation, considering stamina was a question mark after the Hennessy. His age – he's a Gold Cup nipper at six – will put many off.

And what of the Irish Hennessy? People will not store it in their memory because of form rumination – this was all about AP McCoy – but it was encouraging that two sophomore chasers fought out the finish. With Lord Windermere shaping well in third, Carlingford Lough just outstayed Foxrock, whose rate of improvement has been exceptional. The runner-up is not a certainty to go to Cheltenham (at least not for the Gold Cup, as he would have to be supplemented) but both of the first two will have a chance if they make the crossing.

CHAMPION HURDLE It almost seems a given nowadays that Ireland will have serious contenders for the Champion Hurdle. The years that involved Hardy Eustace, Brave Inca, Harchibald and Macs Joy have often been hailed as a golden era for hurdling but one could argue that none was as good as Hurricane Fly, who has won three out of three at Grade 1 level this term but is only fourth favourite for the Champion Hurdle.

Stablemate Faugheen has done nothing but impress this season.

Kitten Rock: interesting Champion Hurdle longshot

Twelve months ago, he was expected to go chasing this term but, perhaps because of the strength of his arsenal, Mullins decided to keep him hurdling. He has been around even-money most of the season to win the Champion Hurdle. Play or lay?

The layers will believe there is reason to take him on: he has won two small-field races as a sophomore hurdler and it is not hard to pick holes in the form. What is eyecatching, however, is that he has improved on Racing Post Ratings on every occasion he has raced. Moreover, he is an easy course winner, only seven years of age, uncomplicated and admirably versatile trip-wise.

Jezki won the race last year but he was all out, with The New One patently unfortunate. Nevertheless, JP McManus's runner has a chance and beware Kitten Rock too. Having slammed Grade 1-winning mare Glens Melody and easily won the Red Mills Trial last time, he looks more than ready to step into truly run combat. He may not be good

enough but he is among the more interesting longshots, with the six-year-old Arctic Fire also worthy of some consideration after pleasing runs at Leopardstown.

CHAMPION CHASE Surely this has the most hazy picture among the big four races, with the true form of Sprinter Sacre and Sire De Grugy far from clear.

The Irish challengers are solid, although it is asking plenty for one of them to win. Pricewise put up Hidden Cyclone, who has good course form, albeit over further, and showed when second to Twinlight at Christmas that he can lie up with a hot two-mile gallop and stay there. His Tied Cottage effort was a career highlight in terms of jumping fluency.

He could well fare better than Champagne Fever, who is shorter in the market. Course form is arguably Champagne Fever's trump card – two wins and a narrow Arkle defeat. He did not stay in the King George before giving Don Cossack a good race in the Kinloch Brae. Two miles looks sharper than ideal but he can jump and has a chance.

WORLD HURDLE More Of That's issues (first with his wind, then a broken blood vessel) have opened up the stayers' hurdle, but even now hope more than confidence will accompany the principal Irish contenders, Lieutenant Colonel and Monksland.

The celebrations will be a sight to behold if Lieutenant Colonel wins

for Sandra Hughes so soon after the death of her father Dessie. She reports the six-year-old to have strengthened nicely since he edged out Jetson at Christmas. That form will hardly suffice at Cheltenham but he is young and progressive.

Monksland has a different profile but, despite being off for two years before his return in that same Leopardstown event, he is only eight. His subsequent Galmoy performance was likeable, even if again that form falls a long way short of what will be required at Cheltenham. Noel Meade insisted the ground was against him but he travelled well and his jumping was absolutely superb off what was a genuine championship pace.

NOVICE CHASES As the major build-up races reached their conclusion in mid-February, Ireland had the favourite for each of the non-handicap novice chases – the Racing Post Arkle, the JLT, the RSA Chase and the National Hunt Chase.

The shortest-priced, of course, is Un De Sceaux at odds-on in the Arkle. Mullins' seven-year-old gets really low at his fences and is exhilarating to watch, although there is still a danger he will get one wrong (remember he fell on his chase debut). As well as the Cheltenham fences, he must also deal with quicker ground than he normally faces and there is a chance he will be taken on up front.

Otherwise, he looks different class to the likes of Josses Hill, whose

Shark Hanlon, trainer of Hidden Cyclone *(Champion Chase)* "The ground drying out [at Punchestown in February] was a big help to him. He jumped great and has a high cruising speed. He'll probably go for the Queen Mother" *Form figures of 1113232F on ground described as yielding or better*

Noel Meade, trainer of Road To Riches *(Gold Cup)* "We changed his whole training regime and diet last spring and he turned inside out from then on. We thought he was a very good horse in bumpers and he's not surprising me now. The Lexus didn't really go to plan, they went very quick up front, and I was thrilled with how he stayed. Going further won't bother him. He's just never stopped improving since we got his diet right" *Form figures of 121211 since last April, with RPR rising from 149 to 172*

What they say

'He gave me the feel of a good one'

Bryan Cooper, rider of Very Wood (*NH Chase*) "He gave me the feel of a good one [at Navan last time]. He got into a lovely rhythm and was jumping great. He'd be some ride in the four-miler [National Hunt Chase] if he went that way" *Won last year's Albert Bartlett on only previous run at Cheltenham*

Barry Geraghty, rider of Special Tiara (*Champion Chase*) "Henry [de Bromhead] told me to let him rip and use his jumping [when he won at Kempton's Christmas meeting]. He definitely stays really well and he's a real two-miler, galloping, jumping and staying, and the jumping is the key with him." *Kempton victory was Special Tiara's first since a Grade 1 novice success at Aintree in April 2013 – fourth that day was Sire De Grugy*

Pick of the bunch
from Ireland

Don Poli Course winner with Gold Cup potential in the long term. Will surely prove difficult to beat whether he goes for the RSA or the National Hunt Chase

Douvan Oozes class over hurdles and potentially better than Vautour, who won the Supreme for the same connections last year

No More Heroes Has to get over his Leopardstown flop but that was clearly not his true form. Looked a class act at Navan previously and will be fresh for the Albert Bartlett

Monksland One for those who like longer prices. Jumped brilliantly at Gowran and might be able to make up for lost time in the World Hurdle

jumping in contrast to Un De Sceaux can be far from economical. Clarcam and Gilgamboa were destroyed by Un De Sceaux at Leopardstown.

The JLT, seemingly, is less straightforward. Vautour hardly touched a fence on his chasing bow at Navan but then flopped at Leopardstown and, even after snaring a poor Grade 2 there in January, Mullins argued he could jump much better. Ruby Walsh said he liked how Vautour jumped but was not totally convincing in his argument. Vautour's course form is certainly a help to his chance and the trip should be no barrier.

Ireland has enviable depth in the JLT as Valseur Lido and Apache Stronghold are strong contenders.

Apache Stronghold in particular looks to have plenty going for him and his willingness to battle in his Flogas win over Valseur Lido was encouraging. The son of Milan jumped brilliantly in defeat to Don Poli at Leopardstown over Christmas when the three-mile distance seemed to suit the winner better. Faster ground is not an issue for Apache Stronghold.

The story goes that Gigginstown probably regard Don Poli, rather than Valseur Lido, as their most suitable RSA Chase horse, although the National Hunt Chase has been mooted. He is seen as their banker whichever race he runs in, and such confidence is not misplaced. He hammered Wounded Warrior and Smashing at Gowran, form that has been strongly endorsed, and he was superb in slamming Apache Stronghold at Leopardstown. He will surely be nothing like the 4-1 available ante-post if he turns up in the RSA.

The aforementioned Wounded Warrior beat another Gigginstown horse, the smart Rule The World, at Naas in January. He has abundant stamina but also class, making him worthy of considerable respect if he tackles the National Hunt Chase.

NOVICE HURDLES Mullins favourites are everywhere and not least in the novice hurdles, which has always been a strong area for him. Supreme Novices' Hurdle hotpot Douvan looked pretty flawless in his Gowran success over Sizing John (subsequent Grade 1 winner) and better again when never off the bridle in the Moscow Flyer at Punchestown. The form can be crabbed to some extent but he has been going off at extremely cramped odds and is clearly working brilliantly at Closutton.

Mullins also has exciting Leopardstown winner Nichols Canyon, third favourite in the race, Shaneshill and possibly Tell Us More, a flashy son of Scorpion who has divided the best of judges. The Dermot Weld-trained Silver Concorde won the Champion Bumper last March and adds to a strong team – it would be a shock if Ireland did not win the Supreme for a tenth time this century.

The Neptune is one of those ante-post markets that is a prisoner to plans of trainers: indeed, in mid-February, it was still 8-1 the field. Outlander is around that price and, while it is clear that No More Heroes disappointed in the Grade 2 they contested in late January at Leopardstown, Outlander would surely have taken a great deal of beating. He is a massive player in the Neptune, with the same connections' Tell Us More also one to be feared if he lines up.

The Albert Bartlett has gone Ireland's way four times in the past six years. The British have some obvious players but Black Hercules and No More Heroes are at the top of the betting. Black Hercules ran a blinder in the Champion Bumper last year and was good in snaring a 3m Grade 3 in December – that was a slog and he did not shirk the battle. No More Heroes' Navan success over Shaneshill illustrated his own willingness to fight; forget his Leopardstown defeat afterwards (bad scope) and he has to be considered. As for the Triumph, we have decent juveniles but nothing really stands out.

OTHER RACES Don Cossack, who looked to have Champagne Fever's measure when that rival departed at the last in the Kinloch Brae at Thurles in January, has long been aimed at the Ryanair Chase. He fell as a novice at Cheltenham but seems stronger this season, both physically and mentally.

If she is ready in time, Annie Power *(below)* will surely assume the mantle of Quevega, for so long an opening-day banker, by winning the Mares' Hurdle.

Since the Bumper's inception, the winner has come over on the boat from Ireland 17 times (from 22 renewals). Incredibly, or perhaps not, Mullins trains six of the first nine in the ante-post market (Bordini, Au Quart De Tour, Up For Review, Pylonthepressure, Bellshill and Stone Hard). Vigil, fifth as a five-year-old last year, could provide Dermot Weld with back-to-back successes in the race, but beware too the Gordon Elliott-trained General Principle, a 22-length winner at Punchestown.

Record of Irish runners in past ten years

Race	Wins	2nd/3rd	Runners	Profit/loss
Supreme Novices' Hurdle	5	4	60	14
Arkle Chase	2	5	35	-19
Ultima Handicap Chase	1	2	14	-6
Champion Hurdle	6	6	51	-10.38
Mares' Hurdle	6	4	30	-17.65
National Hunt Chase	4	11	47	4.25
Novices' Handicap Chase	1	6	28	-18
Neptune Hurdle	5	11	49	-17.5
RSA Chase	4	7	38	-13.75
Champion Chase	4	9	34	7.5
Coral Cup	3	6	50	-6
Cross Country Handicap Chase	8	18	80	-7
Fred Winter Juvenile Hurdle	3	6	61	-4
Champion Bumper	8	12	100	23.5
JLT Novices' Chase	3	1	14	16
Pertemps Handicap Hurdle	2	8	44	18
Ryanair Chase	0	7	28	-28
World Hurdle	1	8	35	-30.5
Stable Plate	0	3	22	-22
Kim Muir Handicap Chase	1	9	39	-26
Triumph Hurdle	2	6	55	-39
County Hurdle	6	8	69	59
Albert Bartlett Novices' Hurdle	3	6	46	31
Gold Cup	3	4	22	13.5
Foxhunter	5	10	47	13
Martin Pipe Handicap Hurdle	2	3	14	4.5
Grand Annual Handicap Chase	4	7	25	12.5
	92	187	1137	-48.03

Vital statistics

Ireland's best and worst

Handicap hurdles are a strong suit and the most profitable race for Ireland is the County Hurdle with six winners (all at double-figure odds) in the past decade. The Pertemps Final and Martin Pipe (both two winners in the past decade) also show a level-stakes profit

Ireland has had eight of the ten winners of the Cross Country Chase, as well as 18 of the other 20 top-three finishers

The Champion Bumper has also yielded eight winners in the past decade (and 17 overall in the race's 22-year history). Willie Mullins has eight wins in the race

The Irish record is excellent in the big novice hurdles with five winners of both the Supreme (plus four places) and the Neptune (11 places) in the past decade

The wider spread of novice chases has favoured Ireland, with three of the four winners of the JLT Novices' Chase (although the exception was last year after the race's elevation to Grade 1 status) and two of the four winners since the National Hunt Chase became a higher-quality event

Tuesday is a strong day – in the past decade Ireland has had six wins in the Champion Hurdle and five in the Supreme (as well as Quevega's six-timer in the Mares' Hurdle)

The only races not won by Ireland in the past decade (Ryanair and Stable Plate) are both on Thursday, by far the most difficult day for the raiders

After a decade without a Foxhunter winner, Ireland finally scored again in 2006 and has added four more winners since (all in the last four years)

What they say

'We don't want to make all in March'

Nicky Henderson, trainer of Peace And Co
(Triumph) "We had to try and get him to settle but it was a fair mess of a race [in the Triumph Hurdle Trial] as they went no gallop. It was hard to get him to settle but we wanted him to learn from it as we don't want to make all in March. It's the first time he has seen another horse on a racecourse" *Four of the last nine Triumph winners went into the race unbeaten over hurdles*

Alan King, trainer of Karezak *(Triumph)*
"He gave the favourite something to think about [when second to Peace And Co at Cheltenham]. The good thing to see was the two of them kept quickening away – they put nine lengths between themselves and the rest. I believe he'll be better in a more strongly run race – but Peace And Co could be exceptional" *Karezak has finished second to leading rivals Peace And Co, Bristol De Mai and Hargam on his last three starts*

Alan King, trainer of Pain Au Chocolat *(Triumph)* "If anything was going to get him beaten [at Sandown] it was the slow pace but he settled well and quickened really nicely. I was delighted with him and he'll head for the Triumph. We could have quite a team for that and it's about time I won it again" *King has two wins and four places from 14 Triumph runners but his last victory was Katchit in 2007*

Success awaits

The Racing Post's regional correspondents pick the best from the major British training centres

LAMBOURN Whichever way you look at the Toby Balding National Hunt Chase, it is easy to reason that Alan King's **Sego Success** is tailor-made for the festival's ultimate stamina test. The fast improver must rank as our region's banker, *writes Rodney Masters*.

Further encouragement can be drawn from the recent history of the race, with King having provided the winner twice in the last seven years (Old Benny in 2008 and Midnight Prayer last year).

The lightly raced Sego Success has won three of his seven races under rules. Two of those successes came this winter when he illustrated his abundance of stamina. At Wetherby in November, off level weights in a beginners' chase, he outpointed If In Doubt, the favourite, who handsomely advertised the form by winning his two subsequent starts, including the Skybet Chase at Doncaster.

After a break over Christmas, Sego Success put up an even better performance to take a Listed chase for novices at Warwick, where he outstayed Grand Vision and Deputy Dan. Importantly, with Cheltenham in mind, he finished strongly in those races at Wetherby and Warwick. All available evidence points to him not only seeing out the longer trip at the festival but thriving for it.

Like Don Poli, who is favourite for the National Hunt Chase, Sego Success also has an entry in the RSA Chase but there is little doubt he would be better suited by the stamina test. If Don Poli lines up against him, so be it. I would be confident of Sego Success beating him.

Dawalan *(below left)* is something of a character and can hit a flat spot during a race, but he is blessed with the rare weapon of being able to produce a burst of speed from the last flight of hurdles and he makes plenty of appeal for the Pertemps Final.

Nicky Henderson's five-year-old switched on that turbo at Aintree

MEMBERS' CLUB YOUR CHELTENHAM SERVICES

Planning your journey to the festival?

Don't forget to stop off at Members' Club en route. We've got the best tipping, analysis, statistics, ratings and special offers around – ensuring you arrive at Cheltenham ready.

Join the best service around from just 40p a day.

RACING POST.com/membersclub

Your Cheltenham guide ❯

What they say

'He'll be suited by a fast-run two miles'

Barry Geraghty, rider of Josses Hill (*Arkle*)
"If we'd won by a neck [at Kempton last time] everyone would have been very happy, instead we lost by a length. We're getting there and he'll be better suited by two miles in a fast-run race as it will give him fewer options" *Eight of the last ten Arkle winners had won at Cheltenham or been placed at the festival before (Josses Hill was second in the 2014 Supreme)*

Ben Pauling, trainer of Smart Freddy (*Novices' Handicap Chase*) "He's missed large spells through injury but has a fantastic attitude. He's got a mark of 136 and there should be a nice opportunity for him to run in the novice handicap chase or the three-mile handicap chase" *The last nine winners of the novice handicap chase were rated 132-142*

Pick of the bunch
from Lambourn

Sego Success Our region's banker. Everything looks right in the National Hunt Chase for this improver with an abundance of stamina

Dawalan Fancied for the Pertemps and a good one for the betting-in-running brigade because he can hit a flat spot before launching a burst of speed from the final flight

Peace And Co Too short for many ante-post punters at 7-4 for the Triumph but latest work confirms he is a class apart

L'Ami Serge Tough and thoroughly professional, he failed to win in six appearances in France but is unbeaten in three races for Nicky Henderson and has a leading chance in the Supreme

in December after looking certain to finish out of the frame and then proved that was no fluke by producing another show of power at Musselburgh in a Pertemps qualifier.

Although well beaten when 7-2 favourite for last season's Fred Winter Juvenile Handicap Hurdle, Dawalan underwent surgery during the summer to improve his breathing and that led to vastly improved form. To such a degree that perhaps at this time next year he will be talked of as a candidate for the Ladbrokes World Hurdle. With the run at Cheltenham in mind, detractors may point to a flat track being more suitable, particularly with the Musselburgh and Aintree wins fresh in the memory, but there is no conclusive evidence to support that. More important to him is good ground, a factor Henderson has emphasised.

It is rare for our region to have a leading contender for the Foxhunter but Warren Greatrex's **Paint The Clouds**, unbeaten in five runs over fences, neatly fits into the slot. It is significant that Sam Waley-Cohen has committed to the ride. If all goes according to plan in his final prep for the festival, Paint The Clouds will be the value against Teaforthree.

He was never off the bit, having quickened impressively from two fences out, when winning the prestigious Champion Hunters' Chase at Stratford last summer and is likely to have too much toe for Teaforthree.

Little went right for **Many Clouds** last season – it was typical of his luck that he was brought down at the 14th fence in the RSA Chase just as he was making a forward move – but his various misfortunes are now forgotten following a glorious winter in which he won the Hennessy Gold Cup and BetBright Cup. A relentless galloper who invariably gives his all, he is now a key player for the Betfred Cheltenham Gold Cup

Coneygree: outstanding chance in RSA Chase if connections decide to take that option

and odds of 9-1 reflect his chance. The worry would be if the ground is quicker than soft because he is likely to be found wanting for pace. He is one of those to back during Cheltenham week if conditions are right.

With his head-down enthusiasm, **Coneygree** is a similar type. Hopefully his team will opt for the RSA Chase rather than the Gold Cup because novices have a poor record in the big one and he would have an outstanding chance in the novice race, for which 5-1 would be fair enough.

WEST COUNTRY If at first you don't succeed – try, try and try again. Those words seem appropriate for **Silviniaco Conti** as he attempts to make it third time lucky in the Betfred Cheltenham Gold Cup, *writes Andrew King.*

Having been an unlucky faller three out when still travelling smoothly in 2013, Silviniaco Conti seemed to be in the right place 12 months ago as he jumped the final fence in front of the chasing pack. Surprisingly he drifted left and was only fourth behind Lord Windermere, beaten just under two lengths. It is hard to say he did not stay considering the distance he was beaten and the fact he appeared to be closing on the principals again up the hill after being straightened up by Noel Fehily.

His two Grade 1 victories this season, following the fitting of cheekpieces, certainly make him the one to beat in this year's renewal. It would be no surprise if he donned a pair of blinkers on the big day in the hope that the headgear can help to end his Cheltenham Festival hoodoo.

As usual the Stan James Champion Hurdle has little interest for this

What they say

'He's always better at this time of year'

Tony McCoy, rider of Holywell (*Gold Cup*) "He's a better horse when ridden positively and he jumped well and won well [at Kelso in February]. I know just what he's capable of and what his trainer is capable of, so he'll improve again on this. He's always a better horse at this time of year and when I went down to school him last week he felt as though he was back to himself" *Form figures of 121241111 from February to May, including wins on both March runs at the festival*

David Pipe, trainer of Un Temps Pour Tout (*World Hurdle*) "He ran a cracker to be beaten less than three lengths behind Saphir Du Rheu in the Cleeve Hurdle on his first start over three miles. That was his first foray into top company against seasoned campaigners and he acquitted himself very well, particularly considering it was his first start since Punchestown last May. He is fully entitled to improve for the run and he holds viable claims in the World Hurdle" *Un Temps Pour Tout has form figures of 1323 in Graded hurdles in Britain and France*

David Bridgwater, trainer of The Giant Bolster (*Gold Cup*) "I was thrilled to bits with him [in the BetBright Cup]. The pace of the race didn't help – he needs to be off the bridle after a mile and he was still cantering after two miles. A bigger field and a stronger pace will bring out the best in him in March and I'm sure he'll be there turning in with a chance again this year" *The Giant Bolster has finished second, fourth and third in three appearances in the Gold Cup, recording the highest RPRs of his career (168 and 170 twice)*

area, with the Paul Nicholls-trained Irving having only the slimmest of chances even before his disappointing run in the Kingwell Hurdle.

With so many question marks hanging over Sprinter Sacre and Sire De Grugy, the Betway Queen Mother Champion Chase looks very open and **Dodging Bullets** could be the one. He comes into the race in great heart having landed his last two Grade 1s – the Tingle Creek at Sandown and Ascot's Clarence House Chase – and boasts winning form at Cheltenham.

Drying ground will hold no terrors for him as he has plenty of pace and the main danger may well come from stablemate **Mr Mole**, who bolted up at Newbury recently.

My original long-term fancy for the Ladbrokes World Hurdle was Un Temps Pour Tout but he did not quite live up to expectations when only third in his prep race at Cheltenham in January, despite looking spot-on beforehand.

He is now passed over in favour of **Zarkandar**, who has been trained

Vibrato Valtat: decent value against Arkle hotpot Un De Sceaux

specifically with this Grade 1 prize in mind since being narrowly chinned at Ascot in December. Paul Nicholls is convinced Zarkandar thrives on going to the races relatively fresh and has purposely given him only two outings this term.

Stablemate Saphir Du Rheu and Un Temps Pour Tout are closely matched on their running in January and Rock On Ruby has to answer stamina questions over three miles.

On the opening day the Irish contingent will be getting stuck into Un De Sceaux in the Racing Post Arkle but festival history is littered with beaten bankers and **Vibrato Valtat** looks decent value against him.

Nicholls' progressive six-year-old has been transformed from a frustrating bridle horse into a smooth-travelling class act this season and he gets better with each run. His defeat at Cheltenham in November can be forgotten as Sam Twiston-Davies and Vibrato Valtat got their wires crossed and his exploits since then give him a sterling chance of turning over the Irish hotpot.

What they say

'We look forward to decent ground'

Harry Fry, trainer of Jollyallan *(Supreme)* "He just got outbattled after the last [at Sandown in January] but it was what we wanted to achieve in terms of getting more experience in him and coming up against a steaming campaigner like Garde La Victoire. Getting into a bit of a battle, whether it was lost or not, will hopefully make more of a man of him with bigger targets in mind. We're looking forward to running him on decent ground" *Fry is looking for his first festival success but oversaw the preparation of 2012 Champion Hurdle winner Rock On Ruby*

Pick of the bunch
from the West

Monetaire One of the season's most unlucky losers after being badly hampered at Cheltenham in November but made amends at Newbury next time. Subsequent rating rise ensures he will get into the handicap of David Pipe's choice

Jollyallan The drying spring ground will bring out the best in him and he is good each-way value for Harry Fry in the Supreme

The Young Master Whether Neil Mulholland sends him for the four-miler or the RSA Chase, he merits close inspection as he is still reckoned to be improving at a rate of knots

What they say

'She's young and going forward'

John Quinn, trainer of Aurore D'Estruval *(Mares' Hurdle)* "I was very happy at Sandown. The ground was barely raceable, but she proved she gets the trip and we know she's better on nice ground. She's a good mare who is young and going forward. She'll go to Cheltenham with a decent chance" *Both first-time winners of the Mares' Hurdle (Whiteoak and Quevega) were aged five*

Nicky Richards, trainer of Simply Ned *(Champion Chase)* "He's a very accurate jumper and he should find more improvement when he gets back on a decent bit of spring ground. Ned won't be too far behind Dodging Bullets, especially on better ground" *Form figures of F21321 with good in the going description*

Pick of the bunch
from the North

Aurore D'Estruval Best on good ground and reckoned to have a sound each-way chance in the Mares' Hurdle

Eduard Has been aimed at the Ryanair Chase from the beginning of the season by Nicky Richards and is reportedly in great form

Diamond King Entered in three handicap hurdles by Donald McCain. Well worth considering as he is thought to be much better than his current mark of 132

THE NORTH Northern yards will field a weaker team than usual but **Aurore D'Estruval** from John Quinn's Malton stable is certainly one with a chance in the OLBG Mares' Hurdle, *writes Colin Russell*.

The ex-French mare proved an instant hit for her new stable last season, winning a weak novice hurdle at Wetherby and going on to finish fifth in the valuable hurdle for four-year-olds at Aintree, and she has improved this term.

She has won Listed mares' hurdles at Wetherby and Sandown, either side of an excellent second to Irving in the stanjames.com Fighting Fifth Hurdle. Quinn has kept her under wraps for the festival since her Sandown run in early January and she has a first-rate each-way chance, given that she is still improving and better ground is expected to suit her.

The other major northern hope in a championship race is **Eduard**, who goes for the Ryanair Chase. He is the flagbearer of the Nicky Richards yard and is still unexposed, having run only six times over fences and 13 times in all.

The seven-year-old has won three and been runner-up in the other three of those six chase starts and his career-best performance came at last year's Scottish Grand National meeting at Ayr when he thrashed the smart Valdez by 20 lengths in the Scottish Future Champion Novices' Chase. He has not added to his tally this season, but he was far from disgraced first time at Carlisle when beaten a length and a quarter by Gold Cup hope Many Clouds, giving 6lb, and on his only other outing

he was just beaten by Wishfull Thinking in the Peterborough Chase at Huntingdon, where a last-fence error cost him his chance.

During the cold weather in late January and early February, Richards sent Eduard to a satellite yard he leases in Newmarket so that he could keep him on the move. He considered a prep race in the Ascot Chase in February but decided against it in order to keep Eduard fresh for Cheltenham. With several of the leading protagonists having been ruled out by injury, the Ryanair looks a weaker affair than usual and Eduard can go well at a fair price.

The Richards-trained **Simply Ned** has a bit to find in the Betway Queen Mother Champion Chase but did have second favourite Dodging Bullets behind him when runner-up to Uxizandre in a Cheltenham conditions race in November. At around 25-1 he is an interesting each-way contender.

Richards also has two unbeaten horses going for the Weatherbys Champion Bumper – dual Newcastle winner **Western Rules** and **Imada**, who won at Ayr on his only outing to date. It is hard to know how they compare against the massed Irish ranks but Richards holds them in high regard.

Donald McCain, whose horses are regularly in the money at the festival, has a weaker team than usual but the unexposed **Diamond King** is fancied to go well in one of the handicap hurdles. His target has yet to be decided but he is considered well handicapped on 132.

Vital statistics

Record of horses wearing headgear

Supreme Nov Hurdle
0 wins-9 runs; £9 loss to £1 stake

Arkle Chase
1-14 (+£20)

Ultima Hcap Chase
3-46 (+£17)

Champion Hurdle
2-16 (+£28)

Mares' Hurdle
0-13 (-£13)

National Hunt Chase
2-45 (-£1)

Novices' Hcap Chase
0-35 (-£35)

Neptune Hurdle
0-10 (-£10)

RSA Chase
0-9 (-£9)

Champion Chase
0-16 (-£16)

Coral Cup
1-47 (-£35)

Cross Country Chase
0-37 (-£37)

Fred Winter Hurdle
3-53 (+£53)

Champion Bumper
0-2 (-£2)

JLT Novices' Chase
1-4 (+£17)

Pertemps Final
3-63 (+£1)

Ryanair Chase
1-16 (-£11)

World Hurdle
0-32 (-£32)

Stable Plate
0-37 (-£37)

Kim Muir
2-66 (-£31.70)

Triumph Hurdle
2-24 (-£13)

County Hurdle
0-48 (-£48)

Albert Bartlett
1-13 (+£31)

Gold Cup
0-19 (-£19)

Foxhunter
2-45 (+£10)

Martin Pipe Hurdle
0-28 (-£28)

Grand Annual
1-32 (+£2)

Statistics from 2005 to 2014 (not including tongue straps)

The key trials

Racing Post analysts Richard Lowther and Dave Orton assess the big winter action

Course winners appeal

Jezki and Saphir Du Rheu are two of the main fancies for the Raceform analysis team

GOLD CUP Silviniaco Conti is a worthy favourite, but there is plenty of value around for those looking to take him on. His wins in the Betfair Chase and the King George, principal Gold Cup trials but major Grade 1s in their own right, represent the best form on offer. After taking a solid edition of the Betfair Chase, when cheekpieces put an edge on him, he didn't need to improve to land his second King George, at the chief expense of Dynaste. Still going well when coming down three from home in the 2013 Gold Cup, he led over the last 12 months ago, only to succumb in that extraordinary finish. There is no reason why he won't be involved once more.

Road To Riches was an impressive winner of the Galway Plate in the summer and has taken the leap into Graded company in his stride. The redoubtable Sizing Europe beat him a head at Gowran in October but he won Down Royal's version of the Champion Chase in dominant fashion and improved again when winning the Lexus at Leopardstown over Christmas. That is obviously high-class form, but the first three were always to the fore and the eight finishers were separated by only twelve and a half lengths.

A few weeks later six of the Lexus field met again in the Hennessy Gold Cup over the same course and distance, with a different outcome. This time Carlingford Lough, a promising fifth in the Lexus, battled home under Tony McCoy to edge out Foxrock (who didn't contest the Lexus and would have to be supplemented for the Gold Cup). Carlingford Lough is admirably tough and still improving, but there are doubts over both his jumping and the bare form of the Hennessy, which wasn't truly run.

Lord Windermere was an eyecatching third in the Hennessy, finding the ground more to his liking than the mud he faced in the Lexus. A remarkable Gold Cup winner in 2014, having been last for much of the trip, he blossoms in the spring and his performances this term have been better than those in the build-up to last year's triumph.

Bobs Worth was bang there over the final fence 12 months ago, only to veer left up the hill and end up with nothing to run with. He took the prize in 2013 on the back of a single previous run that season, but that was a Newbury Hennessy victory whereas his only sighting this term came when last in the Lexus. He will turn up with something to prove but is lightly raced for his age and may well have another big performance in him.

Many Clouds had to be taken seriously as a Gold Cup contender after landing the Hennessy at Newbury off a mark of 151, then added the BetBright Cup at Cheltenham on Trials Day. That length-and-a-half defeat of Smad Place (who was receiving 8lb) leaves him just a little shy of Gold Cup level, with further improvement likely. He jumps proficiently and lacks for nothing in a fight.

Coneygree is an immensely likeable front-runner and may well go for

Vital statistics

Races with the 'festival factor'

Paddy Power Gold Cup
Cheltenham,
November 15, 2014
2m4½f, soft

1 **Caid Du Berlais**
5 10-13
S Twiston-Davies 10-1

2 **Johns Spirit** 7 11-12
R McLernon 8-1

3 **Present View** 6 11-0
B Powell 5-1f

4 **Oscar Whisky** 9 11-12
B Geraghty 6-1

Trainer: Paul Nicholls
Distances: hd, 1¾l, nk
18 ran

Festival pointer One of the best races for finding a festival winner. Last year's first four all made the frame in various festival races (finishing 4222) and Ballynagour (fancied but pulled up in the Paddy Power) won the Byrne Group Plate on his first start since. Four of the first five Ryanair winners came out of this race (and the other was a former Paddy Power winner) but it has not had the same influence in recent years

Seven festival winners have come out of this race in the past ten years

Betfair Chase
Haydock,
November 22, 2014
3m1f, soft

1 **Silviniaco Conti**
8 11-7
N Fehily 100-30

2 **Menorah** 9 11-7
R Johnson 10-1

3 **Dynaste** 8 11-7
T Scudamore 9-2

Trainer: Paul Nicholls
Distances: 2l, 8l
9 ran

Festival pointer Betfair winners to run in the Gold Cup had finishing positions of 012P3PPF (only Kauto Star in 2006-07 has won both in the same season)

Three festival winners in nine years (all in Gold Cup)

Vital statistics

Races with the 'festival factor'

Stanjames.com Fighting Fifth Hurdle
Newcastle,
November 29, 2014
2m, soft

1 **Irving** 6 11-7
  N Scholfield 6-4f

2 **Aurore D'Estruval**
  4 11-0 J Reveley 3-1

3 **Arctic Fire** 5 11-7
  P Townend 9-4

Trainer: Paul Nicholls
Distances: 1¾l, 4l. 6 ran

Festival pointer The key British trial for the Champion Hurdle in recent years, featuring the winners of 2008, 2009 and 2010, the runner-up in 2011, 2012 and 2014 and the third in 2013 (their finishing positions in the Fighting Fifth were 3151111). Only Punjabi (2008-09) has done the Fighting Fifth-Champion in the past 20 years

Four festival winners in the past ten years

Hennessy Gold Cup
Newbury,
November 29, 2014
3m2½f, soft

1 **Many Clouds** 7 11-6
  L Aspell 8-1

2 **Houblon Des Obeaux**
  7 11-12
  A Coleman 50-1

3 **Merry King**
  7 10-7 AP McCoy 14-1

4 **Monbeg Dude**
  9 11-1 P Moloney 25-1

Trainer: Oliver Sherwood
Distances: 3¼l, 1l, 15l
19 ran

Festival pointer Last year's Gold Cup winner Lord Windermere had finished eighth here; before that Denman (2007-08) Bobs Worth (2012-13) completed the Hennessy-Gold Cup double and the 2011 and 2012 Gold Cup runners-up came from this race

Four festival winners in the past ten years

Jezki: will appreciate a stronger pace than he has had in small fields in Ireland

gold following his impressive rout in the Denman Chase at Newbury. Your memory will need to stretch back 41 years to recall the last novice to win (Captain Christy) but not many first-season chasers have taken their chance and Coneygree is an outstanding prospect. Cheltenham will be only his fourth run over fences, however, and his need to go out in front could leave him vulnerable.

Verdict A wide-open Gold Cup. Silviniaco Conti has the best credentials but Lord Windermere won't give up his crown without a fight, with Many Clouds also in the mix *(Richard Lowther)*

CHAMPION HURDLE The opening-day feature is shaping up to be a cracker again. Last season's star novice Faugheen has stretched his unbeaten record with imperious wins in the Ascot Hurdle and the Christmas Hurdle at Kempton. He has been tremendously impressive in almost all his starts and has a huge engine, but has yet to meet a truly top-calibre opponent and an eight-length defeat of Purple Bay at Kempton is not Champion Hurdle form. Faugheen's jumping has improved this season, but he was awkward at the last at Kempton and on the big day he will be travelling at the fastest pace of his life. His raw talent remains untapped, however, and it is not hard to envisage him bounding clear up the hill.

Three key Grade 1 trials in Ireland have featured clashes between last year's winner, Jezki, and Hurricane Fly, the 2011 and 2013 hero. The latter, a stablemate of Faugheen and likely to be rejected by Ruby Walsh, has come out on top each time, beating Jezki in the Morgiana at Punchestown and in the Ryanair and Irish Champion Hurdles at Leopardstown. The Fly is a phenomenal racehorse and one of the slickest jumpers you will ever see, but it is hard to believe he will be

sharp enough to land a third Champion at the age of 11, especially on the quicker spring ground. His last three defeats have all come when there has been some 'good' in the official going description.

A game winner in a first-time hood last March, Jezki was hindered by last-flight errors in the Morgiana and the Irish Champion, and went down by just half a length in the Ryanair after a terrific tussle with Hurricane Fly. Jessica Harrington's star is sure to appreciate a truer gallop than he faced in the small-field trials and will be better suited by the likely ground than Hurricane Fly. He is strongly fancied to turn the tables, provided he can eliminate the mistakes.

The Willie Mullins stable also houses a lively outsider in Arctic Fire, who finished third to Jezki and Hurricane Fly in the Ryanair before splitting the pair in the Irish Champion. He was no match for Irving in a substandard Fighting Fifth at Newcastle in November, but he travels like a dream and the fast pace at Cheltenham will play much more to his strengths. One who needs to be delivered late, he may well run into a place.

British hopes lie principally with second favourite The New One, who thundered home for third a year ago after being badly hampered by the fallen Our Conor early on. Unbeaten since, he has mopped up four races this season, chief among them the International Hurdle at Cheltenham, but the opposition has been second division and he didn't impress in the mud in Haydock's Champion Hurdle Trial. He thrives at Cheltenham and is another who will appreciate quicker ground, but his habit of jumping to his right has become a concern and he cannot afford to give away ground at his hurdles as he has been doing.

Verdict Faugheen is a potential superstar but reigning champion Jezki will be a tough nut to crack and is selected. Arctic Fire can reach a place *(Richard Lowther)*

Vital statistics

Races with the 'festival factor'

888Sport Tingle Creek Chase Sandown, December 6, 2014
2m, soft

1 **Dodging Bullets**
6 11-7
S Twiston-Davies 9-1

2 **Somersby** 10 11-7
AP McCoy 8-1

3 **Hinterland** 6 11-7
N Fehily 12-1

Trainer: Paul Nicholls
Distances: 2½l, 1½l. 10 ran

Festival pointer The key guide to the Champion Chase. Although only six of the 17 to try have won both races since the Tingle Creek became a Grade 1, the Champion Chase winner had run in the Tingle Creek in ten of the past 14 years

Seven festival winners in the past ten years

Caspian Caviar Gold Cup Cheltenham, December 13, 2014
2m5f, good to soft

1 **Niceonefrankie**
8 11-5
A Coleman 16-1

2 **Barrakilla** 7 10-12
P Moloney 9-2jf

3 **Edgardo Sol** 7 11-12
N Fehily 14-1

Trainer: Venetia Williams
Distances: 6l, ½l. 12 ran

Festival pointer None of the festival scorers to come out of this race in the past ten years had won here, although last season's winner Double Ross was a close third in the Grade 1 JLT Novices' Chase. The first three Ryanair Chase winners ran in this race (form figures of 2B3) but none has since. Now it is more likely to be a guide to one of the handicap chases (the latest winner out of the race was Golden Chieftain, third here before winning the 2013 Ultima Handicap Chase)

Six festival winners in the past ten years

Vital statistics

Races with the 'festival factor'

Stanjames.com International Hurdle
Cheltenham, December 13, 2014
2m1f, good to soft

1 **The New One** 6 11-8
   S Twiston-Davies 4-7f

2 **Vaniteux** 5 11-0
   B Geraghty 5-2

3 **Olofi** 8 11-0
   W Hutchinson 25-1

Trainer: Nigel Twiston-Davies
Distances: 4½l, 6l. 8 ran

Festival pointer Rooster Booster (2002-03) is the only winner of this race to land the Champion since Comedy Of Errors (1974-75) but in the past 20 years two who were beaten here went on to take the crown and four of the last six winners to line up in the Champion finished in the first three

Two festival winners in the past ten years

William Hill King George VI Chase
Kempton, December 26, 2014, 3m, good to soft

1 **Silviniaco Conti**
   8 11-10 N Fehily 15-8f

2 **Dynaste** 8 11-10
   T Scudamore 7-1

3 **Al Ferof** 9 11-10
   S Twiston-Davies 7-1

Trainer: Paul Nicholls
Distances: 4½l, 5l. 10 ran

Festival pointer Seven of the last eight festivals have featured at least one winner who had run here. Desert Orchid (1988-89) was the last to complete the King George/Gold Cup double until 2002-2003, since when the double has been done by five of the ten to try (Silviniaco Conti failed last season). Since Desert Orchid, 23 festival winners have come out of this race (in the Gold Cup, Champion Chase or Ryanair Chase)

Eleven festival winners in the past ten years

CHAMPION CHASE AND RYANAIR CHASE The Champion Chase promises an intriguing clash between the last two winners, each of whom has been limited to just a single outing this season.

Sprinter Sacre and Sire De Grugy will cross swords with the fast-emerging Dodging Bullets, who has landed both Grade 1 two-milers in Britain this season, beginning with a defeat of Somersby in the Tingle Creek at Sandown. The addition of a tongue tie was a big plus there and the aid was fitted again as he followed up in Ascot's Clarence House Chase. Paul Nicholls has found the key to Dodging Bullets, who has been very tricky at times, and he looks a solid option.

Much of the interest before the Clarence House focused on the return of Sprinter Sacre, who had been sidelined for 13 months with a heart problem. Would he resume at the height of his powers or blow out completely? In the event there were flashes of the old brilliance as he moved up stylishly on the home turn and Barry Geraghty was far from hard on him when held by the winner, but his RPR was 19lb off his Champion Chase level and there is still significant doubt whether he will be able to reproduce his best in the heat of competition.

Sire De Grugy profited from Sprinter Sacre's absence to rack up a string of wins last season, including a comprehensive victory in the big one, but was sidelined for much of this term with a hip problem. He returned to the fray in the Game Spirit Chase at Newbury, only to dislodge Jamie Moore at the final ditch. He was still in contention at the time and is entitled to come on for the outing.

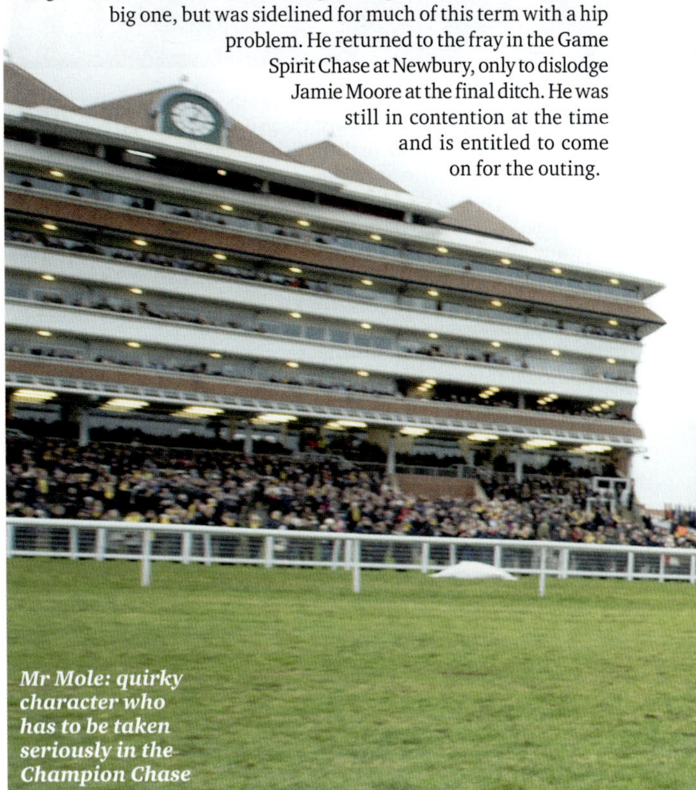

Mr Mole: quirky character who has to be taken seriously in the Champion Chase

Sire De Grugy's departure detracted a little from an excellent showing by Mr Mole, who definitely has to be taken seriously at Cheltenham. This stablemate of Dodging Bullets looked extremely quirky earlier in his career but is knuckling down now and four straight wins will have buoyed his confidence no end.

Hidden Cyclone put himself in the Champion Chase picture with a comfortable win in the Tied Cottage Chase at Punchestown, but he was receiving weight from the placed horses and it was a little way removed from championship form. He ran well at the festival 12 months ago when runner-up to Dynaste in the Ryanair Chase and trainer Shark Hanlon may yet target him at the longer race this year.

The absence through injury of 2014 winner Dynaste makes the Ryanair even more open than usual and the make-up of the field will not become clear until close to the day. Don Cossack looks a worthy favourite, having won all four of his starts this season including a defeat of Boston Bob and Lord Windermere in the Grade 1 John Durkan Memorial at Punchestown. On his latest outing in the Kinloch Brae Chase at Thurles he was upsides Champagne Fever and rallying strongly when the grey fell at the last, leaving him to saunter home. His owner, Michael O'Leary, will be itching to win the race he sponsors.

Like Don Cossack, Champagne Fever holds a variety of entries, but the Ryanair will presumably be his target. He didn't quite stay in the King George but earlier had impressed in a Grade 2 at Clonmel over 2m4f. Prior to his fall at Thurles he had jumped superbly and he was back to his flawless best with an easy win in the Red Mills Chase, again over 2m4f, at Gowran in February.

The 2013 Ryanair winner Cue Card is an obvious candidate. He ran creditably behind Silviniaco Conti in the Betfair Chase and the King George but has yet to produce his best since being partnered by Daryl Jacob. The return to the intermediate trip for the first time in nearly two years will suit him, though.

Verdict With lingering doubts over Sprinter Sacre and Sire De Grugy, Dodging Bullets is a solid Champion Chase option. At the prices, Champagne Fever appeals most in the Ryanair *(Richard Lowther)*

Vital statistics

Races with the 'festival factor'

William Hill.com Christmas Hurdle
Kempton,
December 26, 2014
2m, good to soft

1 Faugheen 6 11-7
R Walsh 4-11f

2 Purple Bay 5 11-7
AP McCoy 11-1

3 Blue Heron 6 11-7
P Brennan 66-1

Trainer: Willie Mullins
Distances: 8l, 9l. 6 ran

Festival pointer The last to do the Christmas/ Champion Hurdle double was Kribensis in 1989-90 (although My Tent Or Yours went close last year when beaten a neck at Cheltenham by Jezki) but four beaten horses in the past 13 runnings have landed the Champion (the most recent was 2011 runner-up Rock On Ruby)

Four festival winners in the past ten years

Lexus Chase
Leopardstown,
December 28, 2014
3m, soft to heavy

1 Road To Riches
7 11-10 B Cooper 4-1

2 On His Own 10 11-10
P Townend 14-1

3 Sam Winner 7 11-10
S Twiston-Davies 7-1

Trainer: Noel Meade
Distances: 1½l, 2l
9 ran

Festival pointer Four of the past ten runnings have featured that season's Gold Cup winner. Two were British raiders who won here (Denman and Synchronised) while the two Irish-trained Gold Cup winners to come out of this race were both beaten here (War Of Attrition was runner-up and Lord Windermere was seventh last season – he filled the same position this season too)

Four festival winners in the past ten years

Races with the 'festival factor'

BoyleSports Hurdle
Leopardstown,
January 18, 2015
2m, soft

1 **Katie T** 6 10-9
  B Hughes 12-1

2 **Modem** 5 10-3
  R Power 20-1

3 **Ted Veale** 8 11-5
  S Clements 33-1

4 **Savello** 9 11-0
  B Cooper 20-1

Trainer: Kevin Prendergast
Distances: 3l, 1¾l, 1l
24 ran

*Festival pointer Five of
the seven Irish-trained
County Hurdle winners
in the past 12 years had
run in this race (only Final
Approach, in 2011, won
both) – one of the other
two ran in the Betfair
Hurdle at Newbury.
Xenophon followed up
victory here by taking the
Coral Cup in 2003*

*Four festival winners in
the past ten years*

**Galliardhomes.com
Cleeve Hurdle**
Cheltenham,
January 24, 2015
3m, soft

1 **Saphir Du Rheu**
  6 11-4
  S Twiston-Davies 3-1

2 **Reve De Sivola**
  10 11-8 D Jacob 4-1

3 **Un Temps Pour Tout**
  6 11-2
  T Scudamore 7-4f

Trainer: Paul Nicholls
Distances: nk, 2½l. 6 ran

*Festival pointer
Principally a World
Hurdle trial (three of the
past seven winners did
the double) but has been
used to prep successfully
for a variety of races –
the Champion Hurdle,
National Hunt Chase and
Ultima Handicap Chase
(twice in the past five
years)*

*Six festival winners in
the past ten years*

WORLD HURDLE With 2014 winner More Of That under a cloud since his tame return in the Grade 2 Long Distance Hurdle at Newbury in November, this looks a wide-open contest. Jonjo O'Neill's enviable festival record and the seven-year-old's superior form are taken into account, so even after all the problems he cannot be ruled out if he lines up back on better ground, but there are obvious reasons to oppose him.

Paul Nicholls has no Big Buck's this season but Zarkandar is a live contender. After a romp in the Grade 1 Grand Prix d'Automne at Auteuil over 3m in November, he was a warm order to score again the following month in the Grade 1 Long Walk at Ascot and looked for a long way as though he would. However, after idling he found the ultra-tough Reve De Sivola too resolute. Zarkandar has finished out of the first four only once in seven starts at Cheltenham and he was a running-on fourth in last year's World Hurdle. His absence since the turn of the year isn't ideal and he's tricky, but he makes each-way appeal.

Nicholls also has Saphir Du Rheu, who jumped to near the top of the ante-post market with a successful return to hurdles in the Cleeve over course and distance in January. He was hugely progressive last season and, with time still on his side, looks a rock-solid contender with the promise of more to come at the trip. David Pipe's Un Temps Pour Tout ran a big race on his belated return when placed in the Cleeve and is entitled to get a little closer at the festival, although he has evidently had his issues.

The 2012 Champion Hurdle winner Rock On Ruby developed into a leading candidate with back-to-back wins over 2m4½f at Cheltenham in December and January. Now ten, having been tried over fences without great success, he first took the well-established Grade 2 Relkeel, won by More Of That in 2014, but it was his weight-carrying success over Nicky Henderson's Vaniteux next time that impressed. He has stamina to prove and no horse older than nine has prevailed since Crimson Embers in 1986.

Ireland's hopes lie mainly with up-and-coming Lieutenant Colonel, who had last year's third At Fishers Cross well beaten when adding a second Grade 1 win to his name with victory over old rival Jetson in the Squared Financial Christmas Hurdle at Leopardstown. The tough six-year-old remains capable of better but must improve around 10lb to figure.

In third that day was Monksland, who caught the eye staying on after a two-year injury layoff. Noel Meade's eight-year-old proved he is back on track when just held by Dedigout next time in the Grade 2 Galmoy at Gowran, where the ground went against him. Monksland was third behind Simonsig in the Neptune Novices' Hurdle on his only previous festival outing in 2013 and could surprise a few back on decent going.

Verdict Title-holder More Of That has a cloud hanging over him and can be opposed. Saphir Du Rheu rates the pick after his Cleeve success over Reve De Sivola. At bigger odds Monksland looks overpriced *(Dave Orton)*

NOVICE CHASES The Arkle Chase is all about the Willie Mullins-trained Un De Sceaux, who has bounced back in tremendous style from a first-time-out fall at Thurles in November. A runaway success at Fairyhouse in December was boosted when runner-up Smashing

Josses Hill: has a lot to prove after unconvincing displays

won next time by a distance, but it was the manner of his bloodless win in the Irish Arkle at Leopardstown the following month that saw him slashed into odds-on favourite. The front-runner was breathtaking in thrashing the progressive Clarcam and is rightly considered a banker by many, remembering he wasn't far off Champion Hurdle class last season. Better going at the festival also promises to be ideal for him and it is not difficult to envisage him taking to Cheltenham.

Vibrato Valtat has not crushed opponents in the same way but has been a revelation himself, having left his limited hurdles form well behind. The Paul Nicholls-trained grey made it four from five over fences when careering away in the Kingmaker Novices' Chase at Warwick in February on deep ground. His hold-up style promises to come into play if the pace collapses and he looks a sound each-way chance, but an RPR of 164+ leaves him with something to find against an on-song Un De Sceaux.

Otherwise credible opposition is thin on the ground, with last year's Supreme Novices' winner Vautour (the favourite's stablemate) looking nailed on to go for the JLT Novices' Chase over 2m4f and Supreme runner-up Josses Hill failing to convince over fences.

Mullins also has a strong hand in the other novice chases. Last year's Martin Pipe Conditional Jockeys' Handicap Hurdle winner Don Poli has taken to fences like a natural and headed ante-post lists for the RSA Chase and National Hunt Chase after a brave win in the Topaz Novice Chase over 3m at Leopardstown's Christmas meeting. He outstayed Apache Stronghold, who went on to land the Grade 1 Flogas Novice Chase at the same venue in December when back down in trip, and will do for many if he takes up his RSA entry.

Coneygree has come back from injury in blinding fashion this season, grinding out a clear-cut win in the Kauto Star Novices' Chase at Kempton on Boxing Day and proving that was no fluke with victory over the big boys in the Grade 2 Denman Chase at Newbury, on his favoured soft ground. He will be a massive player in the RSA if connections can resist the temptation to go for the Gold Cup. However, the front-runner would have a bit to prove on genuinely good ground.

David Pipe's Kings Palace made it 3-3 over fences when winning cleverly at Newbury in February. His previous pair of Cheltenham victories over Sausalito Sunrise give him the best British form apart from Coneygree and he loves the track. His flop in last year's Albert Bartlett Novices' Hurdle came on the back of a much bigger break.

The JLT looks a deep race again. Having disappointed at Leopardstown over Christmas, Vautour got back on track there in January when faced with a simple task in a three-runner Grade 2. He has not looked an absolute natural so far but might take a lot of catching if he is allowed his own way in front.

Apache Stronghold proved himself a high-class performer when denying Valseur Lido, another smart Mullins novice, in the Flogas. He won despite lacking fluency but had a fitness edge on the runner-up and is not certain to confirm form. Expect him to be ridden with plenty of confidence by Paul Carberry.

Ptit Zig is another leading novice chaser for Nicholls, with his Grade 2 course win from Champagne West on New Year's Day being the top British form for the JLT. This former classy hurdler should find the race run to suit and seems sure to go close, although surprisingly the trainer's record in the JLT doesn't inspire.

Verdict Barring accidents Un De Sceaux ought to land the Arkle, although those without ante-post vouchers could do worse than support Vibrato Valtat each-way. Kings Palace has plenty going for him in the RSA, while Vautour should make them all go if he gets into rhythm up front in the JLT *(Dave Orton)*

NOVICE HURDLES Willie Mullins is going for a third successive Supreme Novices' and has the hot favourite in Douvan, who has looked imperious in Ireland since his arrival from France. He sauntered home in a Grade 2 at Punchestown in January that last year's Supreme winner Vautour also won. An inspection of his form suggests he will be tough to beat. His Gowran win in November has worked out very well, with 12-length runner-up Sizing John taking the Grade 1 Future Champions at Leopardstown in December and the fifth, Modem, progressing to finish third in the highly competitive BoyleSports Hurdle in January.

L'Ami Serge easily completed a hat-trick for Nicky Henderson in the Grade 1 Tolworth at Sandown in January, having failed to win previously in France, and that makes him the top British form choice. The festival will be his tenth start and Douvan's camp have a form line through the reliable Killultagh Vic, who ran over a trip short of his best when second to him at Ascot in November.

One who should relish the likely going is Jollyallan, who posted a career-best in defeat when second in a Listed event at Sandown in January. That came on bad ground against battle-hardened Garde La Victoire and the strength of Jollyallan's form suggests he should be closer in the betting.

Mullins' Nichols Canyon came right into the reckoning after an impressive win in the Deloitte in February. That took his form to a new level and he is unbeaten when completing over hurdles. However, the former smart Flat performer seems likely to step up in distance for the Neptune Novices' Hurdle, over a trip he ought to appreciate on good ground. If that materialises, a bold bid to emulate last season's winning stablemate Faugheen is expected.

The Neptune looks more open this year and the leading British hope is Parlour Games, who gave rising trainer John Ferguson a first Grade 1 success when landing the Challow Hurdle at Newbury in December. That followed a Grade 2 success at Cheltenham in November from front-running Blaklion and he has been a revelation for Ferguson considering the mileage he had on the Flat. He has to improve a good deal again, though, and no prep run since the turn of the year is off-putting.

One who comes in under the radar is Irish point winner Kilcrea Vale, who recorded an RPR of 144 with a wide-margin success on his debut for Nicky Henderson at Market Rasen. He appreciates a sound surface and is highly regarded.

Mullins also houses the ante-post leader for the Albert Bartlett Novices' Hurdle in Black Hercules, fourth in last year's Champion Bumper. The form of his December win over 3m at Cork in a recognised trial is sound, with runner-up Alpha Des Obeaux chasing home Douvan back at 2m next time. However, Black Hercules has been absent since and a preference for testing going makes him look vulnerable.

Tea For Two could not have won the Listed Lanzarote Handicap Hurdle at Kempton in January more impressively and that form has substance, although he was beaten at 4-9 in his final prep at Ascot. Stepping up to 3m on a sound surface can bring further improvement.

Nicky Henderson has two live candidates here in Caracci Apache and Vyta Du Roc, who is a course winner over 2m. The former remains unexposed as a stayer and won a key trial when running down Blaklion in a Grade 2 at Doncaster in January.

The juvenile division is exciting and Henderson, rather than Mullins, appears to hold the aces in the Triumph. Peace And Co served up a demolition job at Doncaster on his debut for the stable and cemented his position as favourite on Trials Day at Cheltenham in January. He wasn't so flashy that time, but tactics transpired against him and he still beat a rock-solid yardstick in Alan King's Karezak.

The biggest threat appears to be from his own yard as the JP McManus-owned grey Hargam *(left)* has impressed too. He also beat Karezak (at Cheltenham in December) and should relish the likely good ground.

The Irish juveniles are closely matched. Mullins' tough Petite Parisienne took advantage of her mares' allowance when toppling better-fancied stablemate Kalkir in the Grade 1 Spring Juvenile Hurdle at Leopardstown in February. The Triumph winner has come out of that race for the past three seasons, but an RPR of 136 recorded by the winner is a fair reflection and the Mullins pair need to step up plenty.

Verdict Douvan is hard to oppose in the Supreme, Kilcrea Vale rates value in the Neptune, Tea For Two will appeal strongly if he heads for the Albert Bartlett and Hargam looks a solid each-way alternative to stablemate Peace And Co in the Triumph *(Dave Orton)*

Trainer analysis

Kevin Morley pinpoints the key trainer trends and the jockey-trainer combinations to follow as the top stables chase the big trophies

Nicky Henderson

Festival winners **51** *Last five years* **3/2/7/4/1**

Seven winners at the 2012 festival, four in 2013 but only one from 38 runners last year for Nicky Henderson, who remains the festival's winningmost trainer but has found himself increasingly challenged by Willie Mullins.

Of course it did not help that Henderson went into festival battle last year without two of his star performers. Simonsig, the 2013 Arkle victor, missed the whole of last season through injury while Sprinter Sacre was pulled up on his sole start of the campaign owing to a heart problem. Considering the bulk of Henderson's festival success in recent years has come in the Grade 1 chases, those absences were a major blow.

Henderson still had a reasonably strong team for the championship events but, although Bobs Worth, My Tent Or Yours and Riverside Theatre ran solid races, none was quite good enough to win and the sole success for the yard came with Whisper in the Coral Cup.

While Simonsig's injury problems have continued, at least **Sprinter Sacre** is back in the reckoning for the Champion Chase. There was more than enough promise on his January reappearance to suggest he can regain the crown, although that feat has been achieved just twice before (by Royal Relief in 1974 and Moscow Flyer in 2005).

Sprinter Sacre is clearly Henderson's best hope of success in one of the major championships as Bobs Worth's best days appear to be behind him as he bids to regain the Gold Cup – something that has been accomplished only once (by Kauto Star in 2009). Bobs Worth recorded a Racing Post Rating of 181 in winning the 2013 Gold Cup but 167 is his best since.

Last year's lack of success in the novice events was a surprise given that the yard had won at least one such contest at the previous five festivals. The lack of top-class talent in that division last term is one of the reasons why contenders are scarce for Henderson in the marquee events this year. However, one of Henderson's strengths is the continual turnover and renewal of his racing stock and it was always unlikely that situation would be allowed to persist. Certainly he appears to be stronger in the novice department this term.

His best hope is **Peace And Co** in the Triumph – a contest he has won five times. The French import looked awesome when winning a Grade 2 at Doncaster in December and again at the same level on Cheltenham's

This year's principal Henderson contenders

Bear's Affair *(Pertemps)*, **Beat That** *(World Hurdle)*, **Bivouac** *(Triumph)*, **Blue Fashion** *(World Hurdle)*, **Bobs Worth** *(Gold Cup)*, **Caracci Apache** *(Albert Bartlett)*, **Clean Sheet** *(Martin Pipe)*, **Cup Final** *(Pertemps)*, **Dawalan** *(Coral Cup)*, **Hargam** *(Triumph)*, **Hunt Ball** *(below, Kim Muir)*, **Josses Hill** *(Arkle)*, **Kilcrea Vale** *(Neptune)*, **L'Ami Serge** *(Supreme)*, **Ma Filleule** *(Ryanair)*, **Out Sam** *(Albert Bartlett)*, **Peace And Co** *(Triumph)*, **Polly Peachum** *(Mares' Hurdle)*, **Sign Of A Victory** *(Coral Cup)*, **Snake Eyes** *(Coral Cup)*, **Sprinter Sacre** *(Champion Chase)*, **Theinval** *(Coral Cup)*, **Top Notch** *(Triumph)*, **Utopie Des Bordes** *(Pertemps)*, **Vyta Du Roc** *(Albert Bartlett)*, **Whisper** *(World Hurdle)*

Henderson's Cheltenham record

Festival	Hurdles Handicap			Hurdles Non-handicap			Chases Handicap			Chases Non-handicap			Bumper			Overall		
2010	1/12	8%	3	2/10	20%	7	0/8	0%	-8	0/8	0%	-8	0/0	0%	0	3/38	8%	-6
2011	0/12	0%	-12	1/11	9%	-8.13	0/9	0%	-9	1/10	10%	-5.5	0/1	0%	-1	2/43	5%	-35.63
2012	1/8	13%	33	1/7	14%	-4	1/13	8%	8	4/9	44%	7.73	0/0	0%	0	5/37	14%	44.73
2013	0/8	0%	-8	0/12	0%	-12	1/11	9%	6	3/8	38%	-1.47	0/0	0%	0	4/39	10%	-15.47
2014	1/12	8%	3	0/8	0%	-8	0/10	0%	-10	0/8	0%	-8	0/0	0%	0	1/38	3%	-23
Total	3/52	6%	19	4/48	8%	-25.13	2/51	4%	-13	8/43	19%	-15.24	0/1	0%	-1	17/195	9%	-35.37

Season	Hurdles Handicap			Chases			Bumper			Overall		
10/11	9/51	18%	-8.77	2/39	5%	-30.17	1/6	17%	-1	12/96	13%	-38.29
11/12	8/38	21%	26.03	9/35	26%	24.73	1/1	100%	2	18/74	24%	52.76
12/13	3/46	7%	-38.05	7/34	21%	3.83	0/0	0%	0	10/81	12%	-35.22
13/14	4/41	10%	-3.09	3/33	9%	-24.37	0/4	0%	-3	7/78	9%	-31.46
14/15	3/20	15%	-12.83	0/9	0%	-9	0/1	0%	-1	3/30	10%	-22.83
Total	27/196	14%	-35.07	21/150	14%	-34.97	2/13	15%	-5	50/359	14%	-75.04

Henderson-trained festival winners

1985 First Bout (Triumph), See You Then (Champion), The Tsarevich (Plate) **1986** See You Then (Champion Hurdle), River Ceiriog (Supreme), The Tsarevich (Plate) **1987** Alone Success (Triumph), See You Then (Champion Hurdle) **1989** Rustle (World Hurdle) **1990** Master Bob (Kim Muir), Brown Windsor (Cathcart) **1991** Remittance Man (Arkle) **1992** Flown (Supreme), Remittance Man (Champion Chase) **1993** Travado (Arkle), Thumbs Up (County) **1994** Raymylette (Cathcart) **1997** Barna Boy (County) **1999** Katarino (Triumph), Stormyfairweather (Cathcart) **2000** Tiutchev (Arkle), Stormyfairweather (Cathcart), Bacchanal (World Hurdle), Marlborough (JLT) **2002** The Bushkeeper (Kim Muir) **2005** Liberthine (Plate), Juveigneur (Kim Muir), Trabolgan (RSA) **2006** Non So (Plate), Fondmort (Ryanair), Greenhope (Grand Annual) **2009** Punjabi (Champion Hurdle), Zaynar (Triumph), Andytown (Martin Pipe) **2010** Binocular (Champion Hurdle), Spirit River (Coral Cup), Soldatino (Triumph) **2011** Long Run (Gold Cup), Bobs Worth (Albert Bartlett) **2012** Sprinter Sacre (Arkle), Simonsig (Neptune), Bobs Worth (RSA), Finian's Rainbow (Champion Chase), Une Artiste (Fred Winter), Riverside Theatre (Ryanair), Bellvano (Grand Annual) **2013** Simonsig (Arkle), Rajdhani Express (R4R Novices' Handicap Chase), Sprinter Sacre (Champion Chase), Bobs Worth (Gold Cup) **2014** Whisper (Coral Cup)

Trials Day, and even at this stage he appears to be developing into a potential Champion Hurdle candidate at future festivals. **Hargam** and **Top Notch** add to a strong hand in the Triumph.

L'Ami Serge looks set to feature prominently in the Supreme and **Josses Hill**, runner-up in that event last year, has each-way claims in the Arkle.

Although Henderson has a better strike-rate in the level-weights contests, his handicappers should not be ignored as the level-stakes column is more profitable in those contests, especially over hurdles. Whisper scored at 14-1 in last year's Coral Cup, meaning that none of Henderson's ten handicap winners since 2005 has been returned shorter than 12-1 (and have been as big as 40-1).

Given the prices of his handicap winners it is difficult to predict where he might score in this area, but he has a chance of landing a second successive Coral Cup with the progressive **Dawalan**, while **Snake Eyes** (below) would be one to consider in the County Hurdle.

Bar the Cross Country Chase and the Pertemps Final, Henderson has won every handicap at the festival, including the more recently installed ones such as the Novices' Handicap Chase, Fred Winter Handicap Hurdle and Martin Pipe Conditional Jockeys' Handicap Hurdle.

Paul Nicholls
Festival winners **34** *Last five years* **2/3/2/1/1**

Having relinquished the British trainers' championship to Nicky Henderson in the 2012-13 campaign, Nicholls swiftly regained his title last term but he owed his success less to quality (Silviniaco Conti's King George victory was easily the highlight) and more to the quantity of middle-ranking Saturday winners he amassed.

Once again that did not help him at the festival, where Nicholls has performed well below expectations in the past two years. He usually has around 30 runners at the festival, but whereas he had five winners from 35 in 2009 (the last time he was the meeting's top trainer) he had just one from 30 in 2013 and one from 33 last year.

Nicholls clearly possesses several useful performers but few are top-class and certainly none as smart as the likes of Kauto Star and Denman. One handicap winner and no Grade 1 success at both of the last two festivals lends weight to that view.

He won at least one of the major championship races for six consecutive years from 2007 but has not landed one since 2012 with Big Buck's (World Hurdle) and Rock On Ruby (Champion Hurdle). Kauto Star's 2009 triumph was not only the most recent of Nicholls' four Gold Cup successes, it was also the trainer's last victory in any Cheltenham chase, including handicaps.

Silviniaco Conti bids to break that run and he seems better than ever after defending his King George crown. Twice he has failed in the Gold Cup and has yet to prove Cheltenham is really his course (3F4 from three runs) but the opposition is far from intimidating.

Dodging Bullets has emerged as a leading contender for the Champion Chase, while **Saphir Du Rheu** is taking the Big Buck's route as a failed chaser going for the World Hurdle and will line up alongside **Zarkandar**.

Not only has Nicholls relied on hurdlers for his nine wins at the last five festivals but his handicappers have come increasingly to the fore. Lac Fontana in the County Hurdle was his sole winner last year but he had seconds in the Fred Winter (Katgary) and Pertemps Final (Southfield Theatre) and third in the Martin Pipe (Caid Du Berlais).

The key to finding a Nicholls handicap winner (especially over hurdles) is to look for a young, lightly raced type yet to be exposed to the handicapper. Four of his six handicap hurdle winners were aged four or five (the other two were six) and six of his nine handicap winners overall (chases and hurdles) have carried 10st 10lb to 11st. It is also notable that they are often well fancied – four of the nine have been favourite and only two have been bigger than 12-1.

Nicholls' record also suggests he is most likely to strike in a handicap over two miles, whether it is over fences or hurdles – he has won the County Hurdle four times and the Grand Annual twice. He appears to have strong contenders for both contests this term with **Calipto** for the County and **Solar Impulse** in the Grand Annual. **Mr Mole** was strongly fancied when disappointing in the Grand Annual last year (fell at the last when well beaten) but appears to have turned over a new leaf this season and is set to go for the Champion Chase alongside Dodging Bullets.

Although none of Nicholls' novice chasers could be described as top-notch, he has a solid team this season. **Ptit Zig** has a big chance in the JLT, while **Vibrato Valtat**, **Southfield Theatre** and **Irish Saint** (right) are all open to improvement.

With a stronger team than last year, Nicholls will be disappointed if he fails to strike more than once at the 2015 festival.

Nicholls-trained festival winners

1999 Flagship Uberalles (Arkle), Call Equiname (Champion Chase), See More Business (Gold Cup)
2003 Azertyuiop (Arkle)
2004 Azertyuiop (Champion Chase), Earthmover (Foxhunter), St Pirran (Grand Annual), Sporazene (County)
2005 Sleeping Night (Foxhunter), Thisthatandtother (Ryanair)
2006 Noland (Supreme), Star De Mohaison (RSA), Desert Quest (County)
2007 Denman (RSA), Kauto Star (Gold Cup), Andreas (Grand Annual), Taranis (Ryanair)
2008 Master Minded (Champion Chase), Denman (Gold Cup), Celestial Halo (Triumph)
2009 Master Minded (Champion Chase), Chapoturgeon (Jewson), Big Buck's (World Hurdle), American Trilogy (County), Kauto Star (Gold Cup)
2010 Sanctuaire (Fred Winter), Big Buck's (World Hurdle)
2011 Al Ferof (Supreme), Big Buck's (World Hurdle), Zarkandar (Triumph)
2012 Rock On Ruby (Champion Hurdle), Big Buck's (World Hurdle)
2013 Salubrious (Martin Pipe)
2014 Lac Fontana (County)

This year's principal Nicholls contenders

Benvolio (*Ultima Handicap Chase*), **Bouvreuil** (*Fred Winter*), **Caid Du Berlais** (*Stable Plate*), **Calipto** (*County*), **Ceasar Milan** (*Novices' Handicap Chase*), **Dodging Bullets** (*Champion Chase*), **Hinterland** (*Champion Chase*), **Just A Par** (*Kim Muir*), **Keltus** (*Novices' Handicap Chase*), **Morito Du Berlais** (*Martin Pipe*), **Mr Mole** (*Champion Chase*), **Ptit Zig** (*JLT*), **Rolling Aces** (*Kim Muir*), **Sam Winner** (*Gold Cup*), **San Benedeto** (*Triumph*), **Saphir Du Rheu** (*World Hurdle*), **Silviniaco Conti** (*Gold Cup*), **Sire Collonges** (*Cross Country*), **Solar Impulse** (*Grand Annual*), **Southfield Theatre** (*NH Chase*), **Tara Point** (*Mares' Hurdle*), **Vibrato Valtat** (*Arkle*), **Vivaldi Collonges** (*Pertemps*), **Wonderful Charm** (*Ryanair*), **Zarkandar** (*World Hurdle*)

Nicholls's Cheltenham record		Hurdles Handicap			Hurdles Non-handicap			Chases Handicap			Chases Non-handicap			Bumper			Overall		
Festival	2010	1/6	17%	-1	1/6	17%	-4.17	0/9	0%	-9	0/9	0%	-9	0/1	0%	-1	2/31	7%	-24.17
	2011	0/5	0%	-5	3/7	43%	13.41	0/4	0%	-4	0/12	0%	-12	0/0	0%	0	3/28	11%	-7.59
	2012	0/6	0%	-6	2/11	18%	2.83	0/4	0%	-4	0/9	0%	-9	0/0	0%	0	2/30	7%	-16.17
	2013	1/10	10%	7	0/8	0%	-8	0/4	0%	-4	0/7	0%	-7	0/1	0%	-1	1/30	3%	-13
	2014	1/11	9%	1	0/8	0%	-8	0/5	0%	-5	0/9	0%	-9	0/0	0%	0	1/33	3%	-21
	Total	**3/38**	**8%**	**-4**	**6/40**	**15%**	**-3.93**	**0/26**	**0%**	**-26**	**0/46**	**0%**	**-46**	**0/2**	**0%**	**-2**	**9/152**	**6%**	**-81.93**
Season	10/11	8/45	18%	-8.77				7/50	14%	-6.74				1/2	50%	1.75	16/97	16%	-13.67
	11/12	10/52	19%	3.5				4/43	9%	-29.29				0/1	0%	-1	14/96	15%	-26.79
	12/13	8/47	17%	-8.54				5/38	13%	-3.75				1/4	25%	-1.38	14/89	16%	-13.67
	13/14	5/54	9%	-28.89				6/38	16%	1				0/3	0%	-3	11/95	12%	-30.89
	14/15	3/19	16%	-1.5				4/20	20%	27.5				0/0	0%	0	7/39	18%	26
	Total	**34/217**	**16%**	**-49.87**				**26/189**	**14%**	**-11.28**				**2/10**	**20%**	**-3.63**	**62/416**	**15%**	**-59.11**

Willie Mullins

Festival winners **33** *Last five years* **2/4/3/5/4**

Between 2009 and 2013, the festival's top trainer award had alternated between Mullins and Nicky Henderson but Ireland's champion trainer broke that sequence by retaining the title with four winners at last year's meeting.

Mullins has been a growing force at the festival since 2008 – with at least two winners each year and three top trainer awards – and has overtaken Nicky Henderson and Paul Nicholls in terms of the overall quality at his disposal.

As usual, the perennial Irish champion was particularly strong in the novice division last year when Vautour and Faugheen ran out impressive winners of the Supreme and Neptune respectively. Those victories were supplemented by Quevega's sixth consecutive win in the Mares' Hurdle and Don Poli's success in the Martin Pipe Conditional

Douvan: fancied to start with a bang in the Supreme

Mullins's Cheltenham record

Festival

		Hurdles Handicap			Hurdles Non-handicap			Chases Handicap			Chases Non-handicap			Bumper			Overall		
2010		1/7	14%	14	1/9	11%	-6.5	0/2	0%	-2	0/8	0%	-8	0/3	0%	-3	2/29	7%	-5.5
2011		2/6	33%	10.5	2/9	22%	-3.42	0/1	0%	-1	0/7	0%	-7	0/2	0%	-2	4/25	16%	-2.92
2012		0/3	0%	-3	1/18	6%	-16.43	0/3	0%	-3	1/9	11%	-5	1/2	50%	15	3/35	9%	-12.43
2013		0/11	0%	-11	3/10	30%	0.35	0/4	0	-4	1/7	14%	-3.75	1/3	33%	23	5/35	14%	4.6
2014		1/8	13%	5	3/12	25%	-3.27	0/5	0%	-5	0/9	0%	-9	0/3	0%	-3	4/37	11%	-15.27
Total		4/35	11%	15.5	10/58	17%	-29.27	0/15	0%	-15	2/40	5%	-32.75	2/13	15%	30	18/161	11%	-31.52

Season

		Hurdles Handicap			Hurdles Non-handicap			Chases Handicap			Chases Non-handicap			Bumper			Overall		
10/11		4/15	17%				7.08				0/8	0%	-8	0/2	0%	-2	4/25	16%	-2.92
11/12		2/24	8%				-13.93				2/15	13%	-5.5	1/4	25%	13	5/43	12%	-6.43
12/13		3/23	13%				-12.65				2/15	13%	-6.25	1/3	33%	23	6/41	15%	4.1
13/14		5/25	20%				-1.87				0/15	0%	-15	0/4	0%	-4	5/44	11%	-20.87
14/15		0/1	0%				-1				0/2	0%	-2	0/1	0%	-1	0/4	0%	-4
Total		14/88	16%				-22.37				4/55	7%	-36.75	2/14	14%	29	20/157	13%	-30.12

Jockeys' Handicap Hurdle, a race Mullins also won for Gigginstown in 2011 with Sir Des Champs.

Hurricane Fly (2011 and 2013 Champion Hurdle) remains Mullins' only winner in one of the major championship races and will be back this year, although this time as the apparent second-string behind long-time ante-post favourite Faugheen.

Although **Hurricane Fly** remains difficult to beat in small fields on soft ground in Ireland, his one-paced fourth in the big one last year suggested he was a declining force at the very highest level and he is now 11. Mullins does not seem to have too much to worry about, however, as **Faugheen** is proven at Cheltenham, has travelled over twice this season to win the Coral Hurdle at Ascot and the Christmas Hurdle at Kempton and is open to improvement.

Mullins nearly staged an upset with **On His Own** in last year's Gold Cup and a prominent showing by that one or **Boston Bob** would not be a great surprise in a weak renewal. He has a better chance of landing the Champion Chase with **Champagne Fever**, a previous winner of the Champion Bumper and the Supreme and second in last year's Arkle.

Mullins is strong in the novice races again and has at least one contender prominent in the betting for each contest. **Douvan** (Supreme), **Un De Sceaux** (Arkle), **Don Poli** (RSA or NH Chase), **Shaneshill** (*below,* Neptune), **Vautour** (JLT), **Kalkir** and **Petite Parisienne** (Triumph) and **Black Hercules** (Albert Bartlett) all have solid chances and he seems likely to strike in at least a couple of those races.

The retired Quevega is not around to defend her Mares' Hurdle crown but Mullins has a more than adequate replacement in **Annie Power**, who was a valiant second in last year's World Hurdle.

When analysing Mullins' chances in the level-weights contests, it is worth bearing his mind his superior record with hurdlers compared with chasers. He has had ten winners over hurdles in such contests since 2010, against two over fences.

The strength in depth of the yard has stretched to handicaps in recent years and his hurdlers also fare much better in this respect as he has yet to strike in a handicap chase at the festival. He has had two winners in both the County Hurdle (Thousand Stars in 2010 and Final Approach in 2011) and the Martin Pipe (Sir Des Champs in 2011 and Don Poli in 2014), producing a profit of £15.50 to a £1 level stake in handicap hurdles at the last five festivals.

Both his County Hurdle winners had run in Leopardstown's BoyleSports Hurdle and **Clondaw Warrior**, who was brought down in that contest, appeals as a strong contender. **Killer Crow**, owned by Gigginstown (like Sir Des Champs and Don Poli), appeals for the Martin Pipe.

Mullins has long been fond of the Champion Bumper and usually has more than one representative, with a lesser-fancied runner often obliging. **Au Quart De Tour** has emerged as market leader but it will be worth considering any Mullins runner.

In general, however, it is best to follow the money with Mullins runners. He has had 25 favourites at the past five festivals and 11 obliged (form figures 10113013P121113124114242F), producing a £6.48 level-stake profit with a 44 per cent strike-rate.

Mullins-trained festival winners

1995 Tourist Attraction (Supreme)

1996 Wither Or Which (Bumper)

1997 Florida Pearl (Bumper)

1998 Alexander Banquet (Bumper), Florida Pearl (RSA)

2000 Joe Cullen (Bumper)

2002 Scolardy (Triumph

2004 Rule Supreme (RSA)

2005 Missed That (Bumper)

2007 Ebaziyan (Supreme)

2008 Cousin Vinny (Bumper), Fiveforthree (Neptune)

2009 Quevega (Mares' Hurdle), Mikael D'Haguenet (Neptune), Cooldine (RSA)

2010 Quevega (Mares' Hurdle), Thousand Stars (County)

2011 Hurricane Fly (Champion Hurdle), Quevega (Mares' Hurdle), Final Approach (County), Sir Des Champs (Martin Pipe)

2012 Quevega (Mares' Hurdle), Champagne Fever (Bumper), Sir Des Champs (Jewson)

2013 Champagne Fever (Supreme), Hurricane Fly (Champion Hurdle), Quevega (Mares' Hurdle), Back In Focus (NH Chase), Briar Hill (Bumper)

2014 Vautour (Supreme), Quevega (Mares' Hurdle), Faugheen (Neptune), Don Poli (Martin Pipe)

O'Neill-trained festival winners

1991 Danny Connors (Pertemps)

1995 Front Line (NH Chase)

2000 Master Tern (County)

2002 Rith Dubh (NH Chase)

2003 Inching Closer (Pertemps), Sudden Shock (NH Chase), Spectroscope (Triumph)

2004 Creon (Pertemps), Native Emperor (NH Chase), Iris's Gift (World Hurdle)

2006 Black Jack Ketchum (Albert Bartlett)

2007 Butler's Cabin (NH Chase), Wichita Lineman (Albert Bartlett), Drombeag (Foxhunter)

2008 Albertas Run (RSA)

2009 Wichita Lineman (JLT)

2010 Albertas Run (Ryanair)

2011 Albertas Run (Ryanair)

2012 Alfie Sherrin (JLT), Sunnyhillboy (Kim Muir), Synchronised (Gold Cup)

2013 Holywell (Pertemps)

2014 Holywell (Baylis & Harding Hcap Chase), Taquin Du Seuil (JLT), More Of That (World Hurdle)

Main contenders at this year's festival

Box Office (Fred Winter), **Cloudy Copper** (Ultima Handicap Chase), **Eastlake** (Grand Annual), **Goodwood Mirage** (County), **Holywell** (Gold Cup), **Johns Spirit** (Ryanair), **Join The Clan** (Pertemps), **Merry King** (Ultima), **More Of That** (World Hurdle), **Twirling Magnet** (Ultima)

Jonjo O'Neill

Festival winners **25** *Last five years* **1/1/3/1/3**

O'Neill achieved a personal-best 134 winners last season and the most pleasing aspect must have been the stable's performance at the festival, where three winners from 17 runners confirmed the master of Jackdaws Castle as a trainer who knows how to peak for Cheltenham in March.

He has had only one blank at the meeting since the start of the millennium (that was back in 2005) and what stands out is his impressive 13 per cent strike-rate at this fiercely competitive meeting over the last five years. A level-stakes profit at each of the last three festivals is equally commendable.

The breakdown of his figures shows he is selective in his approach to the level-weights races. Since 2010 he has had just 15 runners in those contests but five of them obliged. He has more ammunition for the handicaps and, while he strikes at a much lower rate in this category, the prices are big enough to keep his backers in front.

Another factor is that his chasers have outperformed the hurdlers at the last five festivals, with seven of his nine winners coming over fences. His record also shows that he excels in staying races – 20 of his 25 festival winners have been in races over three miles or further.

Those factors were evident last year when two of his three winners came over fences (Holywell in the 3m handicap chase and Taquin Du Seuil in the JLT Novices' Chase) while his hurdle winner was over three miles with More Of That in the World Hurdle.

O'Neill's string has not been in quite the same form this season in general but that has not affected the trainer's festival exploits in the past and he can be expected to strike at least once, although there was a major blow with the news that **More Of That**, who disappointed on his only start this term, was unlikely to be ready to defend his crown.

Holywell is another who has been below par. Unlike More Of That, however, the dual festival winner was fit in time to have a prep at Kelso and O'Neill's record in Grade 1 races at this meeting suggests he will be primed for the Gold Cup.

When looking at O'Neill's handicappers, it is best to concentrate on the stayers. **Join The Clan** appears to have been lined up for the Pertemps Final, while **Twirling Magnet** may be one for the Ultima Business Solutions Handicap Chase – O'Neill has won both contests more than once.

O'Neill's Cheltenham record

Festival

	Hurdles Handicap			Hurdles Non-handicap			Chases Handicap			Chases Non-handicap			Bumper			Overall		
2010	0/7	0%	-7	0/2	0%	-2	0/6	0%	-6	1/2	50%	13	0/0	0%	0	1/17	6%	-2
2011	0/4	0%	-4	0/0	0%	0	0/5	0%	-5	1/3	33%	4	0/0	0%	0	1/12	8%	-5
2012	0/4	0%	-4	0/0	0%	0	2/3	67%	19.5	1/2	50%	7	0/0	0%	0	3/9	33%	22.5
2013	1/5	20%	21	0/2	0%	-2	0/6	0%	-6	0/1	0%	-1	0/0	0%	0	1/14	7%	12
2014	0/6	0%	-6	1/1	100%	7.5	1/8	12%	3	1/2	50%	6	0/0	0%	0	3/17	18%	10.5
Total	1/26	4%	0	1/5	20%	3.5	3/28	11%	5.5	4/10	40%	29	0/0	0%	0	9/69	13%	38

Season

	Hurdles Handicap			Hurdles Non-handicap			Chases Handicap			Chases Non-handicap			Bumper			Overall		
10/11		0/15	0%			-15		3/23	13%		-10.38		0/3	0%	-3	3/41	7%	-28.38
11/12		1/8	13%			15		4/14	29%		27.5		0/1	0%	-1	5/23	22%	41.5
12/13		2/16	13%			13.75		0/15	0%		-15		0/0	0%	0	2/31	6%	-1.25
13/14		3/24	13%			-0.75		7/27	26%		24		0/1	0%	-1	10/52	19%	22.25
14/15		1/8	13%			-4.75		1/7	14%		-1		0/1	0%	-1	2/16	13%	-6.75
Total		7/71	10%			8.25		15/86	17%		25.13		0/6	0%	-6	22/163	13%	27.38

Philip Hobbs
Festival winners **18** *Last five years* **2/2/1/0/2**

Prior to last season, numbers had been on the decline at Withycombe but Hobbs bounced back in style in 2013-14. Not only did he break the century barrier with 106 winners, he finished third in the trainers' championship, amassing more than £1.5 million in prize-money, and had two festival winners to boot.

Hobbs may not be as prolific at Cheltenham as some of the other leading trainers but he is a steady scorer, striking at least once at ten of the last 14 festivals and twice at three of the last five. Hurdlers were previously his greatest source of success, with victories just as likely to come in handicaps as they were in novice races. However, that has levelled out in recent years as he has added more wins in chases.

Two of Hobbs's four wins over fences since 2010 came with Balthazar King in the Cross Country in 2012 and 2014 (that one seems likely to miss this year's meeting in favour of a tilt at the Grand National, even though he finished second at Aintree last year after his Cheltenham success). The other two have been with novices – Copper Bleu landed the novice handicap in 2010 and Captain Chris won the 2011 Arkle.

It had been a while since Hobbs landed a handicap hurdle at the meeting but he managed to strike last year with Fingal Bay in the Pertemps Final, giving him his first victory in this category since Monkerhostin's 2004 Coral Cup success.

The Pertemps Final may again represent the stable's best chance of landing a handicap hurdle. **Big Easy** is at his best in these competitive big-field handicaps and should have conditions in his favour.

With three winners from 17 runners since 2010 in contests confined to novices, that is a strong point for Hobbs and **Royal Regatta** looks a likely type for the novice handicap chase or perhaps the Grand Annual. He has outside chances in the RSA with **If In Doubt** and **Sausalito Sunrise**.

Hobbs usually likes to have a crack at the Champion Bumper, having been represented in the race four times in the last five years, and he won in 2011 with Cheltenian. Ascot winner **Wait For Me** and **Wishfull Dreaming**, who took a Cheltenham Listed bumper in January, are two possibles.

Hobbs-trained festival winners

1990 Moody Man (County)

1996 Kibreet (Grand Annual)

2000 What's Up Boys (Coral Cup)

2002 Rooster Booster (County), Flagship Uberalles (Champion Chase)

2003 Rooster Booster (Champion Hurdle), One Knight (RSA)

2004 Monkerhostin (Coral Cup), Made In Japan (Triumph)

2006 Detroit City (Triumph)

2007 Massini's Maguire (Neptune)

2010 Menorah (Supreme), Copper Bleu (Jewson)

2011 Captain Chris (Arkle), Cheltenian (Bumper)

2012 Balthazar King (Cross Country)

2014 Balthazar King (Cross Country), Fingal Bay (Pertemps)

Main contenders at this year's festival

Big Easy (*Pertemps*), **Duke Of Lucca** (*below, Cross Country*), **Garde La Victoire** (*County*), **Hello George** (*Coral Cup*), **If In Doubt** (*RSA*), **Menorah** (*Ryanair*), **Sausalito Sunrise** (*RSA*), **Wishfull Thinking** (*Ryanair*)

Hobbs's Cheltenham record

Festival

	Hurdles Handicap			Hurdles Non-handicap			Chases Handicap			Chases Non-handicap			Bumper			Overall		
2010	0/7	0%	-7	1/2	50%	11	1/10	10%	3	0/1	0%	-1	0/2	0%	-2	2/21	10%	5
2011	0/6	0%	-6	0/3	0%	-3	0/5	0%	-5	1/3	33%	4	1/1	100%	14	2/18	11%	4
2012	0/4	0%	-4	0/2	0%	-2	1/2	50%	4.5	0/4	0%	-4	0/1	0%	-1	1/13	8%	-6.5
2013	0/6	0%	-6	0/2	0%	-2	0/2	0	-2	0/3	0%	-3	0/0	0%	0	0/13	0%	-13
2014	1/11	9%	-5.5	0/3	0%	-3	1/7	14%	-2	0/2	0%	-2	0/1	0%	-1	2/24	8%	-13.5
Total	**1/34**	**3%**	**-28.5**	**1/12**	**8%**	**1**	**3/26**	**12%**	**-1.5**	**1/13**	**8%**	**-6**	**1/5**	**20%**	**10**	**7/90**	**8%**	**-25**

Season

	Hurdles Handicap				Chases Handicap				Bumper			Overall		
10/11	3/30	10%	-11.75		5/33	15%	-7.5		1/4	25%	11	9/67	13%	-8.25
11/12	2/26	8%	-19.2		5/28	18%	-7.84		0/1	0%	-1	7/55	13%	-28.04
12/13	1/22	5%	-16		2/18	11%	-6.27		0/1	0%	-1	3/41	7%	-23.27
13/14	5/32	16%	6.63		5/32	16%	-1.25		0/3	0%	-3	10/67	15%	2.38
14/15	2/9	22%	4.63		7/24	29%	19.47		1/2	50%	3	10/35	29%	27.1
Total	**13/119**	**11%**	**-35.7**		**24/135**	**18%**	**-3.39**		**2/11**	**18%**	**9**	**39/265**	**15%**	**-30.09**

1992 Tipping Tim (JLT)

1993 Gaelstrom
(Neptune), Young Hustler
(RSA)

1994 Arctic Kinsman
(Supreme)

1998 Upgrade (Triumph)

2000 Rubhahunish
(Pertemps)

2004 Fundamentalist
(Neptune)

2008 Ballyfitz (Pertemps)

2009 Tricky Trickster
(NH Chase), Imperial
Commander (Ryanair)

2010 Imperial Commander
(Gold Cup), Baby Run
(Foxhunter), Pigeon Island
(Grand Annual)

2013 The New One
(Neptune), Same
Difference (Kim Muir)

Main contenders at this year's festival

Astracad (*Grand Annual*),
Blaklion (*Albert Bartlett*),
Bristol De Mai
(*Triumph*), **Cogry**
(*NH Chase*),
**Splash
Of Ginge**
(*right, Stable
Plate*), **The New
One** (*Champion
Hurdle*)

Nigel Twiston-Davies
Festival winners **15** *Last five years* **3/0/0/2/0**

With just nine runners at last year's meeting, Twiston-Davies sent out a smaller festival team than usual and his chief hope was The New One in the Champion Hurdle. Unfortunately for the stable's flagbearer, he was hampered by the ill-fated Our Conor at a crucial stage. A powerful surge up the hill to grab third place left connections wondering what might have been but also gave them hope that he would have every chance of making amends next time.

He may have failed to strike at last year's meeting but Twiston-Davies certainly knows how to deliver at the festival when he has the ammunition. He enjoyed his best festival in 2010 with three winners from 21 runners, including Gold Cup victory for Imperial Commander, and 2013 was almost as productive with two winners and five places from 11 runners.

As last year, the trainer's festival is likely to be defined by **The New One's** performance in the Champion Hurdle. He easily represents Twiston-Davies's best chance of landing a Grade 1, although **Splash Of Ginge** has each-way claims in the JLT Novices' Chase, as does **Bristol De Mai** in the Triumph. Course-and-distance winner Splash Of Ginge boasts a similar profile to Double Ross, who was a close third in last year's JLT for the stable, while Twiston-Davies tasted Triumph success with Upgrade in 1998.

Any other victory is likely to come in handicaps and it is worth looking at his stayers with that in mind. Five of his 15 festival winners have been in handicaps, four of which have come over three miles (Ultima Business Solutions Handicap Chase, Kim Muir and twice in the Pertemps Final).

One of his brightest hopes is **Cogry**, an unexposed, staying novice chaser. He is likely to get a low weight if aimed at the Ultima Business Solutions Handicap Chase or the Kim Muir but he is also qualified for the National Hunt Chase, which Twiston-Davies landed in 2009 with Tricky Trickster.

Twiston-Davies's Cheltenham record — Festival

	Hurdles Handicap			Hurdles Non-handicap			Chases Handicap			Chases Non-handicap			Bumper			Overall		
2010	0/4	0%	-4	0/3	0%	-3	1/4	25%	13	2/10	20%	3.5	0/0	0%	0	3/21	14%	9.5
2011	0/3	0%	-3	0/5	0%	-5	0/4	0%	-4	0/4	0%	-4	0/2	0%	-2	0/18	0%	-18
2012	0/3	0%	-3	0/2	0%	-2	0/7	0%	-7	0/1	0%	-1	0/1	0%	-1	0/14	0%	-14
2013	0/3	0%	-3	1/2	50%	2.5	1/4	25%	13	0/1	0%	-1	0/1	0%	-1	2/11	18%	10.5
2014	0/1	0%	-1	0/3	0%	-3	0/3	0%	-3	0/2	0%	-2	0/0	0%	0	0/9	0%	-9
Total	0/14	0%	-14	1/15	7%	-10.5	2/19	11%	12	2/16	13%	-4.5	0/4	0%	-4	5/73	7%	-21

Twiston-Davies's Cheltenham record — Season

	Hurdles			Chases			Bumper			Overall		
10/11	3/31	10%	-9.75	1/43	2%	-22	0/8	0%	-8	4/82	5%	-39.75
11/12	0/20	0%	-20	3/37	8%	-19.75	1/3	33%	3.5	4/60	7%	-36.25
12/13	4/20	20%	8.5	4/32	13%	0.25	0/2	0%	-2	8/54	15%	6.75
13/14	1/17	6%	-15.6	3/33	9%	-13.63	0/4	0%	-4	4/54	7%	-33.23
14/15	3/14	21%	1.82	2/19	11%	-11.25	0/1	0%	-1	5/34	15%	-10.43
Total	11/102	11%	-35.03	13/164	8%	-66.38	1/18	6%	-11.5	25/284	9%	-112.9

Alan King

Festival winners **14** *Last five years* **0/1/0/1/1**

The Barbury Castle trainer enjoyed a golden five-year period at the festival from 2004 to 2008 with ten winners, eight of which came in Grade 1 contests. Although he has struggled to make an impact at the top level since then, he is still likely to turn up the odd festival winner (he has had one in four of the last seven years) and is often competitive (last year he had a winner, two seconds and two thirds from the 14 races in which he was represented).

Three of those most recent four winners were in handicaps, with the other coming in the four-mile National Hunt Chase. He has developed a good record in the latter race, having won with Old Benny in 2008 and Midnight Prayer last year as well as sending out subsequent Scottish National winner Godsmejudge to finish third in 2013. **Sego Success**, who looks nailed on to improve for the step up in distance, is his sole entrant this year.

Most of King's chase wins at the festival have been with novices, not only in Grade 1s and the National Hunt Chase but also in handicaps. He broke his festival duck in 2004 when Fork Lightning landed what is now the Ultima Business Solutions Handicap Chase as a first-season chaser and the novice Oh Crick won the 2009 Grand Annual. Bensalem was in his second season over fences when taking the Ultima Handicap Chase in 2011 but had looked like winning that race as a novice when falling the year before.

Carraig Mor and **Ned Stark** are two unexposed staying novices who could be aimed at the three-mile handicap chase this year.

Although a return to Grade 1 success looks unlikely at this year's festival, King is not without hope. **Balder Succes** and **Uxizandre** (both entered in the Champion Chase and Ryanair) are useful and those races look wide open this year.

The same might be said of the Gold Cup, especially if Silviniaco Conti again fails to shine at Cheltenham, and last year's RSA Chase runner-up **Smad Place** has a shot at some place money.

Ulzana's Raid in the Pertemps Final could be King's best chance of a winner over hurdles.

King-trained festival winners

2004 Fork Lightning (Ultima)
2005 Penzance (Triumph)
2006 Voy Por Ustedes (Arkle), My Way De Solzen (World Hurdle)
2007 My Way De Solzen (Arkle), Katchit (Triumph), Voy Por Ustedes (Champion Chase)
2008 Katchit (Champion Hurdle), Old Benny (NH Chase), Nenuphar Collonges (Albert Bartlett)
2009 Oh Crick (Grand Annual)
2011 Bensalem (Ultima)
2013 Medinas (Coral Cup)
2014 Midnight Prayer (NH Chase)

Main contenders at this year's festival

Balder Succes (*Ryanair*), **Karezak** (*Triumph*), **L'Unique** (*Mares' Hurdle*), **Ned Stark** (*Nov Hcap Chase*), **Ordo Ab Chao** (*Neptune*), **Pain Au Chocolat** (*Triumph*), **Sego Success** (*NH Chase*), **Smad Place** (*Gold Cup*), **Two Rockers** (*Foxhunter*), **Ulzana's Raid** (*Pertemps*), **Uxizandre** (*Champion Chase*), **Valdez** (*left, Grand Annual*)

King's Cheltenham record — Festival

	Hurdles Handicap			Hurdles Non-handicap			Chases Handicap			Chases Non-handicap			Bumper			Overall		
2010	0/8	0%	-8	0/6	0%	-6	0/4	0%	-4	0/3	0%	-3	0/0	0%	0	0/21	0%	-21
2011	0/8	0%	-8	0/4	0%	-4	1/5	20%	1	0/2	0%	-2	0/1	0%	-1	1/20	5%	-14
2012	0/3	0%	-3	0/6	0%	-6	0/4	0%	-4	0/3	0%	-3	0/0	0%	0	0/16	0%	-16
2013	1/5	20%	29	0/4	0%	-4	0/4	0%	-4	0/1	0%	-1	0/0	0%	0	1/14	7%	20
2014	0/3	0%	-3	0/4	0%	-4	0/3	0%	-3	1/5	20%	4	0/0	0%	0	1/15	7%	-6
Total	1/27	3%	7	0/24	0%	-24	1/20	5%	-14	1/14	7%	-5	0/1	0%	-1	3/86	3%	-37

King's Cheltenham record — Season

	Hurdles			Chases			Bumper			Overall		
10/11	2/28	7%	-14	3/20	15%	13	1/4	25%	7	6/52	12%	6
11/12	2/23	9%	-7.25	1/16	6%	-8.5	0/3	0%	-3	3/42	7%	-18.75
12/13	1/22	5%	12	0/12	0%	-12	0/2	0%	-2	1/36	3%	-2
13/14	0/17	0%	-17	2/19	11%	-6.25	0/2	0%	-2	2/38	5%	-25.25
14/15	3/9	33%	20.5	1/5	20%	-2.13	0/2	0%	-1	4/16	25%	16.38
Total	8/99	8%	-5.75	7/72	10%	-15.88	1/13	8%	-2	16/184	9%	-23.63

Pipe-trained festival winners

2007 Gaspara (Fred Winter)

2008 An Accordion (Ultima), Our Vic (Ryanair)

2010 Buena Vista (Pertemps), Great Endeavour (Plate)

2011 Buena Vista (Pertemps), Junior (Kim Muir)

2012 Salut Flo (Plate)

2014 Western Warhorse (Arkle), Dynaste (Ryanair), Ballynagour (Plate)

Main contenders at this year's festival

Alternatif (*Martin Pipe*), **Baltimore Rock** (*Martin Pipe*), **Baraka De Thaix** (*Fred Winter*), **Batavir** (*Pertemps*), **Dell' Arca** (*Coral Cup*), **Easter Meteor** (*Kim Muir*), **Katkeau** (*Pertemps*), **Kings Palace** (*RSA*), **Knight Of Noir** (*Martin Pipe*), **Monetaire** (*Stable Plate*), **Moon Racer** (*Bumper*), **Our Father** (*Ultima Handicap Chase*), **Standing Ovation** (*Kim Muir*), **Un Temps Pour Tout** (*World Hurdle*)

David Pipe
Festival winners **11** *Last five years* **2/2/1/0/3**

At the festivals of 2012 and 2013 combined, David Pipe had just one winner from 55 runners but he enjoyed a dramatic turnaround in fortunes last year with three victories from 21 runners to give him his best Cheltenham to date.

Six of Pipe's seven winners prior to last year had come in handicaps and he again proved his effectiveness in that sphere in 2014 when Ballynagour bolted up in the chase now known as the Brown Advisory & Merriebelle Stable Plate, but what must have pleased him more was the stable's performance in the Grade 1 contests.

Pipe has had some disappointments with fancied Grade 1 runners but he struck twice in such events last year, with Western Warhorse causing an upset in the Arkle and Dynaste justifying favouritism in the Ryanair.

All three of last year's winners came over fences, meaning that seven of his ten festival successes have been in chases. Unfortunately Dynaste is unable to attempt a Ryanair repeat, but Pipe has a Grade 1 opportunity again with **Kings Palace** in the RSA. He disappointed in last year's Albert Bartlett (well beaten when falling at the last) but the course is not a problem as he has won his other four starts at Cheltenham.

The handicap chase in which Pipe excels is the Plate as Ballynagour's victory last year was his third win in the last five years (father Martin landed the same race four times between 1997 and 2002). French import **Monetaire** looks Pipe's strongest contender this year.

Pipe has yet to strike in a Grade 1 hurdle at the meeting but is no stranger to success in handicap hurdles. **Batavir** is prominent in the market for both the Coral Cup and the Pertemps Final – Pipe won the latter race in 2010 and 2011 with Buena Vista.

		Hurdles Handicap			Hurdles Non-handicap			Chases Handicap			Chases Non-handicap			Bumper			Overall		
Festival	2010	1/7	14%	10	0/3	0%	-3	1/9	11%	10	0/2	0%	-2	0/0	0%	0	2/21	10%	15
	2011	1/6	17%	15	0/3	0%	-3	1/9	11%	-4.67	0/4	0%	-4	0/1	0%	-1	2/23	9%	2.33
	2012	0/12	0%	-12	0/5	0%	-5	1/9	11%	-3.5	0/4	0%	-4	0/0	0%	0	1/30	3%	-24.5
	2013	0/6	0%	-6	0/2	0%	-2	0/10	0%	-10	0/4	0%	-4	0/3	0%	-3	0/25	0%	-25
	2014	0/5	0%	-5	0/3	0%	-3	1/10	10%	3	2/3	67%	35	0/0	0%	0	3/21	14%	30
	Total	2/36	6%	2	0/16	0%	-16	4/47	9%	-5.17	2/17	12%	21	0/4	0%	-4	8/120	7%	-2.17
Season	10/11	4/31	13%	20				1/31	3%	-26.67				0/1	0%	-1	5/63	8%	-7.67
	11/12	1/34	3%	-26.5				5/28	18%	6				0/0	0%	0	6/62	10%	-20.5
	12/13	1/24	4%	-16				5/35	14%	6.5				0/4	0%	-4	6/63	10%	-13.5
	13/14	6/27	22%	40.66				3/25	12%	26				1/5	20%	-0.5	10/57	18%	66.16
	14/15	2/16	13%	-6				2/16	13%	-11.63				1/2	50%	1.75	5/34	15%	-15.88
	Total	14/132	11%	12.16				16/135	12%	0.21				2/12	17%	-3.75	32/279	11%	8.62

Donald McCain

Festival winners **6** *Last five years* **2/0/2/0/0**

No trainer has been able to keep up with McCain's number of overall winners in the past two seasons but the quantity coming out of the Cheshire stable has not been matched by the quality and McCain has drawn a blank at both of the last two festivals.

He had a fair record with six festival winners between 2007 and 2012 but the success has dried up. He had a couple of placed runners in handicaps from his 14 runners in 2013 but did not get close to the each-way money with his seven runners last year.

His biggest disappointment in 2014 was Indian Castle, who was a heavily backed favourite for the Kim Muir. However, if the yard is to have a winner at this year's meeting the three-mile handicap chase for amateurs may still be his best hope.

McCain had his first festival winner when Cloudy Lane landed the 2007 Kim Muir and won again with Ballabriggs in 2010, while Super Duty was narrowly denied in 2013.

Corrin Wood may well be the smartest horse in the yard and, while he has been below par this season, his handicap mark has slipped to a level that qualifies him for the Kim Muir.

Diamond King (*right*) is another highly rated by his trainer but who has disappointed this term. He would get a low weight in the County Hurdle or Coral Cup if he made the cut.

It would be interesting if one of McCain's previously disappointing sorts was backed on the day as Son Of Flicka appeared woefully out of sorts before landing a gamble in the 2012 Coral Cup.

McCain-trained festival winners

2007 Cloudy Lane (Kim Muir)

2008 Whiteoak (Mares' Hurdle)

2010 Peddlers Cross (Neptune), Ballabriggs (Kim Muir)

2012 Cinders And Ashes (Supreme), Son Of Flicka (Coral Cup)

Main contenders at this year's festival

Frederic (*Triumph*),
I Need Gold (*NH Chase*),
Starchitect (*Triumph*),
Three Faces West (*Neptune*)

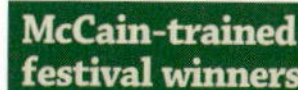

		Hurdles Handicap			Hurdles Non-handicap			Chases Handicap			Chases Non-handicap			Bumper			Overall		
Festival	2010	0/4	0%	-4	1/1	100%	7	1/3	33%	7	0/2	0%	-2	0/0	0%	0	2/10	20%	8
	2011	0/3	0%	-3	0/5	0%	-5	0/4	0%	-3	0/2	0%	-2	0/1	0%	-1	0/15	0%	-15
	2012	1/7	14%	10	1/5	20%	6	0/3	0%	-3	0/4	0%	-4	0/0	0%	0	2/19	11%	9
	2013	0/4	0%	-4	0/3	0%	-3	0/3	0%	-3	0/3	0%	-3	0/1	0%	-1	0/14	0%	-14
	2014	0/3	0%	-3	0/1	0%	-1	0/1	0%	-1	0/2	0%	-2	0/0	0%	0	0/7	0%	-7
	Total	**1/21**	**5%**	**-4**	**2/15**	**13%**	**4**	**1/14**	**7%**	**-3**	**0/13**	**0%**	**-13**	**0/2**	**0%**	**-2**	**4/65**	**6%**	**-19**
Season	10/11	0/14	0%	-14				0/8	0%	-8				0/2	0%	-2	0/24	7%	-24
	11/12	2/24	8%	4				0/8	0%	-8				0/1	0%	-1	2/33	6%	-5
	12/13	1/15	7%	-7.5				2/11	18%	9.25				0/2	0%	-2	3/28	11%	-0.25
	13/14	1/10	10%	5				1/8	13%	7				0/0	0%	0	2/18	11%	12
	14/15	0/2	0%	-2				0/3	0%	-3				0/0	0%	0	0/5	0%	-5
	Total	**4/65**	**6%**	**-14.5**				**3/38**	**8%**	**-2.75**				**0/5**	**0%**	**-5**	**7/108**	**6%**	**-22.25**

(Row label: McCain's Cheltenham record)

Tizzard-trained festival winners

2010 Cue Card (Bumper)

2011 Oiseau De Nuit (Grand Annual)

2013 Golden Chieftain (Ultima Handicap Chase), Cue Card (Ryanair)

Main contenders at this year's festival

Cue Card *(Ryanair)*, **Kingscourt Native** *Albert Bartlett)*, **Sew On Target** *(Grand Annual)*

Colin Tizzard

Festival winners **4** *Last five years* **1/1/0/2/0**

Some bookies would have paid out on Third Intention's fifth place in the Byrne Group Plate but that was the closest Tizzard got to a winner from 12 runners at last year's festival.

The Dorset trainer's hopes were badly hit by injury to stable star Cue Card, who has been the stable flagbearer in recent years – not least at the festival with victories in the 2010 Champion Bumper and 2013 Ryanair, as well as fourth in the 2011 Supreme and second in the 2012 Arkle.

Cue Card has made it back to the track and is set to line up in the Ryanair, having not been entered for the Gold Cup, but the evidence this season suggests he has not returned at quite the same level.

Although Tizzard cannot compete across the board in the Grade 1 events, his yard has become stronger in recent seasons and is not all about Cue Card. In particular, his handicap chasers are worth checking out.

Tizzard has had two festival winners in that category – Oiseau De Nuit in the 2011 Grand Annual and Golden Chieftain in the 2013 running of the 3m handicap chase – and both obliged at huge prices (40-1 and 28-1 respectively), which contribute to a plus in the level-stakes column that no other trainer can match.

This year **Theatrical Star** *(left)* could be aimed at the Kim Muir or the Ultima Business Solutions Handicap Chase and would be particularly interesting on soft ground, while **Theatre Guide** could go for the Ultima or the Brown Advisory & Merriebelle Stable Plate.

A more unexposed staying chaser is **Masters Hill**, who finished a creditable fifth in last year's Albert Bartlett and looks progressive.

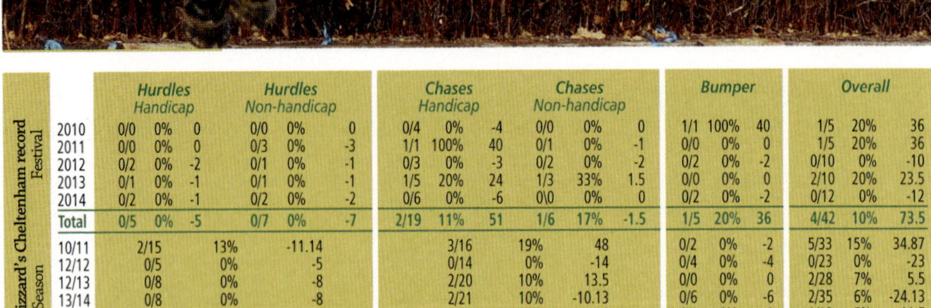

		Hurdles Handicap			Hurdles Non-handicap			Chases Handicap			Chases Non-handicap			Bumper			Overall		
Festival	2010	0/0	0%	0	0/0	0%	0	0/4	0%	-4	0/0	0%	0	1/1	100%	40	1/5	20%	36
	2011	0/0	0%	0	0/3	0%	-3	1/1	100%	40	0/1	0%	-1	0/0	0%	0	1/5	20%	36
	2012	0/2	0%	-2	0/1	0%	-1	0/3	0%	-3	0/2	0%	-2	0/2	0%	-2	0/10	0%	-10
	2013	0/1	0%	-1	0/1	0%	-1	1/5	20%	24	1/3	33%	1.5	0/0	0%	0	2/10	20%	23.5
	2014	0/2	0%	-1	0/2	0%	-2	0/6	0%	-6	0\0	0%	0	0/2	0%	-2	0/12	0%	-12
	Total	**0/5**	**0%**	**-5**	**0/7**	**0%**	**-7**	**2/19**	**11%**	**51**	**1/6**	**17%**	**-1.5**	**1/5**	**20%**	**36**	**4/42**	**10%**	**73.5**
Season	10/11	2/15	13%	-11.14				3/16	19%	48				0/2	0%	-2	5/33	15%	34.87
	12/12	0/5	0%	-5				0/14	0%	-14				0/4	0%	-4	0/23	0%	-23
	12/13	0/8	0%	-8				2/20	10%	13.5				0/0	0%	0	2/28	7%	5.5
	13/14	0/8	0%	-8				2/21	10%	-10.13				0/6	0%	-6	2/35	6%	-24.13
	14/15	0/6	0%	-6				1/12	8%	-4.5				0/1	0%	-1	1/19	5%	-11.5
	Total	**2/42**	**5%**	**-38.14**				**8/83**	**10%**	**32.38**				**0/13**	**0%**	**-13**	**10/138**	**7%**	**-18.26**

Tizzard's Cheltenham record

BET WITH YOUR HEAD

The Racing Post App. It's not just a betting app, it's a knowing-what-to-bet-on app.

Get the most important information, tips and predictions to help you make a swift and savvy bet on the racing from Cheltenham.

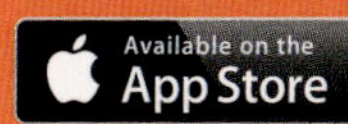

Please gamble responsibly. 18+ www.gambleaware.co.uk

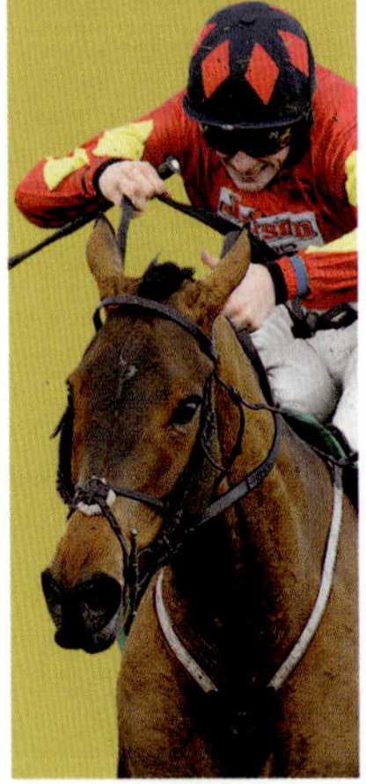

Elliott a growing force
Irish trainer aiming to score for third year in a row

Gordon Elliott's stock at the festival continues to rise. After a double in 2011 with Chicago Grey (NH Chase) and Carlito Brigante (Coral Cup) and victory with Flaxen Flare (Fred Winter) in 2013, he had his first Cheltenham Grade 1 success with Tiger Roll in last year's Triumph and two of his six other runners were placed. His best hopes this year lie with **Bayan**, who bids to improve on his 2014 Coral Cup third, and leading Ryanair contender **Don Cossack**, who was travelling well when falling in last year's RSA.

Prior to 2014, Noel Meade's festival record since 2000 stood at a measly three winners from 117 runners but he was rewarded by a selective approach to last year's meeting with just two runners – Very Wood caused an upset in the Albert Bartlett and Ned Buntline finished runner-up in the Grand Annual. He has realistic hopes with the improving **Road To Riches** (Gold Cup), **Apache Stronghold** (JLT Novices' Chase), **Very Wood** (NH Chase) and **Monksland** (World Hurdle).

Venetia Williams did not even reach a place with her 13 runners last year but it is unwise to dismiss her string. Her six festival winners have all been in handicaps and often at big odds – 50-1 shot Carrickboy landed the Plate in 2013 and Something Wells was 33-1 when winning the same race four years earlier. **Niceonefrankie**, a course-and-distance winner this season, looks likely to be aimed at that race.

Sizing Europe's form figures of 011224 at the festival prove Henry de Bromhead knows how to peak one for Cheltenham. The remarkable 13-year-old seems likely to have another crack at the Champion Chase, although the trainer probably has a better chance of securing prize-money in that race with **Special Tiara**. If anything, he is more likely to cause an upset with one of his up-and-coming novices such as **Sizing John** (Supreme) or **Sizing Granite** (Arkle).

Jessica Harrington takes a selective approach to the festival and it is foolish to dismiss any of her runners, particularly in the Grade 1 contests. **Jezki** proved the point last year when landing the Champion Hurdle and should not be underestimated as he defends his crown. The County Hurdle is a handicap she has won before (Spirit Leader in 2003) and BoyleSports Hurdle runner-up **Modem** looks a solid contender for this year's renewal.

Enda Bolger farmed the Cross Country Chase in its formative years, winning four of the first five runnings. He has not won since that race became more competitive but it still represents his best chance of success, with **Love Rory** and **Quantitativeeasing** his leading hopes from quite a few options. **On The Fringe**, fourth in the 2011 Foxhunter and third last year, could go well in that race again.

Mouse Morris did not strike with any of his four runners last year but none was disgraced and Baily Green probably would have been placed in the Champion Chase but for falling at the fourth-last. Grade

1 contenders look thin on the ground this time but any handicappers making the trip should be noted. He last struck in this category with Fota Island in the 2005 Grand Annual and **Rogue Angel** might be his best chance in something like the Kim Muir. The market can be a good guide (all three of his winners since 2002, from 43 runners, were sent off at single-figure odds).

Tony Martin has had a significant resurgence of late, both overall and at the festival, and is always one to watch in the handicaps. Savello proved the point with his 16-1 victory in last year's Grand Annual, following on from two winners for Martin at the 2013 festival. The trainer's handicap haul also includes Ted Veale (2013 County Hurdle), Dun Doire (2006 Ultima Business Handicap Chase) and Xenophon (2003 Coral Cup). He has County Hurdle possibilities with **Thomas Edison** and **Quick Jack**, while in the Grade 1s he has an each-way shout in the World Hurdle with **Dedigout** (a dual Grade 2 winner since the turn of the year).

John Ferguson achieves plenty during the season with the Flat-bred material at his disposal but has yet to train a festival winner. The closest he has come was second place with New Year's Eve in the 2012 Champion Bumper. His best chance this time appears to lie with Grade 1 Challow winner **Parlour Games** in an open-looking Neptune and he has each-way hopes with novice hurdler **Qewy** (possibly the Supreme) and novice chaser **Three Kingdoms** (possibly the JLT).

Rebecca Curtis had just four runners at last year's meeting but struck with O'Faolains Boy in the RSA Chase, giving her a single winner for the third successive festival, while At Fishers Cross followed his 2013 Albert Bartlett victory with a worthy third in the World Hurdle. All of her festival successes have been with novices but Curtis might have to explore the handicap route more to get on the scoreboard this year.

Tim Vaughan remains a trainer to avoid at Cheltenham. Of his 37 festival runners since 2009, three have finished second but he did not manage a place with any of his eight runners at last year's meeting. It is also worth noting that, in the last five seasons overall, he has not entered the Cheltenham winner's enclosure from 115 attempts.

Gary Moore is hardly the most prolific festival scorer but he managed to bag a Grade 1 last year with Sire De Grugy in the Champion Chase. That was his first success at the meeting since Tikram's 2004 Plate victory. A repeat win for **Sire De Grugy** is possible but he has had injury problems and does not boast the same level of form as last season.

Dermot Weld had a wretched run of 74 consecutive festival losers stretching back to 1990 until Silver Concorde landed last year's Champion Bumper. If he is to strike this year it could be in that race again with **Vigil**, a solid fifth behind his successful stablemate last year, or in the Neptune with Grade 1 Deloitte runner-up **Windsor Park**.

What they say

'I always felt he was the best we'd had'

John Ferguson, trainer of Parlour Games *(Neptune)* "I always felt he was the best we'd had and that he was all class. [In winning the Challow] he did just the same as at Cheltenham last time, which is great. He's a gorgeous horse to have around and is bred like he's in the royal family" *All 14 Challow winners to have run in the Neptune were beaten*

Alan King, trainer of Ordo Ab Chao *(Neptune)* "It was very pleasing he showed his previous effort at Sandown was all wrong [by winning at Cheltenham on Trials Day]. I'm pretty certain he'll run in the Neptune as I'd like to stick to that trip [2m5f] for now. Although he'll get three miles, I don't think we need to be in a rush to go there. I hope he can be very competitive in the Neptune as I think it was very strong form [at Cheltenham] – the second and third are well regarded" *First three at Cheltenham are officially rated 142, 141 and 139*

Nick Gifford, trainer of Generous Ransom *(below, Novices' Handicap Chase)* "We've minded this horse – we've always loved him – and good ground is the key to him. The obvious race is the novice handicap for horses rated up to 140 but he'll have an entry in all the handicaps. I promise he'll be better on better ground" *Form figures of 113 on only previous runs in springtime (March and April)*

Vital statistics

Leading trainers at the festival

Festival award winners

2014	Willie Mullins	4
2013	Willie Mullins	5
2012	Nicky Henderson	7
2011	Willie Mullins	4
2010	Nicky Henderson	3
2009	Paul Nicholls	5
2008	Paul Nicholls	3
2007	Paul Nicholls	4
2006	Paul Nicholls	3
2005	Howard Johnson	3

Total festival winners

Nicky Henderson	51
Paul Nicholls	34
Willie Mullins	33
Jonjo O'Neill	25
Philip Hobbs	18
Edward O'Grady	18
Nigel Twiston-Davies	15
Alan King	14
David Pipe	11
Ferdy Murphy	10
Jessica Harrington	8
Arthur Moore	8
Mouse Morris	7

Willie Mullins has become the dominant festival performer, winning the leading trainer award in three of the last four years

Prior to 2009, Mullins had a total of 12 winners and had never had more than two at a single festival. At the six festivals since, he has added 21 more winners and had at least three winners at five of them

As well as four winners, Mullins had six second places last year (Nicky Henderson was next best with four runners-up)

Henderson's single winner last year was his worst showing since the blanks of 2007 and 2008

Paul Nicholls has had a single winner at each of the last two festivals

Three winners has been the minimum winning total at the past 17 festivals (and at least four have been needed to take the title at six of the ten festivals since the meeting was expanded to four days)

Jockey-trainer pairings to note

Kevin Morley highlights the combinations with good profit and strike-rate figures at the festival

Barry Geraghty/all Irish trainers (12 from 74, 16% strike-rate since 2000) Geraghty has enjoyed plenty of Cheltenham success for Nicky Henderson since becoming stable jockey in 2008 but he failed to strike on any of his 14 mounts for his employer at last year's festival. He still managed to ride three winners in 2014 (losing the top jockey award to Ruby Walsh on number of second places) and that was partly thanks to his enduring links with Ireland. Geraghty was one from three for Irish yards last year, landing the Champion Hurdle with Jezki for strong supporter Jessica Harrington while the other two finished third. Although his outside opportunities have become more scarce since he joined Henderson, he is three from 11 for Irish yards in that period with a 19pt profit (form figures 163132P0133). It is also worth noting that two of last year's winners, Jezki and More Of That in the World Hurdle, were as a 'supersub' on owner JP McManus's second-strings in Grade 1 races.

Conditionals/David Pipe (+16.50pt level stake since 2007) Pipe and stable jockey Tom Scudamore had their best festival in 2014 both collectively and individually but punters should also note the trainer's use of conditionals. Danny Cook, Hadden Frost and Conor O'Farrell have all had their moment in the spotlight for the yard as Pipe took advantage of their allowances. Four winners from 46 runners at a nine per cent strike-rate may not sound great but the figure is distorted by the occasional scattergun approach in the conditionals' handicap hurdle (named after Martin Pipe) and the level-stakes profit of +16.50pt certainly shows the Pipe winners were underestimated by the layers. Kieron Edgar (5lb) and Michael Heard (7lb) are good value for their respective claims and may be the beneficiaries of any Pipe handicap plot this year.

Ruby Walsh/Willie Mullins (Form figures F619011143001FF0611300313 150030P21P11301FP3124114PP02462F since 2008) Walsh was still stable jockey to Paul Nicholls when riding four winners from ten rides for Willie Mullins in 2013 (40%, +26.35pt). In his first festival full-time for Mullins last year, Walsh rode three winners from 14 rides for the stable with those figures taking the jockey's tally to 16 winners from 57 rides for Mullins since 2008 (28%, +26.48pt). The pair look set to add to their impressive statistics this year with Faugheen (Champion Hurdle), Annie Power (Mares' Hurdle) and a raft of smart novices at their disposal.

Tony McCoy/Jonjo O'Neill (Form figures 3U1PFFP121921925320181216PP1 in non-handicaps since 2006) The McCoy/O'Neill partnership is as reliable as they come, especially in the level-weights races where their record is seven winners from 25 runners (28% strike-rate). The pair are also reliable for each-way purposes, as a further six of those runners have finished in the first three. McCoy rode just once for O'Neill in a non-handicap last year and it paid dividends with Taquin Du Seuil landing the JLT Novices' Chase at 7-1. Had the champion jockey not plumped for At Fishers Cross instead of More Of That in the World Hurdle, he would have had another.

Bryan Cooper and Davy Russell/Gigginstown House Stud (Cooper's form figures for all rides at the 2013 meeting 329102511)

Cooper rose to prominence at the 2013 festival, where his three winners from nine rides (33%, +28.00pt) helped to earn him the enviable position as retained rider to the powerful Gigginstown House Stud string. Unfortunately Cooper was unable to make the most of the situation last year as a broken leg sustained in a fall in Wednesday's Fred Winter ruled him out for the last two days. The beneficiary was Davy Russell, the Gigginstown rider prior to Cooper, who had three rides in the maroon and white silks for the remainder of the meeting with two obliging. That took Russell's festival tally for Gigginstown to seven winners from 40 rides (18%, +37.50pt), which was a handy supplement to his Gold Cup success on Lord Windermere. This year it should be Cooper's turn to benefit from Gigginstown's growing presence on the winners' sheet.

Sam Waley-Cohen/Nicky Henderson (Form figures 10890P3P13331033 since 2005)

Much is made of Waley-Cohen's expertise over Aintree's National fences but the amateur also has a decent Cheltenham record and his figures for Henderson stand out. He is three from 16 at the festival for the Seven Barrows trainer (19%, +31.50pt), with Long Run's 2011 victory earning him the rare distinction of being a Gold Cup-winning amateur. It is also worth noting that another six of those rides have rewarded each-way support. The other two wins have come in handicaps over fences (Liberthine in the 2005 Plate and Rajdhani Express in the 2013 Novices' Handicap Chase), where Waley-Cohen's claim proved valuable. He still has a 3lb allowance.

Paul Carberry/all British-based trainers (5 from 28, 18% strike-rate since 1998)

Carberry has had a winner at each of the last two meetings, both for Irish trainers. Solwhit (17-2) in the 2013 World Hurdle and Very Wood (33-1) in last year's Albert Bartlett were returned at decent prices, but so were his winners for British-based trainers over the years (since 1998 he has ridden winners at 10-1, 16-1, 8-1, 14-1 and 20-1 for five different yards). Although best known for his patient riding style, he is just as effective when opting to ride from the front and he is a big draw for his experience and versatility.

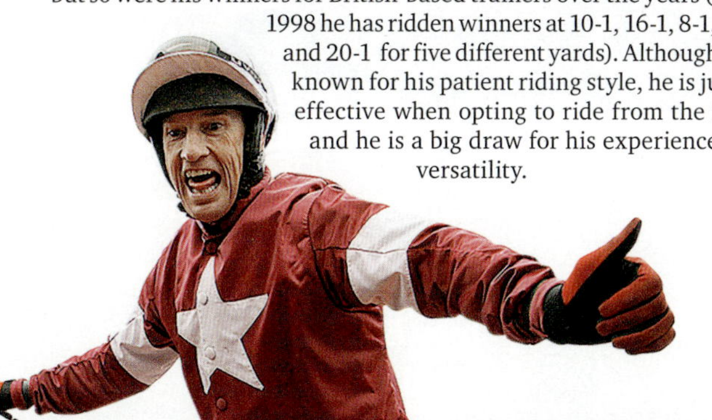

Paul Carberry: big draw for British trainers

Vital statistics

Leading jockeys at the festival

Festival award winners

2014	Ruby Walsh	3
2013	Ruby Walsh	4
2012	Barry Geraghty	5
2011	Ruby Walsh	5
2010	Ruby Walsh	3
2009	Ruby Walsh	7
2008	Ruby Walsh	3
2007	Robert Thornton	4
2006	Ruby Walsh	3
2005	Graham Lee	3

Total festival winners

Ruby Walsh	41
Barry Geraghty	31
Tony McCoy	30
Richard Johnson	20
Robert Thornton	16
Paul Carberry	14
Davy Russell	13
Timmy Murphy	8
Paddy Brennan	6
Jason Maguire	5
Tom Scudamore	5

Four jockeys (Ruby Walsh, Barry Geraghty, Davy Russell and Tom Scudamore) all had three winners last year but Walsh took the leading rider award by virtue of three second places (none of the others had a runner-up)

Walsh has been leading rider eight times – since his first title in 2004 only Graham Lee (2005), Robert Thornton (2007) and Geraghty (2012) have denied him the honours

Twenty-eight of Walsh's 41 winners have been over hurdles or in the Champion Bumper and his last chase winner was Kauto Star in the 2009 Gold Cup

Walsh and Geraghty both have got on the scoreboard at each of the past 13 festivals

Tony McCoy was leading rider in 1997 and 1998 but hasn't won the award since

Walsh, Geraghty and McCoy are the top three jockeys in festival history (next best is Pat Taaffe, Arkle's jockey, with 25)

Tuesday, March 10 (Old Course)

🐎Sky Bet Supreme
Novices' Hurdle

🐎Racing Post Arkle Chase

🐎Ultima Business Solutions
Handicap Chase

🐎Stan James Champion Hurdle

🐎OLBG Mares' Hurdle

🐎Toby Balding
National Hunt Chase

🐎Novices' Handicap Chase

1.30 Sky Bet Supreme Novices' Hurdle   C4/RUK
2m½f   Grade 1   £120,000

Willie Mullins, having won the last two runnings with Champagne Fever and Vautour, has another leading chance with Douvan, who has won both starts for the Irish champion trainer since arriving from France. Although less battle-hardened than the earlier Mullins pair (both of whom had won the Grade 1 Deloitte), Douvan was deemed prepared enough after his Grade 2 win at Punchestown in January (Vautour won the same race before taking in the Deloitte). As usual, Mullins has to juggle his squad (he had 18 entries, more than 20 per cent of the total) and other possibles are Deloitte winner Nichols Canyon, Shaneshill and Alvisio Ville. The chief British contender is the Nicky Henderson-trained L'Ami Serge – also unbeaten since arriving from France, in his case with three wins for his new trainer – while Harry Fry (with Jollyallan) and John Ferguson (Qewy) have realistic hopes of a first festival winner.

Douvan
5 b g; Trainer Willie Mullins
Hurdles form 2111, best RPR 149
Left-handed 21, best RPR 116
Right-handed 11, best RPR 149

Willie Mullins made 18 entries for the Supreme, but this one was all the rage long before then and it seems punters had a fairly good idea which was the No. 1. Two hurdles runs in France last spring yielded a second and a win, but he not surprisingly showed much-improved form on his debut for his new yard, scooting clear on the run-in to beat Sizing John by 12 lengths. The runner-up won an admittedly weak Grade 1 (Mullins-trained odds-on favourite Nichols Canyon unseated early) by more than six lengths next time, so it's hard to crab the form. A step up to Grade 2 company came next in January and Douvan again oozed class as he slammed the 136-rated Alpha Des Obeaux, who was stepping back down from 3m, by just under four lengths. Both Irish runs came in slowly run races in small fields and he's probably going to have to run somewhere between 15 and 20 seconds faster over the same trip at Cheltenham, but that will also be the case for most of his rivals who have been plying their trade on winter ground. Seen as a chaser for the future, but his jumping of hurdles is excellent, leading Mullins to claim he doesn't need any more practice before the big day. Clearly held in the highest esteem and understandably favourite, but already much shorter than stablemate Vautour was at this stage last season and has arguably achieved less – Vautour had won the Grade 1 Deloitte, beating a 150-rated rival.

L'Ami Serge
5 b g; Trainer Nicky Henderson
Hurdles form 323622111, best RPR 152
Left-handed 3236221, best RPR 150
Right-handed 11, best RPR 152

Only a five-year-old, but already had six hurdles runs in France before joining Nicky Henderson this season and lost the lot, some of them in handicaps. The transformation at Seven Barrows was immediate, though, and L'Ami Serge is unbeaten in three and has been impressive every time. He took apart his field in the Gerry Feilden Hurdle off a mark of 132 in November, beating Kilcooley by an easy six lengths and the runner-up gave that form a massive boost with a 23-length handicap victory off 137 next time out. L'Ami Serge then went to Ascot where, in a three-runner race, he toyed with the Willie Mullins-trained Killultagh Vic (close third in a Grade 2 next time). Following that he slammed Jolly's Cracked It by an easy 14 lengths in the Grade 1 Tolworth Hurdle, looking every inch a star of the future. From a trends point of view his failure to win at least 50 per cent of his hurdles starts is a negative, but all the best ex-French horses seem to get beaten a lot early in their careers (Kauto Star lost six out of ten in his native country) and perhaps that shouldn't be held against him. More worrying is that every single one of his runs has come on soft or heavy ground, which he clearly handles very well.

Jollyallan (pictured, green and gold)
6 b g; Trainer Harry Fry
Hurdles form 1112, best RPR 151
Left-handed 1, best RPR 137
Right-handed 112, best RPR 151

Sixth to Shaneshill in the Grade 1 Punchestown bumper at the end of April on only his second racecourse appearance and has since been very progressive over hurdles. A big, raw novice with plenty to learn about jumping, he nonetheless won his first three and seemed to appreciate better ground and a solid pace when seeing off the Willie Mullins-trained Sempre Medici at Kempton over Christmas. That one appears to be some way down the pecking order in that remarkably powerful stable (was a tailed-off seventh of nine in the Grade 1 Deloitte) but it was still a solid performance. Lost nothing in defeat when beaten half a length by the far more experienced Greatwood Hurdle winner Garde La Victoire in the Contenders Hurdle on very sticky ground at Sandown, where he battled all the way to the line. Likely to be seen to best effect on a faster surface and, given his high cruising speed, would not be without a shout if he can brush up his jumping on the day.

Nichols Canyon
5 b g; Trainer Willie Mullins
Hurdles form 11U1, best RPR 150
Left-handed U1
Right-handed 11, best RPR 143

Impressive winner of the Grade 1 Deloitte at Leopardstown, a race Willie Mullins' last two Supreme winners, Champagne Fever and Vautour, also won. However, he was made favourite for the Neptune after that and, with Mullins already having a hot favourite for this, probably goes there. If not he's obviously a major candidate, but he's dealt with in more detail in the Neptune section.

Shaneshill
6 b g; Trainer Willie Mullins
Hurdles form 12, best RPR 148
Left-handed 2, best RPR 148
Right-handed 1, best RPR 134
Cheltenham form 2 (bumper), best RPR 137

At the festival 12 Mar 2014: well placed behind leaders, closed 3f out on inner, ridden to lead over 1f out, headed just inside final furlong, stayed on but held after, finished second, beaten one and a half lengths by Silver Concorde in Champion Bumper

Favourite but found one too good in Silver Concorde for last season's Champion Bumper, although turned that form around at Punchestown the following month, beating his old rival by two lengths. Both hurdles starts this season have come at 2m4f and at long odds-on, but after easily winning the first he was seemingly outstayed by No More Heroes in a Grade 2 at Navan (the winner is expected to take the Albert Bartlett route at the festival). Whether that prompts a change of plan remains to be seen, but he's still much shorter for the Neptune and Mullins clearly has more obvious Supreme candidates. Handles bad ground but will be better on a decent surface.

Qewy

5 b g; Trainer John Ferguson
Hurdles form 31, best RPR 137
Left-handed 31, best RPR 137

Useful Flat performer for John Oxx with a peak rating of 107 following a heavy-ground Listed success over 1m at Leopardstown last April. Hurdles debut third for John Ferguson offered plenty of hope as the two who beat him were previous winners and he duly stepped up on that with a sparkling performance at Newbury in February. Held up in touch by Tony McCoy, he was always travelling strongly and cruised to the front approaching the last before quickening clear for a six-length win. The pace was solid and the fourth and fifth (beaten 11 lengths and 11 and three-quarter lengths) were rated 133 and 130 respectively. Both of those carried penalties but it was hard to argue with the ease of his win. He's by Street Cry, who is not renowned for getting soft-ground performers, but he clearly likes plenty of cut. That said, his best RPR on good to firm on the Flat was only 6lb shy of his best on heavy, and whatever the weather it won't be that fast on day one at Cheltenham. Interesting contender.

Alvisio Ville

5 gr g; Trainer Willie Mullins
Hurdles form 13, best RPR 138
Left-handed 13, best RPR 138
Cheltenham form None

Another with the Neptune entry, but similar price for both races and hard to know where, if anywhere, he'll go. Was heavily supported for the Neptune before 12-length Deloitte defeat and form so far a long way off what is required. Willie Mullins said he didn't expect Nichols Canyon to beat him at Leopardstown, though, so he has clearly been showing a lot at home.

Silver Concorde

7 b g; Trainer Dermot Weld
Hurdles form 24, best RPR 135
Left-handed 24, best RPR 135
Cheltenham form 1 (bumper), best RPR 140
At the festival 12 Mar 2014 held up in midfield, steady progress on inner over 3f out, closed to challenge over 1f out, ridden to lead just inside final furlong, edged right but stayed on well, won Champion Bumper by one and a half lengths from Shaneshill

Very good bumper performer who won last year's Champion Bumper for Dermot Weld before seeing the form turned around by runner-up Shaneshill in the Punchestown version in April. Hasn't been seen too much since then and only scrambled home in a Flat race at Navan in October, before getting turned over at odds of 1-3 at Leopardstown's Christmas meeting (winner only fifth of six to Douvan next time). Stepped into Grade 1 company next time but found wanting, finishing just over 15 lengths behind winner Nichols Canyon in the Deloitte. Needs to improve dramatically for better ground and Cheltenham and as a seven-year-old he would be an older than usual winner of this race as there have been only two of his age (and one aged eight) since 1972. Not certain to travel.

Tell Us More

6 b g; Trainer Willie Mullins
Hurdles form 12, best RPR 145
Left-handed 2, best RPR 145
Right-handed 1, best RPR 130
Cheltenham form None

Easy bumper winner in March 2014 and opened his hurdles account at odds of 1-5 at Gowran in November, after which his trainer said he "could be top drawer". Was surprisingly turned over by 33-1 stablemate McKinley in a 2m4f Grade 1 at Naas in January, when lack of experience may have undone him – also he set a fairly solid pace given the testing nature of the track. Still much shorter in the betting for the Neptune, even though Mullins said he may drop him trip next time.

OTHERS TO CONSIDER

Willie Mullins has been known to change his mind at the last minute but it is surely hard to see him dropping **Outlander** in trip. Warren Greatrex's **Seedling** looked a promising novice in the first half of the season, winning three times including once at Cheltenham, and it is to be hoped the stable will have turned its form around by March (after a fine autumn Greatrex was 0-28 in January and didn't have a runner in the first ten days of February). **Windsor Park** would be worthy of respect if dropped in trip, but that seems unlikely. **Sizing John** is seemingly held by Douvan on early-season form but has won a Grade 1 since and has been kept fresh for spring ground.

Supreme Novices' Hurdle results and trends

	FORM	WINNER	AGE & WGT	Adj RPR	SP	TRAINER	H.Runs	BEST RPR LAST 12 MONTHS (RUNS SINCE)
14	2-111	Vautour D	5 11-7	157^T	7-2j	W Mullins (IRE)	$5^{(18GS)}$	won Gd1 Deloitte Hurdle (2m2f) (0)
13	-1231	Champagne Fever C, D	6 11-7	157^{-13}	5-1	W Mullins (IRE)	$4^{(12S)}$	won Gd1 Deloitte Hurdle (2m2f) (0)
12	-2111	Cinders And Ashes D	5 11-7	152^{-6}	10-1	D McCain	$4^{(19G)}$	won Aintree class 4 mdn hdl (2m1f) (2)
11	-F311	Al Ferof D	6 11-7	146^{-17}	10-1	P Nicholls	$4^{(15G)}$	won Newbury class 3 nov hdl (2m½f) (0)
10	11212	Menorah D, BF	5 11-7	160^{-3}	12-1	P Hobbs	$4^{(18GS)}$	won Kempton class 2 nov hdl (2m) (1)
09	12121	Go Native D	6 11-7	153^{-8}	12-1	N Meade (IRE)	$5^{(20GS)}$	won Punchestown Listed nov hdl (2m) (2)
08	1/711	Captain Cee Bee D	7 11-7	151^{-2}	17-2	E Harty (IRE)	$2^{(22GS)}$	won Punchestown hdl (2m) (0)
07	21	Ebaziyan D	6 11-7	121^{-43}	40-1	W Mullins (IRE)	$2^{(22S)}$	2nd Cork mdn hdl (2m) (1)
06	-3111	Noland C, D	5 11-7	144^{-6}	6-1	P Nicholls	$4^{(20GS)}$	won Exeter Listed nov hdl (2m1f) (0)
05	1143	Arcalis D, BF	5 11-7	150^{-5}	20-1	H Johnson	$4^{(20G)}$	4th Christmas Hurdle Gd1 (2m) (1)

WINS-RUNS: 4yo 0-5, 5yo 5-90, 6yo 4-67, 7yo 1-20, 8yo 0-3, 9yo 0-1 **FAVOURITES:** -£7.75

TRAINERS IN THIS RACE (w-pl-r): Willie Mullins 3-0-16, Paul Nicholls 2-1-11, Noel Meade 1-1-7, Philip Hobbs 1-1-8, Alan King 0-1-4, Brian Ellison 0-0-1, Dermot Weld 0-0-3, David Pipe 0-0-6, Evan Williams 0-0-2, Gary Moore 0-1-3, Gordon Elliott 0-0-1, John Ferguson 0-0-1, John Quinn 0-0-3, Mouse Morris 0-0-2, Nicky Henderson 0-8-16, Nigel Twiston-Davies 0-0-5, Tim Vaughan 0-0-1, Venetia Williams 0-0-1, Warren Greatrex 0-0-1

FATE OF FAVOURITES: 0532534021 **POSITION OF WINNER IN MARKET:** 0204643621

Key trends

🐎 Won at least 50 per cent of hurdle starts, 10/10

🐎 Ran within the last 52 days, 10/10

🐎 Adjusted RPR of at least 144, 9/10

🐎 Won last time out, 8/10

🐎 Previously contested a Graded race, 7/10 (five won, two made the frame)

🐎 Rated within 8lb of RPR top-rated, 7/10 (exceptions between 13lb and 43lb below top-rated)

Other factors

🐎 Ireland has won this 13 times in the past 24 years

🐎 Two winners came via the Flat, where they had earned an RPR between 91 and 110, and neither of the two had won outside minor novice hurdle company

🐎 Seven of the other eight started their careers in bumpers, where they had earned an RPR of at least 110 (last year's winner Vautour started over hurdles)

🐎 Three winners had previously run in the Champion Bumper (Al Ferof second in 2010, Cinders And Ashes fifth in 2011 and Champagne Fever won in 2012)

🐎 In 2013, Champagne Fever became the first Champion Bumper winner to score since Montelado in 1993. Four others tried in between – Cork All Star (seventh), Cousin Vinny (fifth), Dunguib (third) and Cue Card (fourth)

🐎 The last horse to win this after just one hurdle outing was Flown in 1992

🐎 For many years, the shortest-priced Irish runner was often beaten by a compatriot. However, of the last eight to win, six were the most fancied

Notes

Un De Sceaux has created the same sort of buzz as Sprinter Sacre did in the run-up to his Arkle victory in 2012 and Willie Mullins' exciting novice went odds-on after his 15-length demolition job in the Grade 1 Irish Arkle. The only blemish on his record is a fall at the third-last when well clear on his chasing debut at Thurles but he has won his two subsequent starts by 12 lengths and 15 lengths, rocketing to a Racing Post Rating of 171 (the same mark achieved by Sprinter Sacre prior to his Arkle). In most years the Paul Nicholls-trained Vibrato Valtat would be the exciting one but in this instance he is billed more as a solid rival, with more experience than Un De Sceaux and three Graded victories but with 7lb to make up on RPR. Contenders with even more to prove are Irish Arkle runner-up Clarcam and Nicky Henderson's erratic jumper Josses Hill, while Mullins is likely to divert Vautour to the JLT.

Un De Sceaux

7 b g; Trainer Willie Mullins
Chase form F11, best RPR 171
Left-handed 1, best RPR 171
Right-handed F1, best RPR 151
Cheltenham form None

Top-class hurdler last season, although his campaign wasn't to everyone's liking as despite being one of the ante-post favourites for the Champion Hurdle he swerved Cheltenham and stablemate Hurricane Fly for easier pickings in France. Tasted first defeat in ten starts on chase debut in November, but only because he slithered on landing when well clear three out at Thurles, and has since confirmed himself to be something special. He had a fairly straightforward task when getting off the mark at Fairyhouse at odds of 1-5 in December, but it was anything but easy on paper when he was asked to give 10lb to the five-year-old 156-rated Clarcam in the Grade 1 Frank Ward Solicitors Arkle Novice Chase at Leopardstown in January. He turned in a jaw-dropping performance that day, making all as usual, attacking his fences with relish and winning with his head in the chest by 15 lengths. The Racing Post Rating of 171 he earned was identical to that awarded to Sprinter Sacre when he won the Game Spirit on his Arkle warm-up three years ago and that one was sent off at odds-on to beat the likes of Cue Card, Menorah and Al Ferof at Cheltenham, which he did with ease. That run puts Un De Sceaux a mile clear of almost everything likely to take him on and, with one possible exception, he is unlikely to face anything of the calibre of the horses Sprinter Sacre had to deal with. That Thurles fall aside, he has a faultless profile and it's hard to see what can beat him given a clear round. Has done virtually all of his racing on very soft ground but trainer not worried on that score.

Vibrato Valtat

6 b g; Trainer Paul Nicholls
Chase form 12111, best RPR 164
Left-handed 121, best RPR 164
Right-handed 11, best RPR 156
Cheltenham form 2 (chase), best RPR 147

Paul Nicholls has a couple of horses this season who seem to have been transformed from gutless loser into potential star and this is definitely one of them. The six-year-old has always had plenty of talent, but having been heavily backed for the Swinton Hurdle at Haydock at the end of last term, he cruised up to join the leaders on the run-in and then didn't seem to want to go past. It was a similar story on his seasonal return over hurdles at Cheltenham and, after having a big class edge when winning at Warwick on his chase debut, he found less than expected when second to Dunraven Storm in a Grade 2 back at Cheltenham. The ride Sam Twiston-Davies gave him that day split opinion as many blamed him for leaving his run too late, but plenty who had followed him closely were prepared to accept that the horse was the one to blame. However, since then his performances have been flawless as he had to put his head down and battle twice in the space of three weeks in December, first to gain revenge over Dunraven Storm in the Grade 1 Henry VIII at Sandown and then when beating Three Kingdoms in a Grade 2 at Kempton. Both those runs left him way short of what Un De Sceaux had done, but he took his form to a new level with an on-the-bridle victory giving 3lb to four-timer-seeking and 153-rated Top Gamble (promising but did make a few mistakes) in the Grade 2 Kingmaker at Warwick. The RPR he earned there (164) would make him favourite in a normal year and, even though there might be a small field, the tactical battle between him and the front-running Un De Sceaux promises to be fascinating.

Josses Hill

7 b g; Trainer Nicky Henderson
Chase form 212, best RPR 153
Left-handed 1, best RPR 153
Right-handed 22, best RPR 150
Cheltenham form 2 (hurdles), best RPR 150
At the festival 11 Mar 2014: in touch, pushed along to challenge for places approaching last, stayed on to take 2nd final 110yds, no chance with winner, finished second, beaten six lengths by Vautour in Supreme Novices' Hurdle

Top-class novice hurdler for Nicky Henderson last season and, having finished a respectable second to Vautour in the Supreme, slammed Sgt Reckless by six lengths in a Grade 2 at Aintree. Was always seen as a chaser by connections and has achieved a pretty high level in three starts despite being far from foot perfect. The chances are he ran into one of the best British novices around in Paul Nicholls' Ptit Zig at Ascot in December, so it was no disgrace to go down by nine lengths over a trip (2m3f) that might have been against him in soft ground, but he was awkward at several of his fences. Beat another Nicholls-trained runner in Solar Impulse at Doncaster on his next start in January, gradually warming to his task without looking a complete natural. It's arguable that he jumped his best on his third outing at Kempton over 2m4½f, but he still lost his rhythm after reaching for the ninth, and a three-quarter-length defeat getting

11lb from Third Intention had to go down as disappointing, although the trip was again probably at the end of his stamina range. Barry Geraghty has not lost faith in him, though, and says a strong pace at 2m at Cheltenham will bring out the best in him. It needs to, though – while a top RPR of 153 would be pretty respectable heading into a normal Arkle, this one looks far from normal. No denying his talent, but backers will be holding their breath at every fence.

Vautour

6 b g; Trainer Willie Mullins
Chase form 121, best RPR 153
Left-handed 121, best RPR 153
Cheltenham form 1 (hurdles) 158
At the festival 11 Mar 2014: made most, quickened between last 2, big jump last, ran on well to draw clear run-in, impressive, won Supreme Novices' Hurdle by six lengths from Josses Hill

Superb novice hurdle season culminated in victories in the Supreme and another Grade 1 at Punchestown, and looks likely to be at least as good over fences. Dealt with in more detail in Thursday's JLT section as he is surely unlikely to take on stable's red-hot favourite here.

Clarcam

5 b g; Trainer Gordon Elliott
Chase form 2112, best RPR 146
Left-handed 2112, best RPR 146
Cheltenham form F (hurdles)
At the festival 12 Mar 2014: chased leaders, took slight advantage and travelling okay when fell 2 out in Fred Winter Juvenile Handicap Hurdle

Decent juvenile hurdler last season, who was going like a winner when coming down two out in the Fred Winter off a mark off 133. Subsequent Grade 1 second at Aintree suggests he was well treated at Cheltenham and has done even better over fences this season. Not disgraced when eight-length second to Vautour on his debut at Navan in November, he then got off the mark easily back at the same track a couple of weeks later. It was still a major surprise when he had a below-par Vautour 17 lengths behind him in the Grade 1 Racing Post Novice Chase at Leopardstown over Christmas and the joint runner-up (with Ted Veale) has since proved that form all wrong. Only got a distant view of Un De Sceaux's backside in receipt of 10lb back at Leopardstown in January and won't have that weight-for-age allowance in March. Best RPR of 146 at odds with Irish handicapper's mark of 154 (dropped 2lb for latest effort) and mountain to climb if he reopposes. Hard to see where else he'd go given his handicap mark, though, and Gordon Elliott says he's most likely to take his chance.

Sgt Reckless (below)

8 b g; Trainer Mick Channon
Chase form 1, best RPR 140
Left-handed 1, best RPR 140
Cheltenham form 04 (bumper and hurdle)
At the festival 13 Mar 2013: always in midfield, in touch but ridden 3f out, weakened 2f out, finished 13th, beaten 33 lengths by Briar Hill in Champion Bumper
11 Mar 2014: held up in rear, still last about 13 lengths off the pace approaching 3 out, ridden and headway when hung left before last, edged left run-in when staying on, finished well, finished fourth, beaten seven and a half lengths by Vautour in Supreme Novices' Hurdle

Pretty useful novice hurdler for Mick Channon last season when he finished in the first four in Grade 1/2 events at all three major spring festivals, albeit beaten a fair way each time. Doesn't like soft ground at all, so chase experience by the start of

February had been limited to just one outing three months earlier at Uttoxeter, where he jumped well and won easily. Otherwise has been well out of his depth in the Christmas Hurdle behind Faugheen (last of five finishers) and won a Lingfield Polytrack maiden by an easy five lengths. Clearly has the ability to make a decent chaser in the right conditions.

OTHERS TO CONSIDER

It really is hard to know what else is likely to turn up as this is sure to feature the hottest favourite of the festival and a small field. Connections of **Gilgamboa** have already said he is unlikely to travel after he finished a distant last of three behind Un De Sceaux and Clarcam at Leopardstown and they are hardly like to change their minds after his shock Flyingbolt defeat in February, while John Ferguson's **Three Kingdoms**, closely matched with Vibrato Valtat on Kempton form, was said by Tony McCoy to need further after just reeling in Solar Impulse at Doncaster last time. **Court Minstrel** took surprisingly well to chasing early in the season but hates soft ground and hasn't been seen for a while (trainer Evan Williams suggests he may wait for Aintree). **Gitane Du Berlais** impressed at Sandown, but that was 2m4½f in soft ground and it's hard to see her dropping back in trip.

Arkle Chase results and trends

	FORM	WINNER	AGE & WGT	Adj RPR	SP	TRAINER	C.Runs	BEST RPR LAST 12 MONTHS (RUNS SINCE)
14	1-261	**Western Warhorse**	6 11-4	148^{-23}	33-1	D Pipe	1$^{(9GS)}$	won Doncaster class 3 nov ch (2m3f) (0)
13	11-11	**Simonsig** C, D	7 11-7	174^{T}	8-15f	N Henderson	2$^{(7S)}$	won Kempton Gd2 nov ch (2m) (0)
12	3-111	**Sprinter Sacre** D	6 11-7	179^{T}	8-11f	N Henderson	3$^{(6G)}$	won Newbury Gd2 ch (2m1f) (0)
11	22221	**Captain Chris** C, D	7 11-7	163^{-4}	6-1	P Hobbs	4$^{(10G)}$	2nd Sandown Gd1 nov ch (2m4½f) (1)
10	41111	**Sizing Europe** C, D	8 11-7	170^{T}	6-1	H de Bromhead (IRE)	4$^{(12GS)}$	won Leopardstown Gd1 nov ch (2m1f) (0)
09	-1222	**Forpadydeplasterer** D	7 11-7	160^{-6}	8-1	T Cooper (IRE)	4$^{(17GS)}$	2nd Gd1 Dr PJ Moriarty Nov Ch (2m5f) (0)
08	-1112	**Tidal Bay** C, BF	7 11-7	160^{T}	6-1	H Johnson	4$^{(14GS)}$	won Carlisle class 3 nov ch (2m4f) (2)
07	21211	**My Way De Solzen** C, D	7 11-7	161^{-1}	7-2	A King	5$^{(13S)}$	won Haydock Gd2 nov ch (2m4f) (0)
06	-1111	**Voy Por Ustedes** D	5 11-2	164^{-5}	15-2	A King	4$^{(14GS)}$	won Wincanton Gd2 nov ch (2m) (0)
05	-2213	**Contraband** C, D	7 11-7	161^{T}	7-1	M Pipe	4$^{(19G)}$	3rd Uttoxeter Gd2 nov ch (2m) (0)

WINS-RUNS: 5yo 1-17, 6yo 2-29, 7yo 6-49, 8yo 1-20, 9yo 0-4, 10yo 0-1, 12yo 0-1 **FAVOURITES:** -£6.74

TRAINERS IN THIS RACE (w-pl-r): Alan King 2-0-5, Nicky Henderson 2-2-8, David Pipe 1-0-4, Henry de Bromhead 1-0-1, Philip Hobbs 1-2-6, Tony Martin 0-0-1, Evan Williams 0-0-1, Gary Moore 0-0-1, Mouse Morris 0-1-2, Nigel Twiston-Davies 0-0-1, Noel Meade 0-1-4, Paul Nicholls 0-1-12, Tom George 0-0-2, Venetia Williams 0-0-3, Willie Mullins 0-1-8

FATE OF FAVOURITES: 0023F04112 **POSITION OF WINNER IN MARKET:** 2522334118

Key trends

🐎SP no bigger than 8-1, 9/10

🐎Aged five to seven, 9/10

🐎Finished in the first two on all completed chase starts, 9/10 (exception no worse than third)

🐎Rated within 6lb of RPR top-rated, 9/10

🐎Adjusted RPR of at least 160, 9/10

🐎Three to five runs over fences, 8/10 (both exceptions had less)

🐎RPR hurdle rating of at least 153, 8/10

Other factors

🐎Six had previously won a 2m-2m1f Graded chase (no race has proved a reliable guide)

🐎Seven winners had previously run at the festival, showing mixed form in a variety of hurdle races

🐎Two French-bred horses have scored and a French-bred has finished in the first three on six occasions

Notes

Benvolio (centre): possible runner for Paul Nicholls, who has never won this race

The top handicap chase of the festival usually goes to a fancied, up-and-coming chaser – five of the last seven winners had run no more than six times over fences beforehand. Last year Holywell (joint-third in the market at 10-1, aged seven and with only five previous chase runs) fitted the profile. If there is an upset, it is most likely to come from a more seasoned chaser but that is a fairly rare occurrence.

Only two favourites have won since 1977 but the race usually goes to a fancied runner, with 11 of the past 16 winners sent off at 10-1 or lower. The longest-priced winners since 1999 were Chief Dan George (33-1 in 2010) and Joes Edge (50-1 in 2007) and it is also notable they were the only winners in that period from the double-figure age band. Four of the five winners at 20-1 or more in the past 20 years were aged ten or above.

Younger winners tend to be well fancied – 12 of the last 14 winners were aged seven, eight or nine, with nine of those 12 younger winners sent off no bigger than 8-1.

Course form in the current season is worth noting and most winners have a previous good run at Cheltenham on their record (Holywell had won the Pertemps Final at the previous year's festival) – the only winner in the past ten years without any previous course form was the Irish-trained Dun Doire in 2006. Two of the past ten winners had run well in this race the year before.

Second-season chasers have traditionally done well and, after many years without a victory by a raw novice, there have been four novice winners in 11 years (Holywell was the latest and was the highest-rated novice winner, off a mark of 145).

Since 1983 no winner has had a mark above 150. Unguided Missile made all under 11st 10lb in 1998 when rated 149 in an uncompetitive renewal, but since then only two winners have carried more than 10st 12lb.

Paul Nicholls, whose established handicappers tend to be over-weighted by the time of the festival, has never won this race. Third is the closest he has come from ten runners in the past decade. His best chance is likely to be with a novice.

Nicky Henderson's runners are more noteworthy. Although his last winner was Marlborough in 2000, six of his 17 runners since then have finished second or third (including last year's runner-up Ma Filleule).

Ultima Business Solutions Handicap Chase results and trends

	FORM	WINNER	AGE & WGT	OR	SP	TRAINER	C.Runs	BEST RPR LAST 12 MONTHS (RUNS SINCE)
14	32U11	Holywell C, D	7 11-6	145^{-9}	10-1	J O'Neill	5$^{(23GS)}$	won Doncaster class 4 nov ch (3m) (0)
13	P3633	Golden Chieftain D	8 10-2	132^{-1}	28-1	C Tizzard	14$^{(24S)}$	won Worcester class 3 hcap ch (2m4f) (5)
12	-PF75	Alfie Sherrin (1oh) D	9 10-0	129^{-5}	14-1	J O'Neill	6$^{(19G)}$	7th Kempton class 3 hcap ch (2m4½f) (0)
11	F2-52	Bensalem C, BF	8 11-2	143^{T}	5-1	A King	5$^{(19G)}$	fell Festival Handicap Chase (3m½f) (3)
10	-3701	Chief Dan George D	10 10-10	142^{-6}	33-1	J Moffatt	9$^{(24GS)}$	won Doncaster class 2 hcap ch (3m) (0)
09	9-121	Wichita Lineman C, D	8 10-9	142^{T}	5-1f	J O'Neill	3$^{(21GS)}$	won Chepstow class 3 nov ch (3m) (0)
08	3-P61	An Accordion D	7 10-12	143^{-6}	7-1	D Pipe	6$^{(14GS)}$	won Doncaster Listed hcap ch (3m) (0)
07	76-78	Joes Edge	10 10-6	130^{-8}	50-1	F Murphy	17$^{(23GS)}$	13th Cheltenham Gold Cup (3m2½f) (4)
06	11111	Dun Doire D	7 10-9	129^{-9}	7-1	T Martin (IRE)	9$^{(21GS)}$	won Gowran hcap ch (3m) (0)
05	03F43	Kelami D	7 10-2	133^{-9}	8-1	F Doumen (FR)	19$^{(20G)}$	3rd Haydock Gd3 hcap ch (3m4½f) (0)

WINS-RUNS: 6yo 0-14, 7yo 4-36, 8yo 3-44, 9yo 1-48, 10yo 2-35, 11yo 0-23, 12yo 0-6, 13yo 0-2 **FAVOURITES:** -£4.00

FATE OF FAVOURITES: 0P2312F020 **POSITION OF WINNER IN MARKET:** 5203102703

OR 121-133 5-3-47, **134-148** 1-24-141, **149-161** 0-3-24

Key trends

🐎 Aged seven to ten, 10/10

🐎 Officially rated 129-145, 10/10

🐎 Carried no more than 11st 2lb, 9/10

🐎 Won over at least 3m, 9/10

🐎 Top-three finish on either or both of last two starts, 8/10

🐎 No more than nine runs over fences, 7/10

🐎 Ran no more than five times that season, 7/10

Other factors

🐎 Alfie Sherrin in 2012 was the first to win from out of the handicap since Maamur in 1996

🐎 Seven winners had run at a previous festival, four recording at least one top-four finish

🐎 Four winners had run well (two placing, one falling when going well and one sixth) in a handicap at Cheltenham earlier in the season. Bensalem, the 2011 winner, had run well in a Grade 2 hurdle at the course (and fallen when going well in this race the year before)

🐎 There have been two winning favourites in the past 30 years – Antonin in 1994 and Wichita Lineman in 2009

🐎 Three winners had won a Class 1 handicap chase

🐎 This was once seemingly an impossible task for novices but three of the past ten winners have been first-season chasers

Notes

Willie Mullins has the ante-post favourite for all four Grade 1 races on what could be a crackerjack opening day for the Irish champion trainer and, whatever happens in the others, he will make the headlines if he is successful here. Having won twice in the past four years with Hurricane Fly, Mullins has developed the next potential star in Faugheen, who won the Neptune last year (like other top-notch Champion Hurdle winners before him) and has made himself a solid favourite with two decisive victories this season. Interestingly, both runs have been in Britain (latterly in the Grade 1 Christmas Hurdle) and that has left the resurgent Hurricane Fly to mop up three Grade 1s in Ireland (beating Jezki, last year's Champion Hurdle winner, each time). Jezki, though, turned around the Irish form last year and it remains doubtful that the 11-year-old Hurricane Fly can be the force of old at Cheltenham. The chief British contender once again is The New One, arguably unlucky in last year's race and with five straight wins since. This promises to be some race.

Faugheen

7 b g; Trainer Willie Mullins
Hurdles form 1111111, best RPR 169
Left-handed 11, best RPR 155
Right-handed 11111, best RPR 169
Cheltenham form 1, best RPR 155
At the festival 12 Mar 2014: prominent, tracked leader after 6th, not fluent next, led and mistake 3 out, drew clear before last, ridden out, won Neptune Investment Management Novices' Hurdle by four and a half lengths from Ballyalton

Incredibly exciting hurdler with a flawless record, having won his sole point, a bumper (by 22 lengths from subsequent Supreme runner-up Josses Hill) and seven hurdles. He started over 2m6f as a novice, went up to 3m to win a Grade 3 at Limerick, dropped back to 2m5f to win the Neptune and then came right back to 2m to run away with the Herald Champion Novice Hurdle at Punchestown in April by 12 lengths. At every trip he has never looked remotely like getting beaten and he began this season's campaign in similar style, laughing at a group of essentially stayers in the Ascot Hurdle over 2m3½f in November before dropping back to 2m for the Grade 1 Christmas Hurdle and cantering all over his rivals for another bloodless win at Kempton. There really is no telling how good he could be, but if you wanted to pick holes in his form it's not that hard to do when you take into account he is little better than even-money for

the Champion Hurdle and has yet to take on a horse with anything like serious claims for the big one. From a trends point of view, he has yet to post a high Topspeed figure, his 141 falling a full 10lb below what most recent winners had achieved. Then there's the horses he has beaten. His best piece of form came in the Christmas Hurdle, when he thumped Purple Bay by eight lengths. The runner-up carried a rating of 161 then (since dropped 2lb) but that was a questionable figure given it was earned by winning an early-season handicap when he had a fitness advantage over his rivals and was ridden by a 7lb claimer. Purple Bay certainly didn't look like a 161 horse at Kempton, where for a long time he didn't seem able to go with the hectic pace set by Blue Heron. Still, it's impossible not to be impressed by a horse who doesn't just win but destroys every horse he comes up against and Blue Heron franked the Kempton form by beating Irving in the Kingwell in February, albeit having been given a much better and less aggressive ride. Universally fancied to have Ruby Walsh in the saddle, although it can't be an easy choice given Hurricane Fly's continued dominance in Ireland. Going straight to Cheltenham from Kempton, which is an unusual prep, but it didn't stop Rock On Ruby in 2012 or Bobs Worth from winning the Gold Cup from a longer layoff and that should not be a concern.

The New One with trainer
Nigel Twiston-Davies: chief
British hope against the Irish
raiders led by Faugheen

The New One

7 b g; Trainer Nigel Twiston-Davies
Hurdles form 111212112311111, best RPR 173
Left handed 111212131111, best RPR 173
Right handed 121, best RPR 171
Cheltenham form (all races) 16121131, best RPR 173
At the festival 14 Mar 2012: tracked leaders, ridden and outpaced 2f out, hung left over 1f out, rallied final 100yds, no impression on front three, finished sixth, beaten six lengths by Champagne Fever in Champion Bumper
13 Mar 2013: tracked leaders, not fluent 2 out, driven to lead approaching last, ran on strongly run-in, won Neptune Investment Management Novices' Hurdle by four lengths from Rule The World
11 Mar 2014: tracking leaders when badly hampered and dropped to 7th 3rd, effort to close after 3 out, ridden approaching 2 out and one pace, rallied under pressure approaching last, stayed on well for 3rd final 50yds, closing on leading duo but always held, finished third, beaten two and three-quarter lengths by Jezki in Champion Hurdle

Ultra-consistent and top-class hurdler, whose only finish out of the frame in 19 starts came when he was sixth in the 2012 Champion Bumper. Returned the following season with an impressive novice campaign that culminated in victory in the Neptune – surprisingly a better breeding ground for future Champion Hurdle winners than the Supreme – and a second in open company to Zarkandar in the 2m4f Grade 1 Aintree Hurdle. Jumping is sometimes his Achilles heel and it cost him victory in the 2013 Christmas Hurdle when a blunder at the last allowed My Tent Or Yours to get up to win. However, defeat in the Champion Hurdle last season was not his fault as the ill-fated Our Conor fell right in front of him, stopping him in his tracks. Given time to recover, he had made up most of the lost ground heading to three out but then appeared to get outpaced before flying home for third after the last. The general consensus is that he should have won and he is unbeaten in five starts since, although the way he has been campaigned has been a little disappointing. That's partly due to a programme that encourages the best horses to stay away from each other, but The New One is by some way the best 2m hurdler trained in Britain and for him to swerve both early-season British Grade 1s in search of easier pickings is hardly good for the sport. Was probably at his most impressive this term when, back at Cheltenham, he gave 8lb and an easy beating to Vaniteux in the StanJames.com International. Things were not so straightforward last time when he had to battle to get past the 149-rated Bertimont at Haydock after jumping out to his right several times, but that was on desperate ground and he still displayed the willing attitude he is renowned for. Sound claims of making up for last season's near miss.

Jezki (pictured, winning last year)

7 b g; Trainer Jessica Harrington
Hurdles form 111131112411223, best RPR 173
Left-handed 111324123, best RPR 173
Right-handed 111112, best RPR 168
Cheltenham form 831
At the festival 14 Mar 2012: midfield, headway to chase leaders 4f out, ridden over 2f out, kept on same

pace final furlong, finished eighth, beaten 12 lengths by Champagne Fever in Champion Bumper
12 Mar 2013: midfield, headway to track leaders 3 out, effort and switched left when mistake last, stayed on same pace final 75yds, finished third, beaten two and three-quarter lengths by Champagne Fever in Supreme Novices' Hurdle
11 Mar 2014: took keen hold, tracked leaders, not fluent 4 out, slight lead 2 out, edged left and ridden approaching last, stayed on well under pressure run-in, all out, won Champion Hurdle by a neck from My Tent Or Yours

Another super-consistent and top-class hurdler, but one who has won only two of his last seven starts, largely because he keeps running into Hurricane Fly at Leopardstown. However, he got it right when it mattered in last season's Champion Hurdle when, discarded by Tony McCoy, he scored by a neck under Barry Geraghty from the McCoy-ridden My Tent Or Yours. Whether he'd have won if The New One had not been hampered is another matter, but Jezki confirmed it was no fluke when beating fourth-placed Hurricane Fly by a similar margin (three and a quarter lengths) in the Racing Post Champion Hurdle at Punchestown in May. That made it 2-2 between the new kid on the block and The Fly, but it's now 5-2 in the veteran's favour after three more Grade 1 outings at Leopardstown. Jezki was second in the first two and they would all have been reasonably close because he looked booked for second before making a bad mistake at the last in the Irish Champion Hurdle in January. Despite those defeats Jezki is expected by most to turn the form around with Hurricane Fly back at Cheltenham, largely because he's the younger horse and will be far happier in a strongly run race and on better ground. Needs to step up on performances so far this term but every chance he will.

Hurricane Fly

11 b g; Trainer Willie Mullins
Hurdles form 1121113111111311111111142111, best RPR 173
Left-handed 1211111311111411, best RPR 173
Right-handed 1113111111121, best RPR 173
Cheltenham form 1314, best RPR 173
At the festival 15 Mar 2011: Held up in touch, steady headway to track leaders 2 out and soon travelling well, driven to take slight lead last, ridden and edged right run-in, held on all out, won Champion Hurdle by a length and a quarter from Peddlers Cross
13 Mar 2012: held up in rear, headway 3 out, went 3rd 2 out and soon driven, kept on under pressure run-in but no impression on leading duo, finished third, beaten five and a half lengths by Rock On Ruby in Champion Hurdle
12 Mar 2013: tracked leaders, not fluent and nudged along after 4th, pressed leaders 2 out, led soon after, driven and edged right to stands rail run-in, ran on strongly, won Champion Hurdle by two and a half lengths from Rock On Ruby
11 Mar 2014: not fluent 1st, tracking leaders when left in close 2nd 3rd, strong challenge 2 out, stayed upsides until edged left and no extra into 3rd approaching last, outpaced into 4th final 50yds, finished fourth, beaten five lengths by Jezki in Champion Hurdle

True legend of the game having run in 27

consecutive Grade 1 races and extended his world record to 22 Grade 1 victories with three successes over last year's Champion Hurdle winner Jezki this season. The last two successes came at his beloved Leopardstown, where he is now unbeaten in ten starts and, although he has had to work hard each time, he keeps pulling it out. His latest effort in January's Irish Champion Hurdle was all about guts as he seemed to be off the bridle a long way out, but he powered his way to the front jumping the last and looked to have taken his great rival's measure before that one made a hash of it and backed out of it. The big question, of course, is whether at the age of 11 he can go back to Cheltenham and regain the Champion Hurdle for a remarkable second time. At the age of ten last season he fell five lengths short when fourth to Jezki and, despite his two titles, he has always given the impression his wins at Cheltenham came despite the track rather than because of it. For his first Champion Hurdle he was all out to beat Peddlers Cross and it's hard to believe he wouldn't have toyed with that one at Leopardstown. Perhaps it's simply the ground as Hurricane Fly is obviously well at home on a soft surface but maybe lacks the pace these days to do it on a faster surface. If it comes up soft, though, Ruby Walsh may well have a hell of a decision to make between the favourite and the horse of a lifetime. That the possibility of a third Champion Hurdle is being seriously entertained is remarkable enough given that at the end of last season he was a 33-1 chance to win it again. The head (and trends) says he won't have it in him to emulate Sea Pigeon and Hatton's Grace, who both won at the age of 11, but the hearts of many will be willing him on even if the money is riding on something else.

Arctic Fire

6 b g; Trainer Willie Mullins
Hurdles form 1S34212332, best RPR 165
Left-handed 142332, best RPR 165
Right-handed S312, best RPR 152
Cheltenham form 2, best RPR 150
At the festival 14 Mar 2014: in rear, steady headway from 2 out, quickened to track leaders approaching last, driven to lead with 1f to run, headed closing stages, finished second, beaten half a length by Lac Fontana in County Hurdle

In normal circumstances a career-best last-time-out Racing Post Rating of 165 would entitle a horse to serious consideration, but he is only the third string for his stable and a general 16-1 shot. He does, however, have quite a nice profile, having shown easily his best form as a novice at the time when second in last season's County Hurdle off a mark of 141. That was on good ground, which he hasn't yet had this season, and he is improving judging by his placings behind Hurricane Fly on his last two starts. He may have been a shade fortunate to grab second in the Irish Champion, but that was still another step up and he promises to be well suited by the return to Cheltenham and a decent surface. Far from a complete no-hoper, although his failure to win at all this season would be a negative and he has yet to win a Graded race of any description.

OTHERS TO CONSIDER

It's very hard to see where the dangers to the top five in the betting are going to come from as there were only 16 left at the last entry stage and the next two in the betting were **Un De Sceaux** and **Annie Power**, who presumably have no chance of lining up unless both Faugheen and Hurricane Fly suffer mishaps. The Edward O'Grady-trained **Kitten Rock** was roundly shortened by the bookies afer winning the Red Mills Trial Hurdle at Gowran in February, but with Abbyssial falling two out when looking a threat, he was left to stroll home 12 lengths clear of a 127-rated four-year-old, so it's hardly Champion Hurdle form. On the same day Paul Nicholls' **Irving** failed to enhance his outside chances when beaten by Blue Heron in the Kingwell at Wincanton. A tactical race did not suit but, having looked a potentially top novice last season and won the Grade 1 Fighting Fifth this term, he simply doesn't appear anywhere near good enough now. The same can be said of Nicky Henderson's pair **Vaniteux** and **Sign Of A Victory** (big drifter and well beaten in the Kingwell), **Purple Bay** (doesn't have tactical speed to lay up), **Garde La Victoire** (good handicapper but that's all), **Tiger Roll** (bitterly disappointing since Triumph win, well beaten in Red Mills Trial), **Bertimont** and **Plinth** (pacemaker).

Champion Hurdle results and trends

	FORM	WINNER	AGE & WGT	Adj RPR	SP	TRAINER	H.Runs	BEST RPR LAST 12 MONTHS (RUNS SINCE)
14	-1124	**Jezki** D	6 11-10	169^{-8}	9-1	J Harrington (IRE)	10$^{(9GS)}$	2nd Gd1 Ryanair Hurdle (2m) **(1)**
13	1-111	**Hurricane Fly** CD	9 11-10	177^{T}	13-8f	W Mullins (IRE)	19$^{(9S)}$	won Gd1 Irish Champion Hurdle (2m) **(0)**
12	23-12	**Rock On Ruby** C, D	7 11-10	170^{-7}	11-1	P Nicholls	6$^{(10G)}$	2nd Gd1 Christmas Hurdle (2m) **(0)**
11	1-111	**Hurricane Fly** D	7 11-10	172^{-2}	11-4f	W Mullins (IRE)	11$^{(11G)}$	won Gd1 Irish Champion Hurdle (2m) **(0)**
10	3-531	**Binocular** D	6 11-10	171^{-2}	9-1	N Henderson	10$^{(12GS)}$	won Sandown Listed hdl (2m½f) **(0)**
09	1-1F3	**Punjabi** D, BF	6 11-10	168^{-8}	22-1	N Henderson	12$^{(23GS)}$	won Gd1 Punchestwn Champ Hdl (2m) **(3)**
08	-1321	**Katchit** CD	5 11-10	166^{-8}	10-1	A King	12$^{(15GS)}$	won Gd2 Kingwell Hurdle (2m) **(0)**
07	444-1	**Sublimity** D	7 11-10	146^{-31}	16-1	J Carr (IRE)	5$^{(10S)}$	4th Gd1 Supreme Nov Hdl (2m½f) **(2)**
06	11311	**Brave Inca** CD	8 11-10	172^{T}	7-4f	C Murphy (IRE)	20$^{(18GS)}$	won Gd1 Punchestwn Champ Hdl (2m) **(4)**
05	12331	**Hardy Eustace** CD	8 11-10	174^{T}	7-2jf	D Hughes (IRE)	16$^{(14G)}$	won Gd1 Champion Hurdle (2m½f) **(5)**

WINS-RUNS: 5yo 1-28, 6yo 3-36, 7yo 3-24, 8yo 2-19, 9yo 1-8, 10yo 0-5, 11yo 0-6, 12yo 0-4, 13yo 0-1 **FAVOURITES:** £1.38

TRAINERS IN THIS RACE (w-pl-r): Nicky Henderson 2-6-15, Willie Mullins 2-1-8, Jessica Harrington 1-1-4, Paul Nicholls 1-1-8, Edward O'Grady 0-0-3, Nigel Twiston-Davies 0-2-3, Philip Hobbs 0-0-4

FATE OF FAVOURITES: 1160301314 **POSITION OF WINNER IN MARKET:** 1165971415

Key trends

🐎Ran within the past 51 days, 9/10

🐎Aged between six and nine, 9/10

🐎Adjusted RPR of at least 166, 9/10

🐎Ten to 20 runs over hurdles, 8/10 (both exceptions had fewer starts)

🐎Topspeed of at least 151, 8/10

🐎Rated within 7lb of RPR top-rated, 8/10

🐎Had won either a Grade 1 hurdle or a Grade 3 handicap hurdle, 7/10

🐎Won a Grade 1 or 2 hurdle that season, 7/10

🐎Won last time out, 7/10

Other factors

🐎Only Binocular (2010) had an unplaced effort in the form figures for that season

🐎Katchit (2008) broke a long-standing trend when he became the first five-year-old to win since See You Then in 1985. In the intervening years 73 had failed while 19 have come up short since

🐎Jezki, Rock On Ruby, Binocular, Punjabi, Sublimity and Hurricane Fly (for 2011) had not won at the festival, although the first-named quartet had made the frame there

🐎In 2012, Rock On Ruby became only the fourth winner in the past 30 years who had not run since the turn of the year

🐎The last horse aged ten or more to win was Sea Pigeon in both his winning years (1980 and 1981)

Notes

This race is newly promoted to Grade 1 status, which seems a little unfair on Quevega immediately after the record-breaking six-time winner departed the scene (all her victories were classed as Grade 2, although there is no doubt she was a Grade 1 performer). Quevega's sterling service has left a legacy in the upgrading of the race and the first beneficiary might be erstwhile stablemate Annie Power, who did not oppose her last year (when she had the edge on official ratings) but instead went for the World Hurdle and finished runner-up to More Of That. That form puts her a long way ahead in this division (12lb on Racing Post Ratings) and she will be expected to take over as the new banker for the Willie Mullins stable. A leg problem has kept her off the track this season but Mullins remains hopeful of making the festival – as he used to do with the fragile Quevega, who had a prep run only once in six years. John Quinn's five-year-old Aurore D'Estruval has emerged as the most serious rival – and it is interesting to note Quevega was five when she first won the contest, as was inaugural winner Whiteoak – while Mullins also has last year's runner-up Glens Melody, who gave Quevega quite a scare on that occasion. There are a number of solid British-trained mares, including the Nicky Henderson-trained Polly Peachum, Carole's Spirit (Robert Walford) and Bitofapuzzle (Harry Fry), but they will have a lot to find if Annie Power turns up on top form.

Mares' Hurdle results

	FORM	WINNER	AGE & WGT	Adj RPR	SP	TRAINER	H.Runs	BEST RPR LAST 12 MONTHS (RUNS SINCE)
14	1/11-	**Quevega** CD	10 11-5	171[T]	8-11f	W Mullins (IRE)	16[(16GS)]	won Gd1 Punchestown World Hdl (3m) (0)
13	/111-	**Quevega** CD	9 11-5	168[T]	8-11f	W Mullins (IRE)	14[(19S)]	won Gd1 Punchestown World Hdl (3m) (0)
12	1/1-1	**Quevega** CD	8 11-5	168[T]	4-7f	W Mullins (IRE)	12[(19G)]	won Gd1 Punchestown World Hdl (3m) (0)
11	3911-	**Quevega** CD	7 11-5	166[T]	5-6f	W Mullins (IRE)	10[(14G)]	won Gd2 Mares' Hurdle (2m4f) (1)
10	11-39	**Quevega** CD	6 11-5	168[T]	6-4f	W Mullins (IRE)	8[(17G)]	3rd Gd1 Punchestown Champ Hdl (2m) (1)
09	19-31	**Quevega** D	5 11-3	156[-4]	2-1f	W Mullins (IRE)	5[(21GS)]	won Punchestown hdl (2m4f) (0)
08	23121	**Whiteoak**	5 11-0	139[-23]	20-1	D McCain	5[(13GS)]	won Ascot class 3 nov hdl (2m) (0)

WINS-RUNS: 4yo 0-3, 5yo 2-23, 6yo 1-37, 7yo 1-28, 8yo 1-18, 9yo 1-7, 10yo 1-3 **FAVOURITES:** £5.36

TRAINERS IN THIS RACE (w-pl-r): Willie Mullins 6-1-8, Donald McCain 1-0-5, Alan King 0-1-3, Charlie Mann 0-0-1, Colin Bowe 0-0-1, David Pipe 0-0-3, Evan Williams 0-0-1, Fergal O'Brien 0-0-1, Gordon Elliott 0-0-1, Harry Fry 0-0-1, Henry Daly 0-0-1, Jamie Snowden 0-0-2, Jarlath Fahey 0-0-1, John Quinn 0-0-1, Kim Bailey 0-0-2, Martin Keighley 0-0-1, Jessica Harrington 0-0-4, Neil Mulholland 0-0-1, Nicky Henderson 0-2-8, Oliver Sherwood 0-0-1, Paul Nicholls 0-0-2, Paul Webber 0-0-5, Tim Vaughan 0-0-2

FATE OF FAVOURITES: 3111111 **POSITION OF WINNER IN MARKET:** 7111111

Notes

4.40 Toby Balding National Hunt Chase — RUK

4m *Listed* *Amateur riders' novices' chase* *£85,000*

The Young Master: leading chance if he runs here in preference to the RSA Chase

Recent changes to the race conditions have made this more of a 4m RSA Chase in quality and that means the big yards have a greater chance of producing the winner. It is notable that three of the past four winners had the highest official rating in the field (the other top-rated, Shotgun Paddy last year, was beaten a neck).

At the entry stage, the highest-rated this year is The Young Master on a mark of 151. The next five are Southfield Theatre (149), Royal Player (147), Sego Success (143), Shantou Magic (143) and Return Spring (142). The Young Master, Southfield Theatre and Sego Success are particularly interesting.

This is Jonjo O'Neill's best race at the festival with five wins, although he has not been successful in the six years since the race conditions were comprehensively revised – the closest he has come from six runners is fourth place with 4-1 favourite Can't Buy Time in 2009.

With more of an accent on quality, the race is starting to lose its reputation for producing big-priced winners. In the decade before the conditions changed, half of the winners were returned at 25-1 or bigger, whereas under the new conditions the biggest-priced winner has been 14-1 and the other four winners all came from the top five in the betting.

All bar two of the winners since 1990 had been first or second in at least one of their latest two outings, with the exception achieving it three runs before this race. Four of the last ten winners had a good run at Cheltenham that season to their credit, while two more in that period had run well over 3m at the course in a previous season (finishing first or second).

Winning form over at least 3m is significant, but punters have to try to work out whether a chaser who is a bit one-paced at the end of 3m will relish the extra mile of this test, although there are signs that the class factor is starting to make this a more predictable betting heat.

Irish amateur riders have won this race eight times in the past 13 runnings, although there have been only three Irish-trained winners in that period.

NH Chase results and trends

	FORM	WINNER	AGE & WGT	Adj RPR	SP	TRAINER	C.Runs	BEST RPR LAST 12 MONTHS (RUNS SINCE)
14	61U21	**Midnight Prayer**	9 11-6	154[-12]	8-1	A King	4[(15GS)]	won Warwick class 3 nov ch (3m2f) **(0)**
13	/2111	**Back In Focus**	8 11-6	161[T]	9-4f	W Mullins (IRE)	3[(16GS)]	won Leopardstown Gd1 nov ch (3m) **(0)**
12	321P1	**Teaforthree**	8 11-6	161[T]	5-1f	R Curtis	5[(19G)]	won Chepstow class 3 nov ch (3m) **(2)**
11	11F25	**Chicago Grey** C	8 11-6	163[T]	5-1f	G Elliott (IRE)	9[(16G)]	2nd Cheltenham class 2 nov ch (3m1½f) **(1)**
10	-2951	**Poker De Sivola**	7 11-6	145[-8]	14-1	F Murphy	11[(18G)]	2nd Kelso class 3 hcap ch (3m1f) **(3)**
09	42212	**Tricky Trickster**	6 11-11	140[-18]	11-1	N Twiston-Davies	3[(19GS)]	2nd Chelt class 2 nov hcap ch (2m5f) **(0)**
08	27322	**Old Benny**	7 11-7	135[-18]	9-1	A King	3[(20GS)]	2nd Newbury class 2 nov ch (3m) **(0)**
07	11430	**Butler's Cabin** C	7 12-0	131[-20]	33-1	J O'Neill	7[(19GS)]	won Aintree class 3 hcap ch (2m4f) **(4)**
06	15361	**Hot Weld**	7 11-11	113[-32]	33-1	F Murphy	4[(22G)]	3rd Wetherby class 4 nov ch (3m1f) **(2)**
05	-22F4	**Another Rum**	7 11-7	123[-24]	40-1	I Duncan (IRE)	4[(20G)]	4th Navan Gd3 nov ch (3m) **(0)**

WINS-RUNS: 6yo 1-26, 7yo 5-71, 8yo 3-47, 9yo 1-28, 10yo 0-9, 11yo 0-1, 12yo 0-2 **FAVOURITES:** £5.25

TRAINERS IN THIS RACE (w-pl-r): Alan King 2-1-8, Gordon Elliott 1-0-2, Ian Duncan 1-0-1, Nigel Twiston-Davies 1-0-7, Rebecca Curtis 1-0-1, Willie Mullins 1-1-7, Tony Martin 0-1-2, Charlie Longsdon 0-0-3, Colin Tizzard 0-0-2, David Pipe 0-1-5, Donald McCain 0-0-6, Emma Lavelle 0-1-2, Henry Daly 0-0-4, Kim Bailey 0-0-1, Mouse Morris 0-1-4, Martin Keighley 0-0-2, Noel Meade 0-0-2, Paul Nicholls 0-1-7, Philip Hobbs 0-0-3, Tom George 0-0-3, Venetia Williams 0-1-4

FATE OF FAVOURITES: 53F5451110 **POSITION OF WINNER IN MARKET:** 0004571114

Key trends

🐎Ran at least three times over fences, 10/10

🐎Finished first or second in a chase over at least 3m, 9/10

🐎Top five-finish last time out, 9/10 (exception unplaced in Class 1 chase)

🐎Aged seven or eight, 8/10 (exceptions one older and one younger)

🐎Had won over at least 3m (hurdles or chases), 9/10

🐎Finished first or second on either or both of last two starts, 8/10

Other factors

🐎The six winners between 2005 and 2010 had an adjusted RPR of 113-145. The last four were 154-163

🐎Since a change in the conditions of the race nine years ago, all bar one winner had a hurdles RPR of at least 119

🐎Three winners had run and won in handicap company

🐎Three winners since 2002 have worn headgear, two of which were trained by Jonjo O'Neill

🐎Four winners since 2003 started 25-1 or bigger

🐎The three winners between 2011 and 2013 were outright favourites (Chicago Grey, Teaforthree and Back In Focus) – the last to oblige before them was Keep Talking in 1992

🐎Jonjo O'Neill landed this contest five times between 1995 and 2007

🐎Paul Nicholls has never won this race despite strong representation

Notes

5.15 Novices' Handicap Chase
2m4½f · Listed · £60,000 · RUK

In common with the other festival handicaps, this race has seen an upward shift in ratings that has put the accent on quality and increased the difficulty of getting a run.

In its first six years this race was run on the New Course over 2m5f, but then it moved to the Old Course over half a furlong less and the last four winners carried the biggest weights so far successful. The last three winners were officially rated 142, 140 and 137, whereas only one of the first seven winners was rated above 135. The ceiling mark is now 140 and the ratings spread has become quite narrow (131-140 for last year's 19 runners).

All ten winners had shown smart form and nine had finished first or second last time out. Six of the ten had won no more than once. Three winners had run at Exeter that season, while four had run at the previous year's festival and two of the last four winners had run at Cheltenham that season. All ten winners arrived with a minimum of three runs over fences, with only the Irish-trained Finger Onthe Pulse not having won over fences.

Winners have been prominent in the betting, with eight sent off at odds between 9-2 and 12-1 (all those were in the first five in the market).

The Nick Gifford-trained Generous Ransom looks a likely type, having risen to a mark of 136 after his Cheltenham victory on Trials Day in a 2m5f novice handicap chase.

Novices' Handicap Chase results and trends

	FORM	WINNER	AGE & WGT	OR	SP	TRAINER	C.Runs	BEST RPR LAST 12 MONTHS (RUNS SINCE)
14	32121	**Present View** D	6 11-7	137[-1]	8-1	J Snowden	4[(19GS)]	won Kempton class 3 hcap ch (2m4½f) (0)
13	-2F17	**Rajdhani Express** D	6 11-7	140[T]	16-1	N Henderson	5[(20S)]	won Kempton class 3 hcap ch (2m4½f) (1)
12	12111	**Hunt Ball** D	7 12-0	142[-4]	13-2f	K Burke	9[(20G)]	won Kempton class 3 hcap ch (2m4½f) (0)
11	31591	**Divers** D	7 11-4	132[-6]	10-1	F Murphy	4[(20G)]	won Musselburgh class 3 nov ch (2m4f) (0)
10	-1321	**Copper Bleu**	8 11-1	139[-3]	12-1	P Hobbs	3[(20G)]	won Exeter class 4 ch (2m1½f) (0)
09	9-F21	**Chapoturgeon**	5 10-11	135[-2]	8-1	P Nicholls	3[(20GS)]	won Doncaster class 2 nov ch (2m½f) (0)
08	-3F22	**Finger Onthe Pulse** D	7 10-12	135[-7]	9-1	T Taaffe (IRE)	4[(20GS)]	2nd Leopardstown Gd2 nov ch (2m5f) (0)
07	221F2	**L'Antartique** D	7 10-11	133[-16]	20-1	F Murphy	6[(19GS)]	won Bangor class 4 nov ch (2m4½f) (2)
06	6-221	**Reveillez** D	7 10-11	133[-1]	9-2f	J Fanshawe	3[(18G)]	2nd Exeter class 4 nov ch (2m3½f) (2)
05	FF212	**King Harald** (2oh) D	7 10-4	123[T]	9-1	M Bradstock	5[(19G)]	2nd Wetherby Gd2 nov ch (3m1f) (0)

WINS-RUNS: 5yo 1-16, 6yo 2-38, 7yo 6-77, 8yo 1-43, 9yo 0-16, 10yo 0-4, 11yo 0-1 **FAVOURITES:** £3.00

FATE OF FAVOURITES: P10F005150 **POSITION OF WINNER IN MARKET:** 2103254183

OR 123-130 1-4-18, **131-140** 8-23-155, **141-148** 1-3-22

Key trends

- Top-two finish last time out, 9/10
- Officially rated 132-142, 9/10
- Won over at least 2m2f, 9/10
- Aged six or seven, 8/10
- Carried no more than 11st 4lb, 7/10 (last three winners the exceptions)
- Finished in the first four all completed starts over fences, 8/10
- No more than one win over fences, 7/10

Other factors

- Five winners had fallen at least once over fences
- Three winners had contested novice hurdles at the previous year's festival
- Three winners had hurdle RPRs of at least 144, two in the 130s and four in the 120s
- Two winners had been placed in Grade 2 novice chases
- Only two winners have started longer than 12-1 (outside first five in the market)

Wednesday, March 11
(Old Course)
Neptune Investment Management Novices' Hurdle
RSA Chase
Coral Cup
Betway Queen Mother Champion Chase
Glenfarclas Cross Country Chase
Fred Winter Juvenile Handicap Hurdle
Weatherbys Champion Bumper

1.30 Neptune Investment Novices' Hurdle   C4/RUK
2m5f   Grade 1   £120,000

Once again Willie Mullins is strong in this event, both historically (three wins, a second and three thirds in the past seven runnings) and in terms of the ammunition available to him (he had 24 of the 109 entries). His embarrassment of riches means he might well end up with more than one representative and he is likely to have the favourite, as he has in four of the past six years (those favourites finished 1331). Victory in the Grade 1 Deloitte edged Nichols Canyon into pole position for Mullins in this race, assuming Douvan goes for the Supreme, and the Irish champion trainer has more options with Outlander, Shaneshill and Tell Us More. The chief British challenger appears to be the John Ferguson-trained Parlour Games, who will try to overcome the hoodoo for Challow winners in this race, while Nicky Henderson (who tends not to be so strongly represented here and has won only once, with Simonsig in 2012) has the promising but inexperienced Kilcrea Vale.

Nichols Canyon
5 b g; Trainer Willie Mullins
Hurdles form 11U1, best RPR 150
Left-handed U1, best RPR 150
Right-handed 11, best RPR 143
Cheltenham form None

Trained by John Gosden on the Flat and earned a rating of 113 in that sphere following Listed victories over 1m6f at Ascot and just short of 2m at Saint-Cloud. Was always likely to take high rank if handling the winter game and duly won first two hurdles starts with the minimum of fuss following a year off before unseating early when odds-on for the Grade 1 Future Champions Novice Hurdle at Leopardstown. Showed that mishap didn't have any lasting effect when given an aggressive ride by Ruby Walsh to land the all-important Grade 1 Deloitte back at Leopardstown in February, beating Windsor Park and well-touted stablemate Alvisio Ville with a bit in hand. The last two runnings of the Deloitte have been won by Willie Mullins' subsequent Supreme heroes Champagne Fever and Vautour, and the trainer said he would not be worried about going back in trip, although he has favourite Douvan for that (different owner) and this appears the more likely target for a horse who clearly stays very well and might improve again for 2m5f. All best Flat form on bad ground, but it wasn't far off good at Leopardstown, so it may not be an issue.

Parlour Games
7 ch g; Trainer John Ferguson
Hurdles form 1210211, best RPR 148
Left-handed 211, best RPR 148
Right-handed 1102, best RPR 142
Cheltenham form 1, best RPR 146

Decent Flat performer with a peak rating of 99 in that sphere who has made a good fist of novice hurdling despite trying the winter game at a relatively late stage. Stayed 1m6f on the Flat and started off over 2m over hurdles but, having found the Galway Hurdle too much for him in July and then been outpaced by Blue Heron at Kempton in October, he was stepped up in trip to 2m5f with excellent results. He took a Grade 2 at Cheltenham in November from Blaklion, using his superior Flat speed in the closing stages of a slowly run race, and then proved it was no fluke in a more strongly run Grade 1 Challow Hurdle. He once again made smooth headway from the rear and this time proved he had the courage to go with his ability as he held on well to win by a neck from Vyta Du Roc, with Blaklion back in third. That form puts him up there with the best of those likely to run, but he's hardly a standout on it and it remains to be seen how much improvement he has in him. Winners of his age are rare, with French Holly's victory in 1998 the only win by a horse older than six (he was seven) since Brown Lad scored at the age of eight in 1974.

Outlander

7 b g; Trainer Willie Mullins
Hurdles form 121, best RPR 143
Left-handed 1, best RPR 143
Right-handed 12, best RPR 142
Cheltenham form None

Another seven-year-old near the head of the market and entered in all three novices, having tried his hand at 2m-3m from three outings. Won a soft race very easily over 2m on his debut after 18 months off the track since his bumper season, but then beaten a neck by Martello Tower in three-runner Grade 3 over 3m at Limerick. Gained his revenge at the intermediate trip at Leopardstown in January, beating Martello Tower by three and a quarter lengths, but more than a suspicion that one or two of his rivals were well below form. That definitely appeared to be the case with No More Heroes, who had beaten Shaneshill quite comfortably the time before but was never travelling and was reported to have scoped badly afterwards. Age a negative and, according to Racing Post Ratings, was only the fifth best of his powerful stable among the entries, so questionable whether he deserves his place in the market.

Tell Us More

6 b g; Trainer Willie Mullins
Hurdles form 12, best RPR 145
Left-handed 2, best RPR 145
Right-handed 1, best RPR 130
Cheltenham form None

Trainer very complimentary about him after he won his opening maiden hurdle at Gowran and he was sent off at odds-on stepped up in trip at Naas in January, but was turned over by a 33-1 stablemate. He still showed improved form and may have gone off a shade too fast in front, although Mullins said he might drop him in trip next time. By promising young jumps sire Scorpion and in reality should have little difficulty with the trip, especially on better ground.

Shaneshill (below, left)

6 b g; Trainer Willie Mullins
Hurdles form 12, best RPR 148
Left-handed 2, best RPR 148
Right-handed 1, best RPR 134
Cheltenham form 2 (bumper), best RPR 137
At the festival 12 Mar 2014: well placed behind leaders, closed 3f out on inner, ridden to lead over 1f out, headed just inside final furlong, stayed on but held after, finished second, beaten one and a half lengths by Silver Concorde in Champion Bumper

Yet another Mullins performer with entries in all three novice races. Yet to finish out of the first two in all starts and second when favourite to Silver Concorde in last season's Champion Bumper, confirming his liking for decent ground. Seemingly outstayed by the Albert Bartlett-bound No More Heroes over 2m4f in the Grade 2 Navan Novice Hurdle in December and had not returned to the track by the beginning of February. Obviously very talented, though, and boasts better form than a couple of Mullins horses ahead of him in the betting.

Kilcrea Vale

5 b g; Trainer Nicky Henderson
Hurdles form 1, best RPR 144
Right-handed 1, best RPR 144
Cheltenham form None

Point winner in May who subsequently went for £100,000 at the sales and joined Nicky Henderson. Just the one start to go on so far, but it was an impressive one as Kilcrea Vale proved very strong in the betting and powered 26 lengths clear of Novirak in a 2m3f event at Market Rasen. The runner-up was rated in the high 80s on the Flat and had been a promising third on his hurdles debut (behind subsequent Morebattle winner Glingerburn), so it was a pretty sparkling effort from Kilcrea Vale and it earned him an RPR of 144. To put that into perspective, it's just 6lb shy of what Nichols Canyon was awarded when winning the Grade 1 Deloitte in February, so any small improvement would put him up there with the best. This race normally goes to something

with more experience (eight of the last ten winners having run at least three times over hurdles) and, having been pulled out of a couple of possible engagements in early February, time is running out for him to get some more. Interesting if he makes the line-up all the same.

Windsor Park
6 b g; Trainer Dermot Weld
Hurdles form 142, best RPR 147
Left-handed 142, best RPR 147

Showed some decent bumper form last season and again on return in August when winning at Galway before being switched to the Flat and winning twice more, the last time back at Galway when he thrashed a 90-rated rival by nearly ten lengths. December's maiden hurdle victory at Leopardstown was straightforward enough, but it didn't work out particularly well and Windsor Park disappointed next time when only fourth in a Grade 2 won by Outlander. Slight suspicion that he, and favourite No More Heroes, were some way below their best that day, and he at least proved so when running second to Nichols Canyon in the Grade 1 Deloitte at Leopardstown in February. Was held up that day while the winner made all, but there was no hanging around and no obvious reason to think he'll turn the form on its head.

Alvisio Ville
5 gr g; Trainer Willie Mullins
Hurdles form 13, best RPR 138
Left-handed 13, best RPR 138
Cheltenham form None

Big horse who was third in his sole French bumper but made a big impression on his debut for Willie Mullins when scoring by five and a half lengths at Leopardstown over Christmas. Suddenly became all the rage for this in the run-up to the Grade 1 Deloitte Hurdle back at Leopardstown in February and he was sent off at 11-10 favourite there despite boasting form some way from the best in the line-up. He tried to go with winner and stablemate Nichols Canyon turning for home but was left behind and beaten 12 lengths into third. Whether it was lack of experience or stamina was hard to tell and he is in the Supreme (and the Albert Bartlett) but Willie Mullins said he

didn't expect Nichols Canyon to beat him, so it might not be wise to rule him out yet. That said, he looks for all the world like a chaser of the future.

Ordo Ab Chao
6 b g; Trainer Alan King
Hurdles form 1141, best RPR 142
Left-handed 1, best RPR 142
Right-handed 114, best RPR 132
Cheltenham form 1, best RPR 134

Fourth in the Grade 2 bumper at Aintree's Grand National meeting and held in high regard by Alan King. Won first two hurdles starts in weak company at Huntingdon (four-and-a-half-length runner-up in second outing was subsequently beaten 36 lengths by Kilcrea Vale) and seemed to be found out when only fourth of five to Vyta Du Roc in Sandown's Grade 2 Winter Novice Hurdle in December. However, resumed progress with a battling win from Albert Bartlett fancy Value At Risk at Cheltenham on Trials Day, although wandered near the finish and was all out to score by three-quarters of a length. Also in the three-miler, but said to want the ground no faster than good to soft.

OTHERS TO CONSIDER

As always the final line-up is hard to predict this far in advance, especially when it comes to Willie Mullins. Others he could run include **McKinley**, who shocked stablemate Tell Us More at Naas but then ran poorly in the Deloitte, Black Hercules (though he is favourite for the Albert Bartlett), recent Warwick scorer **Arbre De Vie** and **Milsean**. The Paul Nicholls-trained **Vago Collonges** travelled really well when third to Ordo Ab Chao at Cheltenham in January and, if he ever finds as much as he often promises to, could be interesting. It would be a surprise if the likes of **L'Ami Serge** and **Jollyallan** came here instead of the Supreme, but **Vyta Du Roc,** whose form (close second to Parlour Games) would entitle him to consideration, could easily come here rather than go for the Albert Bartlett over a trip he hasn't yet tried. **Definitly Red**, on the other hand, will probably go the 3m route after a game win over that trip at Haydock in February.

Neptune Novices' Hurdle results and trends

	FORM	WINNER	AGE & WGT	Adj RPR	SP	TRAINER	H.Runs	BEST RPR LAST 12 MONTHS (RUNS SINCE)
14	1111	**Faugheen**	6 11-7	156^T	6-4f	W Mullins (IRE)	3$^{(15G)}$	won Limerick Gd3 nov hdl (3m) (0)
13	-1112	**The New One** CD, BF	5 11-7	162^{-1}	7-2	N Twiston-Davies	4$^{(8GS)}$	2nd Cheltenham Gd2 nov hdl (2m4½f) (0)
12	1121	**Simonsig**	6 11-7	160^T	2-1f	N Henderson	3$^{(17G)}$	2nd Sandown Gd2 nov hdl (2m4f) (1)
11	-4131	**First Lieutenant**	6 11-7	152^{-8}	7-1	M Morris (IRE)	4$^{(12G)}$	won Leopardstown Gd1 nov hdl (2m) (0)
10	111	**Peddlers Cross**	5 11-7	155^{-1}	7-1	D McCain	2$^{(17G)}$	won Haydock Gd2 nov hdl (2m½f) (0)
09	21111	**Mikael D'Haguenet**	5 11-7	160^{-4}	5-2f	W Mullins (IRE)	7$^{(14GS)}$	won Punchestown Gd2 nov hdl (2m) (0)
08	153-1	**Fiveforthree**	6 11-7	141^{-9}	7-1	W Mullins (IRE)	1$^{(15GS)}$	won Fairyhouse mdn hdl (2m) (0)
07	21U53	**Massini's Maguire** CD	6 11-7	145^{-8}	20-1	P Hobbs	9$^{(15GS)}$	won Cheltenham class 2 nov hdl (2m5f) (3)
06	1F221	**Nicanor**	5 11-7	147^{-17}	17-2	N Meade (IRE)	5$^{(17G)}$	won Leopardstown Gd3 nov hdl (2m4f) (0)
05	121	**No Refuge** D	5 11-7	152^T	17-2	H Johnson	3$^{(20G)}$	won Warwick Gd2 nov hdl (2m5f) (0)

WINS-RUNS: 4yo 0-5, 5yo 5-53, 6yo 5-66, 7yo 0-25, 8yo 0-1 **FAVOURITES:** -£1.00

TRAINERS IN THIS RACE (w-pl-r): Willie Mullins 3-5-12, Donald McCain 1-0-2, Mouse Morris 1-2-6, Nicky Henderson 1-0-10, Nigel Twiston-Davies 1-0-7, Noel Meade 1-1-6, Philip Hobbs 1-0-2, Tony Martin 0-0-1, Alan King 0-1-7, Ben Case 0-0-1, Colin Tizzard 0-0-2, Dermot Weld 0-1-3, David Bridgwater 0-0-1, David Pipe 0-0-5, Emma Lavelle 0-0-1, Evan Williams 0-0-1, Henry de Bromhead 0-0-1, John Ferguson 0-0-2, Jonjo O'Neill 0-1-3, Nick Williams 0-2-2, Paul Nicholls 0-2-6, Rebecca Curtis 0-0-1, Venetia Williams 0-0-2, Warren Greatrex 0-0-2

FATE OF FAVOURITES: 5250133131 **POSITION OF WINNER IN MARKET:** 4484144121

Key trends

🐎 Aged five or six, 10/10

🐎 Won at least 50 per cent of hurdle runs, 9/10

🐎 Adjusted RPR of at least 145, 9/10

🐎 Rated within 9lb of RPR top-rated, 9/10

🐎 Finished first or second on all completed starts over hurdles, 8/10

🐎 Scored over at least 2m4f, 8/10

🐎 Started career in Irish points or bumpers, 8/10

🐎 At least three runs over hurdles, 8/10

🐎 Won a Graded hurdle, 8/10

Other factors

🐎 Only two winners had previously run in the Champion Bumper – Fiveforthree finished fifth in the 2007 running and The New One was sixth in 2012

🐎 Three of the last ten favourites have obliged (Mikael D'Haguenet 2009, Simonsig 2012, Faugheen 2014) – in that period only one winner has started bigger than 17-2

Notes

An already fascinating race gained more intrigue with Coneygree's sparkling success in the Denman Chase at Newbury, where he defeated more seasoned campaigners in some style on only his third run over fences. That confirmed him as one of the leading contenders for this race but gave trainer Mark Bradstock and the owners the dilemma of whether to go for the Gold Cup in an open year. Coneygree is not the only one with Gold Cup potential, if not this season then next, as the David Pipe-trained Kings Palace (also with three wins out of three over fences) has always been highly rated and has excellent Cheltenham form, apart from his disappointing effort in last year's Albert Bartlett. Willie Mullins also has exciting prospects with Don Poli, who seems likely to spearhead his challenge (Valseur Lido and Vautour are other possibles from his yard but may go for other races). With The Young Master, Apache Stronghold and Southfield Theatre also in the frame (but again with other options), this is shaping up into a high-class contest.

Kings Palace (right)

7 b g; Trainer David Pipe
Chase form 111, best RPR 156
Left-handed 111, best RPR 156
Cheltenham form (all) 11F11, best RPR 156
At the festival 14 Mar 2014: led, headed after 4th, remained chasing leader until regained lead 8th, headed after 2 out, soon weakened, 5th and well beaten when fell last in Albert Bartlett Hurdle

Looked a potential superstar as a staying novice hurdler last autumn, with three front-running victories on the spin, the last two at Cheltenham by wide margins, and was subsequently sent off at just 5-2 for the Albert Bartlett. Again he set out to make all in a big field but was a sitting duck turning for home and already beaten when taking a heavy fall at the last. It's possible he had to go a bit harder than he would have liked in such a big field, but that clearly wasn't his form and he was back on track at the start of this season as a novice chaser. He made a sparkling debut when beating previous winner Sausalito Sunrise by four lengths at Cheltenham in November and, while he was getting 5lb that day, he showed the benefit of a run when beating the same horse by seven lengths back there in December, despite an 8lb turnaround at the weights. Warmed up for this in a two-runner novice at Newbury in February and gave his backers a scare with a couple of uncharacteristically slow jumps and one bad blunder before coming back on the bridle to win with plenty in hand. It's probably not wise to read too much into that, but the worry is that he will again be a sitting duck for those played later in the day. That said, he was happy enough to take a lead on his chase debut, so if Tom Scudamore can get him settled he might not need to make it. He certainly goes well at Cheltenham and on decent ground.

Don Poli

6 b g; Trainer Willie Mullins
Chase form 11, best RPR 154
Left-handed 1, best RPR 154
Right-handed 1, best RPR 147
Cheltenham form (hurdle) 1, best RPR 153
At the festival 14 Mar 2014: held up in rear, headway 3 out, driven to challenge after 2 out, slight lead last, driven clear final 110yds, won Martin Pipe Conditional Jockeys' Handicap Hurdle by four and a half lengths from Thomas Crapper

Useful novice hurdler who followed the same path as top-class stablemate Sir Des Champs by going down the handicap route on his first festival visit and winning the Martin Pipe Conditional Jockeys' Handicap Hurdle. Was well on top at the end there and might not have been at his best when runner-up by three-quarters of a length to Beat That at Punchestown the following month, although it was hardly bad form. Chase campaign started well with two victories in November and December, the latter coming in the Grade 1 Topaz Novice Chase by three lengths from Apache Stronghold. He hadn't been seen again by the beginning of February but the form received the perfect boost when Apache Stronghold beat Don Poli's stablemate Valseur Lido in the Grade 1 Flogas Novice Chase at Leopardstown's big trials meeting. Was at one point nominated for the National Hunt Chase, for which he is still ante-post favourite, but it will be a surprise if he doesn't follow the Grade 1 route given the strength of his form and won't be far off market leader if he does.

Coneygree

8 b g; Trainer Mark Bradstock
Chase form 111, best RPR 169
Left-handed 11, best RPR 169
Right-handed 1, best RPR 159
Cheltenham form (hurdles) 113, best RPR 148

Decent staying novice hurdler a couple of seasons ago when reckoned to have more potential than his useful half-brother Carruthers, but then had to miss 22 months with injury. Was withdrawn on vet's advice from intended chase debut at lowly Plumpton, so had to go deeper on his first run, making it in a Grade 2 at Newbury, where he was well supported and jumped superbly to beat Dell' Arca by just under two lengths. That was over 2m4f but stamina was always going to be his thing and so it proved when he stepped up to 3m for the Grade 1 Feltham at Kempton over

Christmas and ran his rivals ragged with a 40-length victory. That race wasn't without incident and the odds-on favourite departed early, but Coneygree proved the form's worth when stepped into open company for the Denman Chase at Newbury, where he again made all, jumped like a stag and stayed on far too strongly for Hennessy runner-up Houblon Des Obeaux, winning by seven lengths. Clearly handles soft ground very well, but it wasn't that deep at Kempton and he boasts comfortably the best form of any staying novice. Also entered in the Gold Cup, though, and connections are giving that serious thought, so hardly an ante-post proposition.

The Young Master

6 b g; Trainer Neil Mulholland
Chase form 111d1, best RPR 154
Left-handed 11, best RPR 136
Right-handed 11d, best RPR 154
Cheltenham form 1, best RPR 136

Has been one of the racing stories of the season, not least because he ran away with a race for which he was ineligible and had to be disqualified. That is far from the only reason, though. Bred to win mile races on the Flat, he proved next to useless in his first year on the racetrack and little more than moderate until the end of 2013 when he suddenly developed the winning habit, winning four on the trot on the Flat and over hurdles from December of that year to February 2014. Then came a chase campaign,

which began last September with a 27-length win in a weak four-runner novice event at Worcester. Thrown straight into handicap company next time, he again made short work of the opposition, beating subsequent winner Charingworth by four and a half lengths off a mark of 121. Then came trainer Neil Mulholland's almighty faux pas of entering and running him in the Badger Ales Trophy (although the BHA must shoulder some of the blame for not spotting it), in which he bolted up by seven lengths off 130 despite not being qualified as he had yet to run in three chases. With the trainer fined £300, the race taken off him and the handicapper hitting him with a 14lb rise, things looked likely to get harder, but he was always in control when beating Hennessy runner-up Houblon Des Obeaux at Ascot in December, since when he has been put aside for this. He won't need to improve much to take a hand, but if trends are your thing he'd be easy enough to discard as having a Flat career is a definite no-no. He also hasn't contested a Graded chase, had far too many runs over hurdles and is younger than a usual winner. Then again, there's nothing usual about him and he does keep winning.

Valseur Lido

6 b g; Trainer Willie Mullins
Chase form 112, best RPR 158
Left-handed 1, best RPR 154
Right-handed 11, best RPR 158
Cheltenham form (hurdle) 0, best RPR 145
At the festival 11 Mar 2014: tracked leaders, niggled along approaching 2 out, outpaced between last 2, checked slightly after last, kept on run-in, finished 10th, beaten 11 and a half lengths by Vautour in Supreme Novices' Hurdle

Marginally shorter for the JLT on Thursday and, having yet to try 3m, is dealt with in that section.

Southfield Theatre

7 b g; Trainer Paul Nicholls
Chase form 1121, best RPR 156
Left-handed 12, best RPR 153
Right-handed 11, best RPR 156
Cheltenham form (bumper/hurdle) 41342, best RPR 152
At the festival 13 Mar 2014: midfield, headway on outer approaching 2 out, led before last, hard pressed run-in, headed post, finished second, beaten a nose by Fingal Bay in Pertemps Final

Tough and consistent handicap hurdler last season, who was beaten by an agonising nose in the Pertemps Final having led over the last, and wound up that campaign with a short-head victory off a mark of 150 at Sandown. Progress over fences has been as swift as you would expect from a Paul Nicholls-trained novice, with two easy victories coming in October and November, including in the Rising Stars Novices' Chase at Wincanton. His unbeaten run came to a surprising end at odds of 4-11 in a three-runner contest at Newbury in November, but he was giving 7lb to the winner and jumped poorly out of ground softer than he really cares for, and he was back on track at Exeter in February when beating Melodic Rendezvous at Exeter dropping back to 2m3½f. The runner-up had some good hurdles form to his name over shorter, but does stay and looked to be going very well three out, so it was impressive the way Southfield Theatre pulled out more. He'll be better on good ground over 3m and has never run a bad race at Cheltenham, so has plenty going for him.

Ptit Zig

6 b g; Trainer Paul Nicholls
Chase form 1111F, best RPR 165
Left-handed 11, best RPR 165
Right-handed 11F, best RPR 160
Cheltenham form (all) 361, best RPR 165
At the festival 13 Mar 2013: in touch, hit 4th, headway 3 out, went 2nd well before last, no impression on winner and stayed on same pace after last, finished third, beaten six and a quarter lengths by Flaxen Flare in Fred Winter Juvenile Handicap Hurdle
11 Mar 2014: hit 1st, in touch, blundered 4 out, weakened before 2 out, finished sixth, beaten 14 and a half lengths by Jezki in Champion Hurdle

Second-best British novice chaser on the figures (behind Coneygree) going into the festival and has all three options. Most likely to head for the JLT, though, so dealt with in Thursday's section.

Very Wood (right)

6 b g; Trainer Noel Meade
Chase form 1PP1, best RPR n/a
Left-handed P1, best RPR n/a
Right-handed 1P, best RPR 117
Cheltenham form (hurdle) 1, best RPR 153
At the festival 14 Mar 2014: held up, steady headway after 3 out, ridden and switched left to go close 2nd approaching last, led soon after flight, stayed on well to draw clear final 110yds, won Albert Bartlett Hurdle by four and a half lengths from Deputy Dan

Was a 33-1 shot when winning last season's Albert Bartlett Novices' Hurdle and was promising to be at least as big for the RSA after being pulled up twice following a workmanlike winning debut over fences in October. However, he was rumoured to be working well again before lining up for the Grade 2 Ten Up Novice Chase at Navan in February and so it proved as he put in a strong staying performance to score by four and a quarter lengths from Noble Emperor. That means he is back on track and, as a past festival winner who obviously goes well on good ground, he has to be respected. Three previous Albert Bartlett winners went on to score at the festival again and two of those – Weapon's Amnesty and Bobs Worth – did so in the RSA.

Sausalito Sunrise

7 b g; Trainer Philip Hobbs
Chase form 122F, best RPR 151
Left-handed 122, best RPR 151
Right-handed F
Cheltenham form (all) 3622, best RPR 151
At the festival 14 Mar 2014: midfield, headway 8th, chased leaders 3 out, weakened 2 out, no danger when hampered last, finished sixth, beaten 40 lengths by Very Wood in Albert Bartlett Novices' Hurdle

Fair staying novice hurdler, although a distant sixth to Very Wood in the Albert Bartlett hinted at limitations. Has already turned out better as a chaser, putting on a good display when winning on his debut and running well despite twice being put in his place by Kings Palace art Cheltenham. Fell in the Grade 1 Feltham at Kempton over Christmas, but was in the process of running well behind Coneygree (two lengths down when exiting at the 12th).

OTHERS TO CONSIDER

Grade 1 Flogas Novice Chase winner **Apache Stronghold** was confirmed for the JLT after his Leopardstown success, so it would be a surprise if Noel Meade changed his mind, and **Vautour** is another who is surely JLT-bound. Skybet Chase winner **If In Doubt** earned an RPR of 157 at Doncaster and would surely not be anywhere near a 33-1 chance if taking his chance. The same can be said of Willie Mullins' mare **Gitane Du Berlais**, who was impressive at Sandown at the end of January, while his other mare **Vroum Vroum Mag** has been doing it well against her own sex. The Reynoldstown at Ascot featured a pitiful field this season and winner Ainsi Fideles was not even entered for this. Second-placed **Deputy Dan** is, but his jumping needs to be a lot better.

RSA Chase results and trends

	FORM	WINNER	AGE & WGT	Adj RPR	SP	TRAINER	C.Runs	BEST RPR LAST 12 MONTHS (RUNS SINCE)
14	4-2P1	O'Faolains Boy D	7 11-4	160^{-9}	12-1	R Curtis	3$^{(15G)}$	won Gd2 Reynoldstown Nov Ch (3m) (0)
13	22123	Lord Windermere	7 11-4	155^{-10}	8-1	J Culloty (IRE)	5$^{(11GS)}$	3rd Gd1 Dr PJ Moriarty Nov Ch (2m5f) (0)
12	1-132	Bobs Worth C, D	7 11-4	172^{-6}	9-2	N Henderson	3$^{(9G)}$	3rd Gd1 Feltham Nov Ch (3m) (1)
11	21411	Bostons Angel D	7 11-4	160^{-13}	16-1	J Harrington (IRE)	5$^{(12G)}$	won Gd1 Dr PJ Moriarty Nov Ch (2m5f) (0)
10	3F122	Weapon's Amnesty C, D	7 11-4	160^{-15}	10-1	C Byrnes (IRE)	5$^{(9G)}$	2nd Leopardstown Gd1 nov ch (3m) (1)
09	-8131	Cooldine	7 11-4	166^{-3}	9-4f	W Mullins (IRE)	3$^{(15GS)}$	won Gd1 Dr PJ Moriarty Nov Ch (2m5f) (0)
08	-1211	Albertas Run CD	7 11-4	164^{-3}	4-1f	J O'Neill	4$^{(11GS)}$	won Gd2 Reynoldstown Nov Ch (3m) (0)
07	-1111	Denman C, D	7 11-4	170^{T}	6-5f	P Nicholls	4$^{(17GS)}$	won Newbury class 2 nov ch (3m) (0)
06	-1231	Star De Mohaison	5 10-8	159^{-7}	14-1	P Nicholls	4$^{(15G)}$	3rd Cheltenham Gd2 nov ch (2m5f) (1)
05	P-122	Trabolgan BF	7 11-4	162^{-3}	5-1	N Henderson	3$^{(9G)}$	2nd Gd1 Feltham Nov Ch (3m) (1)

WINS-RUNS: 5yo 1-5, 6yo 0-19, 7yo 9-63, 8yo 0-23, 9yo 0-12, 11yo 0-1 **FAVOURITES:** £0.45

TRAINERS IN THIS RACE (w-pl-r): Paul Nicholls 2-1-12, Willie Mullins 1-2-12, Alan King 0-1-2, Colin Tizzard 0-0-5, David Pipe 0-0-4, Donald McCain 0-0-3, Gordon Elliott 0-1-2, Mouse Morris 0-1-2, Mark Bradstock 0-0-1, Nigel Twiston-Davies 0-1-5, Noel Meade 0-0-1, Oliver Sherwood 0-0-1, Philip Hobbs 0-1-2, Tom George 0-1-1, Venetia Williams 0-0-2

FATE OF FAVOURITES: 2P11155442 **POSITION OF WINNER IN MARKET:** 4011157248

Key trends

🐎 Did not run on the Flat 10/10

🐎 Top-three finish last time out, 10/10

🐎 Last ran between 24 and 53 days ago, 10/10

🐎 Ran at least three times over fences, 10/10

🐎 Contested a Graded chase (six won, four placed), 10/10

🐎 Six to 12 hurdles and chase runs, 10/10

🐎 Rated less than 11lb off RPR top-rated, 8/10

🐎 Chase RPR of at least 150, 9/10

🐎 Aged seven, 9/10

Other factors

🐎 Of the combined 45 chase starts of winners, none had finished outside the first three (two had fallen). However, only Denman was unbeaten over fences

🐎 Eight winners had previously run at the festival – four ran in the Albert Bartlett (1P14), one in the Neptune (2) and three in the Bumper two years previously (207)

🐎 Nine five-year-olds have run in the last 21 years – one won, four were placed, two were unplaced and two fell. The winner, Star De Mohaison in 2006, received a 10lb weight-for-age allowance, which has since been cut to 2lb

Notes

2.40 Coral Cup (Handicap Hurdle) C4/RUK
2m5f Grade 3 £80,000

Older handicappers dominated this race in the early years, but increasingly the winners come from the younger age range – nine of the past 14 have been aged five or six, and eight of the last ten winners were second-season hurdlers. That inevitably means the winners are coming here with fewer runs on their record (six of the last seven were in single figures over hurdles).

In-form runners do best, with 11 of the winners in the race's 21-year history having scored on their previous run and four more finishing in the first three. Good handicap form is essential and three winners have come out of the past nine runnings of the Betfair Hurdle. On the Irish front the BoyleSports Hurdle in January and the Boyne Hurdle over this trip at Navan in mid-February are worth checking.

Only one favourite has won, but the form factor means eight of the past ten winners were in the first six in the betting. Twelve of the winners had landed a handicap that season and most had not been overraced that season (two to four runs). This is a high-quality handicap and seven winners were rated at least 137 – in the past decade it is notable that three of the seven winners rated 140-plus were Irish-trained. High weights are not necessarily a barrier to success, although only two of the British-trained winners carried more than 11st 2lb.

Ireland has had seven winners and only Xenophon, 4-1 favourite in 2003, was heavily fancied. The other six Irish winners were returned at between 11-1 and 16-1.

Coral Cup results and trends

	FORM	WINNER	AGE & WGT	OR	SP	TRAINER	H.Runs	BEST RPR LAST 12 MONTHS (RUNS SINCE)
14	-3312	**Whisper** C, D, BF	6 11-6	153^{-4}	14-1	N Henderson	9$^{(28G)}$	2nd Ffos Las class 2 hcap hdl (2m4f) (0)
13	-2241	**Medinas**	6 11-10	148^{-3}	33-1	A King	9$^{(28GS)}$	won Ffos Las class 2 hcap hdl (2m4f) (0)
12	-9090	**Son Of Flicka**	8 10-6	135^{T}	16-1	D McCain	22$^{(28G)}$	2nd Martin Pipe Cond Hcp Hdl (2m4½f) (5)
11	2-102	**Carlito Brigante** (2ow)	5 11-0	142^{-10}	16-1	G Elliott (IRE)	9$^{(22G)}$	2nd Fairyhouse hdl (2m) (0)
10	1-510	**Spirit River** C	5 11-2	141^{-1}	14-1	N Henderson	5$^{(28G)}$	won Chelt class 3 hcap hdl (2m1f) (1)
09	-4511	**Ninetieth Minute**	6 10-3	140^{T}	14-1	T Taaffe (IRE)	8$^{(27GS)}$	won Thurles Listed hdl (2m) (0)
08	12-71	**Naiad Du Misselot** D	7 10-13	130^{-7}	7-1	F Murphy	5$^{(24GS)}$	won Haydock class 2 hcap hdl (2m4f) (0)
07	23521	**Burntoakboy** D	9 9-12	128^{T}	10-1	R Newland	27$^{(28GS)}$	won Leicester class 3 hcap hdl (2m4½f) (0)
06	50121	**Sky's The Limit**	5 11-12	144^{-12}	11-1	E O'Grady (IRE)	8$^{(30G)}$	won Fairyhouse hdl (2m2f) (0)
05	-1626	**Idole First**	6 10-10	131^{-1}	33-1	V Williams	8$^{(29G)}$	2nd Uttoxeter class 3 hcap hdl (2m) (1)

WINS-RUNS: 5yo 3-57, 6yo 4-71, 7yo 1-54, 8yo 1-43, 9yo 1-27, 10yo 0-13, 11yo 0-5, 12yo 0-2 **FAVOURITES:** -£10.00

FATE OF FAVOURITES: 0F00000205 **POSITION OF WINNER IN MARKET:** 0442667705

Key trends

🐎Not run for at least 32 days, 10/10

🐎Won between 2m2f and 2m6f over hurdles, 9/10

🐎Scored at Class 3 or higher, 9/10

🐎Won a race earlier in the season, 9/10 (five won last time out)

🐎Aged five to seven, 8/10

🐎Officially rated 130 to 148, 8/10

🐎Five to nine hurdle runs, 8/10

🐎No more than four runs that season, 8/10

🐎Carried no more than 11st 2lb, 7/10

Other factors

🐎None of the last ten winners was out of the handicap – the only two to score when wrong at the weights were Olympian (1993) and Top Cees (1998)

🐎The two winners to have had more than nine hurdle runs had 22 and 27 starts

🐎Only one outright and one joint-favourite have won in the race's 21-year history

This is going to remain a guessing game until the race gets under way, with clouds of uncertainty swirling around 2013 winner Sprinter Sacre and Sire De Grugy, who took the crown in his absence last year. Sprinter Sacre is the class act at his best – his winning performance was rated 17lb better than Sire De Grugy's – but there remains a big question mark over his ability to return to that level after the heart problem that kept him off for 13 months and a comeback at Ascot in January that divided opinion. Sire De Grugy has also had problems and his belated reappearance at Newbury in February ended with Jamie Moore being unseated at the third-last fence. Even if one or both of those was ruled out, there would be just as many questions over which of the others might take the title. Dodging Bullets won the Tingle Creek and then beat the returning Sprinter Sacre, while trainer Paul Nicholls has another contender in the once wayward but seemingly reformed Mr Mole, who won the race in which Sire De Grugy unseated. The chief Irish challengers are dual festival winner Champagne Fever and Hidden Cyclone, although as with several contenders there is the alternative of the Ryanair Chase.

Sprinter Sacre (right)

9 b/br g; Trainer Nicky Henderson
Chase form 1111111111P2, best RPR 190
Left-handed 1111111, best RPR 190
Right-handed 111P2, best RPR 179
Cheltenham form (all) 3111, best RPR 190
At the festival 15 Mar 2011: tracked leaders, led just before 3 out, joined 2 out but still going strongly, ridden when hit last, immediately headed and faded, finished third, beaten five and a quarter lengths by Al Ferof in Supreme Novices' Hurdle
13 Mar 2012: jumped well, raced keenly in 3rd, quickened to lead on bridle 4 out, still on bit approaching 2 out, shaken up after last as 2nd tried to close, never any danger, eased closing stages, impressive, won Arkle Chase by seven lengths from Cue Card
13 Mar 2013: tracked leaders, went 2nd travelling smoothly 4 out, upsides next and soon led, came clear before 2 out, never off bridle, impressive, won Champion Chase by 19 lengths from Sizing Europe

Brilliant chaser two seasons ago when laying claim to being the best of his and any other generation over two miles. Almost every one of his races was won in a canter by a wide margin and he achieved the rare feat of winning at the Cheltenham, Aintree and Punchestown festivals in the space of six weeks, although he had to work much harder than usual in the final leg. Whether that punishing schedule was too much for him is hard to tell, but there were rumours he hadn't worked with his usual relish in the run-up to last season's reappearance and he was pulled up before the eighth fence in the Desert Orchid Chase just before Christmas, a heart problem being the diagnosis. That was it for the campaign as Nicky Henderson was never happy with him afterwards and it was beginning to look as though we would never see him again until he got the green light to run in the Grade 1 Clarence House Chase at Ascot in January. A Newbury gallop, which included jumping five fences down the back straight with veteran Tanks For That, was enough to persuade connections he was ready for competitive action and, although he'd have been a lot shorter in his pomp, he was heavily backed on the day down to 4-6 favouritism. He didn't bring home the money, though, finishing a three-length second to Dodging Bullets for his first chase defeat when completing and, if anything, his performance asked more questions than it answered. Just for a brief spell down the back straight he grabbed hold of the bit and looked like the superstar we'd all been hoping to see, but he couldn't sustain his effort in the home straight and wasn't given too hard a time. The run proved he is still a Grade 1 performer and if he comes on only a few pounds for that he remains the one to beat, but will he? The legendary Big Buck's returned from a similar layoff last season, albeit after a different problem and at a more advanced age, and he found no improvement. Likely better ground at Cheltenham will be a plus, but how Sprinter Sacre will respond when it starts to hurt at the end of a race is now open to question and a horse who has had just one completed start in 22 months brings plenty of risks at around the 11-4 mark.

Dodging Bullets

7 b g; Trainer Paul Nicholls
Chase form 111245311, best RPR 174
Left-handed 12453, best RPR 162
Right-handed 1111, best RPR 174
Cheltenham form (chase) 143, best RPR 162
At the festival 16 Mar 2012: held up, headway approaching 3 out, strong challenge before last, not quicken run-in, kept on under pressure but always held, finished fourth, beaten four lengths by Countrywide Flame in Triumph Hurdle
12 Mar 2013: raced in midfield on outer, headway to chase leaders approaching 3 out, weakened before 2 out, finished ninth, beaten 50 lengths by Champagne Fever in Supreme Novices' Hurdle
11 Mar 2014: took keen hold, chased leaders, ridden after 3 out, kept on same pace under pressure from 2 out, finished fourth, beaten five lengths by Western Warhorse in Racing Post Arkle

A great advertisement for the talents of champion trainer Paul Nicholls, who has

turned a once soft-looking performer into a top-notcher who would be favourite in any normal year following Grade 1 victories in the Tingle Creek and Clarence House Chases. A 1m-1m2f performer on the Flat, he spent two seasons as a novice hurdler, finishing fourth in the Triumph on only his second outing, but only ninth in the following season's Supreme behind Champagne Fever. Last season's novice chase campaign began well with three comfortable wins and a neck second to Module in the Game Spirit, but not for the first time he lost his form in the spring, finishing a never-nearer fourth in the Arkle and a tailed-off last at Aintree. There has always been a question mark over how robust he is as until this season he had won five times from October to December but was 0-8 from January on. That all changed this year when he supplemented a career-best Tingle Creek victory at Sandown with an even better performance at Ascot and he appears to be the coming force. His Cheltenham form is patchy, but he certainly acts on the track and deserves every respect.

....

Sire De Grugy

9 ch g; Trainer Gary Moore
Chase form 12141112111111U, best RPR 174
Left-handed 2141121U, best RPR 173
Right-handed 111111, best RPR 174
Cheltenham form 221, best RPR 173
At the festival 12 Mar 2014: held up towards rear and confidently ridden, steady headway from 4 out to track leaders 3 out, travelling well when challenged next, led soon after, driven clear run-in, won Champion Chase by six lengths from Somersby

Good novice chaser two seasons ago without suggesting he was going to make the progress he did last year when, taking advantage of the absence of Sprinter Sacre, he proved far and away the best 2m chaser around by winning the Tingle Creek, Clarence House and Champion Chases by an aggregate of 21 lengths. Was not at his best after a long season when successful again at Sandown in April but still went into summer quarters as the horse seen as most likely to dominate again. Unfortunately he became the second Champion Chase winner in a row to become beset by problems, a hip injury preventing him from running in any of the mid-season highlights this term. He made his long-awaited return in the Betfair Price Rush Chase (Game Spirit) at Newbury in February with conflicting reports as to what was expected, his jockey Jamie Moore reckoning he was fit enough to win and his trainer father Gary saying he was the least fit he'd ever had him. Hopefully Gary was nearer the mark as Sire De Grugy neither travelled nor jumped with his usual alacrity and, following a mistake four out, he was already beaten when unseating at the next. There has to be a major question mark over him now, but it's too early to write him off.

Champagne Fever (below)

8 gr g; Trainer Willie Mullins
Chase form 132614F1, best RPR 167
Left-handed 32, best RPR 161
Right-handed 1614F1, best RPR 167
Cheltenham form (all) 112, best RPR 164
At the festival 14 Mar 2012: prominent, led after 1f, made rest, ridden when pressed over 1f out, kept on well and in control towards finish, won Champion Bumper by a length and a quarter from New Year's Eve 12 Mar 2013: led, ridden and headed narrowly last, rallied gamely to regain lead final 110yds, soon edged right, stayed on well towards finish, won Supreme Novices' Hurdle by half a length from My Tent Or Yours 11 Mar 2014: led after 1st, pushed along approaching 2 out, ridden approaching last, hard pressed final 110yds, kept on gamely, headed last stride, finished second, beaten a head by Western Warhorse in Racing Post Arkle

Really tough grey who last season came within a head of winning three different 2m championship races at the festival, his second to Western Warhorse in the Racing Post Arkle following on from victories in the Champion Bumper and Supreme Novices' Hurdle. Despite all this he has always been considered a stayer in the making and much was expected of him when, after opening his campaign with a straightforward 2m4f victory at Clonmel in November, he was upped to 3m for the first time in the King George. If you take figures into account it would be hard to argue that he didn't stay as a ten-and-a-half-length fourth to Silviniaco Conti represented a career-best on RPRs, but the way he travelled and finished surely suggests he found the trip too far. He tanked along behind Silviniaco Conti for at least two miles but didn't seem able to go on from between three out and two out and lost two places from the last to the line. Dropped back to 2m4f for a Grade 2 at Thurles next time, he was in the process of running a fine race but looked set to be outstayed by Don Cossack when falling at the last, something of a surprise given how well he normally jumps. He showed no ill effects, though, as his jumping was flawless in the Grade 2 Red Mills Chase at Gowran in February, a race he won in comfortable fashion. That will have set him up perfectly for another crack at Cheltenham, but his target remains uncertain. Better ground at the festival would certainly give him a chance of staying the 2m5f of the Ryanair, but a horse with such a good 2m record on the course is surely worth a shot at the big one and market support suggests that's the route he may take.

Mr Mole

7 br g; Trainer Paul Nicholls
Chase form 132F1111, best RPR 171
Left-handed 12F11, best RPR 171
Right-handed 311, best RPR 157
Cheltenham form (all) 3F, best RPR 144

At the festival 14 Mar 2014: midfield, not fluent and lost place 4th, not fluent 3 out, headway approaching 2 out, keeping on but no impression on leaders disputing 7th when fell last in Grand Annual Chase won by Savello

Has long been well regarded but proved a bit of a nutcase over hurdles and in his first season over fences and it's hard to believe the progress he has made since falling when well beaten (around seventh at the time) in last season's Grand Annual Chase off a mark of 147. Had a confidence-boosting victory in weak company at Newton Abbot to close last season, making all to win by three and a half lengths, and those tactics were adopted on his first two starts of this campaign as he twice beat Brick Red, the first time in a conditions chase at Exeter and next time on 3lb worse terms in a handicap at Sandown. That saw him inch his way up to a mark of 155, but his form was some way short of Champion Chase standard until he lined up in the Betfair Price Rush Chase at Newbury and, despite showing his quirky side by jinking to his left and losing ten lengths at the start, he cantered his way into the lead four out and strolled to a 13-length victory over Upsilon Bleu. With both Sire De Grugy and Uxizandre looking well below their best it is possible to question the form, but Nicholls had been telling anyone who would listen how much Mr Mole had blossomed since his last run and it might not be wise to argue with an RPR of 171. It won't need much improving upon to make him a major player.

Hidden Cyclone

10 b g; Trainer John Joseph Hanlon
Chase form 131186F213222FF21, best RPR 165
Left-handed 13186F13222, best RPR 165
Right-handed 122FF1, best RPR 165
Cheltenham form 32, best RPR 165
At the festival 13 Mar 2014: tracked leader to 3rd, stayed prominent, went 2nd again 12th, slight lead 13th, driven and stayed on approaching 2 out, headed after last and wandered run-in but kept on well, not going pace of winner, finished second, beaten two and a quarter lengths by Dynaste in Ryanair Chase

Decent performer at his peak who has run right up to his best form in two previous visits to Cheltenham, finishing third giving 13lb to Johns Spirit in the 2013 Paddy Power Gold Cup and second to Dynaste in last season's Ryanair when outstayed after the last. Confirmed he is still at the peak of his powers when a comfortable five-length winner of the Tied Cottage back at 2m at Punchestown in early February and has been nibbled at each-way prices for this. In reality, though, he was entitled to win at the weights at Punchestown and he is a ten-year-old with a peak RPR of just 165. To have any chance of winning he'd have to run a career-best to the tune of at least 10lb and that is simply hard to see.

Uxizandre

7 b g; Trainer Alan King
Chase form (all left-handed) 11521418U, best RPR 166
Cheltenham form 21, best RPR 166
At the festival 13 Mar 2014: led, ridden after 3 out, hard pressed after 2 out, joined last, gamely held slight lead until headed final 75yds, kept on, not going pace of winner, finished second, beaten three-quarters of a length by Taquin Du Seuil in JLT Novices' Chase

Defeat of Simply Ned and Dodging Bullets at Cheltenham in November suggested last year's JLT runner-up and Aintree winner could prove a force at 2m, but he has disappointed since. It might have been a case of the travelling which saw him run a shocker at Leopardstown in December, and he was better behind Mr Mole at Newbury in the Betfair Price Rush Chase until unseating at the last. Was 12 lengths down at the time having made the running, so needs to improve, although he did come to life on good ground last year.

OTHERS TO CONSIDER

There are probably six solid contenders in an open year, but there could be a sizeable field and **Simply Ned** is entitled to make the line-up should Nicky Richards want to send him down. Second to Balder Succes in a 2m Grade 1 at Aintree in April, his runner-up spot to Uxizandre at Cheltenham in November is his best piece of form and does need improving upon. **Somersby** still has plenty of class despite his age and will probably run again, but it's hard to see him playing anything more than a bit part and the same can be said of **Special Tiara**, who bounced back to form at Kempton but won't get an easy lead at Cheltenham. Sizing Europe might show up, but he's 13 now and not really up to it any more, although plenty will be happy to clap him back in wherever he finishes.

Champion Chase results and trends

	FORM	WINNER	AGE & WGT	Adj RPR	SP	TRAINER	C.Runs	BEST RPR LAST 12 MONTHS (RUNS SINCE)
14	12111	**Sire De Grugy** D	8 11-10	178^T	11-4f	G Moore	11$^{(11G)}$	won Gd1 Clarence House Ch (2m1f) (0)
13	11-11	**Sprinter Sacre** CD	7 11-10	182^T	1-4f	N Henderson	7$^{(7GS)}$	won Gd1 Victor Chandler Ch (2m1f) (0)
12	21-12	**Finian's Rainbow** D, BF	9 11-10	171^{-9}	4-1	N Henderson	7$^{(8G)}$	2nd Gd1 Victor Chandler Ch (2m1f) (0)
11	3-223	**Sizing Europe** CD	9 11-10	170^{-9}	10-1	H de Bromhead (IRE)	9$^{(11G)}$	3rd Punchestown Gd2 ch (2m) (0)
10	-2141	**Big Zeb** D	9 11-10	171^{-19}	10-1	C Murphy (IRE)	13$^{(9G)}$	won Navan Gd2 ch (2m) (2)
09	12-11	**Master Minded** CD	6 11-10	191^T	4-11f	P Nicholls	12$^{(12GS)}$	won Gd1 Champion Chase (2m) (3)
08	-2U11	**Master Minded** D	5 11-10	173^{-4}	3-1	P Nicholls	8$^{(8GS)}$	won Gd2 Game Spirit Ch (2m1f) (0)
07	2-21U	**Voy Por Ustedes** CD	6 11-10	174^{-9}	5-1	A King	9$^{(10GS)}$	won Kempton Gd2 ch (2m) (1)
06	-5431	**Newmill** D	8 11-10	159^{-23}	16-1	J Murphy (IRE)	8$^{(12G)}$	won Thurles Gd2 ch (2m4f) (0)
05	-1111	**Moscow Flyer** CD	11 11-10	185^T	6-4f	J Harrington (IRE)	22$^{(8G)}$	won Gd1 Tingle Creek Chase (2m) (1)

WINS-RUNS: 5yo 1-1, 6yo 2-10, 7yo 1-12, 8yo 2-27, 9yo 3-22, 10yo 0-14, 11yo 1-8, 12yo 0-2 **FAVOURITES:** -£1.14

TRAINERS IN THIS RACE (w-pl-r): Nicky Henderson 2-1-7, Paul Nicholls 2-1-15, Alan King 1-1-3, Gary Moore 1-0-1, Henry de Bromhead 1-2-5, Mouse Morris 0-1-2, Mick Channon 0-1-2, Tom George 0-1-2, Willie Mullins 0-0-4

FATE OF FAVOURITES: 1FF2140211 **POSITION OF WINNER IN MARKET:** 1632145211

Key trends

- Won over at least 2m1f, 10/10
- At least seven runs over fences, 10/10
- No older than nine, 9/10
- Adjusted RPR of at least 170, 9/10
- No more than 9lb off RPR top-rated, 8/10
- Grade 1 chase winner, 8/10
- Won Graded chase last time out, 7/10

Other factors

- Five winners had previously won at the festival
- Five winners were French-bred. In the past ten years 33 French-breds have run, yielding another two seconds and four thirds

Notes

Balthazar King won this race for the second time last year (after his 2012 victory) and still he is the only British-trained horse to have broken the Irish stranglehold.

Ireland's chief exponent Enda Bolger had four of the first five winners. Although his grip has loosened, Bolger has had the runner-up in three of the six runnings he didn't win and his strong team is the starting point for punters, although Willie Mullins is a growing force.

Previous good form in this specialist discipline is important and the best guides are the two handicaps run over course and distance in November and December (won by the British-trained Balthazar King and Any Currency this season – they were the one-two in this race last year) and the PP Hogan Memorial Chase at Punchestown in February. Three PP Hogan winners went on to take this race, while Big Shu was second at Punchestown before winning here. Big Shu's trainer Peter Maher won the PP Hogan this year with Ballyboker Bridge.

Most winners had scored at Punchestown or Cheltenham (or at least had run well around this unusual course) and two more to look out for are Sire Collonges and Uncle Junior.

Eight of the ten winners have come from the first three in the betting and none of those was sent off bigger than 13-2.

Cross Country results and trends

FORM		WINNER	AGE & WGT	OR	SP	TRAINER	C.Runs	BEST RPR LAST 12 MONTHS (RUNS SINCE)
14	P-111	**Balthazar King** CD	10 11-12	150^{-5}	4-1	P Hobbs	21$^{(16GS)}$	won Cheltenham cl 2 hcap ch (3m½f) **(1)**
13	-F742	**Big Shu**	8 10-5	136^{-10}	14-1	P Maher (IRE)	7$^{(16GS)}$	2nd Punchestwn cross-country ch (3m) **(0)**
12	15P00	**Balthazar King** C	8 10-9	139^{-3}	11-2	P Hobbs	13$^{(16GF)}$	won Cheltenham cl 2 hcap ch (3m½f) **(4)**
11	4-138	**Sizing Australia**	9 10-9	140^{-7}	13-2	H De Bromhead (IRE)	17$^{(15GF)}$	3rd Chelt cross-country ch (3m7f) **(0)**
10	70454	**A New Story** (4oh)	12 9-7	135^{-3}	25-1	M Hourigan (IRE)	48$^{(16G)}$	3rd Cork National hcap ch (3m4f) **(4)**
09	1-421	**Garde Champetre** CD	10 11-12	150^{-4}	7-2	E Bolger (IRE)	15$^{(16GS)}$	won Chelt cross-country ch (3m7f) **(0)**
08	9-9F1	**Garde Champetre**	9 10-13	129^{T}	4-1	E Bolger (IRE)	11$^{(16GS)}$	won Punchestwn cross-country ch (3m) **(0)**
07	-2341	**Heads Onthe Ground**	10 10-2	126^{-9}	5-2f	E Bolger (IRE)	14$^{(16S)}$	won Punchestwn cross-country ch (3m) **(0)**
06	5P-31	**Native Jack**	12 10-8	126^{T}	7-2jf	P Rothwell (IRE)	16$^{(16GS)}$	won Punchestwn cross-country ch (3m) **(0)**
05	10114	**Spot Thedifference** CD	12 11-12	143^{-12}	4-1	E Bolger (IRE)	30$^{(16GS)}$	won Chelt cross-country ch (3m7f) **(0)**

WINS-RUNS: 6yo 0-2, 7yo 0-5, 8yo 2-22, 9yo 2-29, 10yo 3-33, 11yo 0-29, 12yo 3-23, 13yo 0-12, 14yo 0-3, 15yo 0-1 **FAVOURITES:** -£4.25

FATE OF FAVOURITES: F116254P03 **POSITION OF WINNER IN MARKET:** 2112293372

Key trends

Won over at least 3m, 10/10

Trained in Ireland, 8/10

Officially rated 126-143, 8/10

Won or placed in a cross-country race at Cheltenham or Punchestown, 9/10 (exception carried out when set to place)

Carried no more than 10st 13lb, 7/10 (all three exceptions carried top weight)

Top-four finish last time out, 8/10

Other factors

JP McManus and Enda Bolger have teamed up for four of the winners

Three winners had taken the PP Hogan at Punchestown in February, while 2013 winner Big Shu was runner-up in that event

Only 11 British-trained runners have made the first four, although last year the home team had first, second and fourth

Ireland has had a 1-2-3-4 four times and in 2009 had the first nine finishers

The two winners officially rated higher than 143 were both rated 150 and were winning the race for the second time (Garde Champetre in 2009 and Balthazar King in 2014)

4.40 Fred Winter Juvenile Handicap Hurdle　RUK
2m½f　Grade 3　£75,000

This has quickly become a competitive contest, drawing the second rank of juvenile hurdlers from the Triumph Hurdle, and runners from the big stables are always worth noting (Paul Nicholls, Nicky Henderson and David Pipe have all had a winner). Nicholls and Pipe have identical records in the past five years – one winner, two runners-up, a third and a fourth from ten runners. Alan King, perennially well stocked in the juvenile department, has yet to win this race but has had a placed horse the last three times he has tried.

Nine of the ten winners were rated between 124 and 133 (the exception was What A Charm off 115). Seven of the winners were weighted to carry at least 10st 13lb.

Winning form is virtually essential, with only two of the three Irish-trained winners starting as maidens. Five of the other seven winners had scored last time out (the three Irish winners were beaten in Grade 1/2 hurdles on their run before Cheltenham, as was Une Artiste in 2012). Seven of the ten winners were having their fourth start over hurdles.

Getting a horse handicapped is the real skill and winning at a low level seems the key, with three of the winners coming off victories at Folkestone, Southwell and Taunton. Even 2007 winner Gaspara, who had just taken the Imperial Cup, was 8lb well in under her 4lb penalty.

French-breds have done well, with four wins in ten runnings (a French-bred has finished first or second in the last three runnings). They mature early and generally need fewer runs to be ready. Bouvreuil and Baraka De Thaix – French-breds trained by Nicholls and Pipe respectively – were prominent in the ante-post market when the race was priced up prior to the weights being announced.

Fred Winter Handicap Hurdle results and trends

	FORM	WINNER	AGE & WGT	OR	SP	TRAINER	H.Runs	BEST RPR LAST 12 MONTHS (RUNS SINCE)
14	1216	**Hawk High** D	4 11-1	130⁻¹²	33-1	T Easterby	4(24G)	won Warwick class 4 hdl (2m) (1)
13	125	**Flaxen Flare** D	4 10-8	127⁻⁵	25-1	G Elliott (IRE)	3(24GS)	5th Leopardstown Gd1 nov hdl (2m) (0)
12	11114	**Une Artiste** D	4 10-8	127⁻⁶	40-1	N Henderson	3(24G)	won Haydock class 2 hdl (2m) (1)
11	757	**What A Charm**	4 10-6	115⁻³	9-1	A Moore (IRE)	3(23G)	7th Fairyhouse Gd2 nov hdl (2m) (0)
10	531	**Sanctuaire** D	4 11-2	127⁻⁹	4-1f	P Nicholls	3(24G)	3rd Auteuil hdl (2m2f) (1)
09	52111	**Silk Affair** (5x)	4 10-4	125⁻¹²	11-1	M Quinlan	5(22GS)	won Sandown cl 3 nov hcap hdl (2m4f) (1)
08	531	**Crack Away Jack** D	4 11-10	133⁻²²	14-1	E Lavelle	3(22GS)	won Sandown class 3 nov hdl (2m½f) (0)
07	22111	**Gaspara** (4x) D	4 10-11	130ᵀ	9-2jf	D Pipe	10(24GS)	won Sandown Listed hcap hdl (2m½f) (0)
06	4P1	**Shamayoun** D	4 11-3	124⁻⁷	40-1	C Egerton	3(24GS)	won Southwell class 4 nov hdl (2m) (0)
05	225	**Dabiroun**	4 11-4	124⁻⁴	20-1	P Nolan (IRE)	3(24G)	2nd Limerick mdn hdl (2m) (2)

FAVOURITES: -£2.25 **FATE OF FAVOURITES:** 0012414300 **POSITION OF WINNER IN MARKET:** 9014415000

Key trends

By a sire who won a Group 1 on the Flat, 9/10

Officially rated 124 to 133, 9/10

Beaten in first two starts over hurdles, 7/10 (last three winners the exceptions)

Won at least one of last two starts, 7/10

Set to carry at least 10st 13lb, 7/10

Other factors

Only five of the 42 horses rated 120 or less made the frame

Six winners had earned a Flat RPR of at least 85; the other four were unraced on the Flat

Four winners were French-bred

Three winners were ridden by jockeys able to claim (two conditionals, one amateur)

Two winners had yet to win over hurdles

The annual certainty with this event is that Ireland, and Willie Mullins in particular, will hold the strongest hand, but as it is one of the late-closing races the picture does not come into sharper focus until much closer to raceday. Mullins played one of his early cards when Bordini won at Punchestown and Navan before Christmas and then in early January he appeared to trump that with Au Quart De Tour, who won by five lengths on his bumper debut at Fairyhouse. He also has dual winner Pylonthepressure in the same colours of Rich Ricci's wife Susannah, as well as Up For Review and Bellshill for Andrea and Graham Wylie and Balko Des Flos, Stone Hard and Valerian Bridge among the Gigginstown House Stud possibles. Vigil, second favourite when fifth last year, remains eligible and is set to represent Dermot Weld (who won last year with Silver Concorde). Among the British hopefuls are Moon Racer (trained by David Pipe), Wait For Me (Philip Hobbs), See The World (Emma Lavelle), Barters Hill (Ben Pauling) and Supasundae, an intriguing possible for leading Flat trainer Andrew Balding.

Au Quart De Tour
5 b g; Trainer Willie Mullins
Bumper form (right-handed) 1, best RPR 111

Has been favourite since making a winning debut at Fairyhouse in January, after which trainer Willie Mullins said he expected a lot of improvement as the horse had shown nothing at home so far. Was a five-length winner of that nine-runner contest, but fifth, sixth and eighth have been tailed off since and an RPR of 111 is pretty low compared with what a lot of his rivals will boast. To put that into context, Mullins had three contenders last season and all went into it with an RPR at least 21lb superior to Au Quart De Tour. Time for him to run again before the big one, but not much.

Bordini
5 b g; Trainer Willie Mullins
Bumper form 11, best RPR 132
Left-handed 1, best RPR 132
Right-handed 1, best RPR 119

Dual bumper winner in November and December and arguably boasts a better profile than stablemate Au Quart De Tour as he beat a few previous winners easily in his second bumper to earn an RPR of 132. Third and fifth have already scored over hurdles, so the form looks strong enough even if there were only six runners. Trainer said he'd look to give him another run before sending him to the festival but lengthy absence has never been much of a worry for this race.

Up For Review
6 br g; Trainer Willie Mullins
Bumper form 1 (left-handed), best RPR 125

Impressive ten-length winner of what was probably a decent bumper at Leopardstown's Christmas meeting (third ran to similar level when third next time and fifth won) and plenty to like about the way he did it. Seemed to set a strong enough pace and quickened at the end of it, after which he was another nominated for this by Willie Mullins, who said: "I'd say he's a fair sort, he has everything."

Vigil
6 b g; Trainer Dermot Weld
Bumper form 2151, best RPR 134
Left-handed 151, best RPR 134
Right-handed 1, best RPR 119

Second favourite and fifth in last season's Champion Bumper behind lesser-fancied stablemate Silver Concorde and was expected to make a hurdler this season, but has evidently been laid out for another crack at this. Has run only once since, picking up the Willie Mullins-trained Bellshill inside the final furlong to win by a length. Runner-up was a four-year-old but had been given an easy time of it up front. Clearly still has last year's ability and obviously boasts some of the best form.

Moon Racer (below, left)
6 b g; Trainer David Pipe
Bumper form 11, best RPR 131
Left-handed 1, best RPR 131
Right-handed 1, best RPR 118
Cheltenham form 1, best RPR 131

Won valuable Fairyhouse bumper by seven and a half lengths at odds of 50-1 last spring, but there didn't seem to any fluke about it and he subsequently went for £225,000 at the sales and joined David Pipe. Debut for new stable came at Cheltenham, hinting at a possible tilt for this and Moon Racer could not have been more impressive, making all and quickening clear for a 12-length win. Runner-up subsequently a lot closer when second to Definitly Red in a Listed bumper back at the track and has also won over hurdles. No surprise he's the shortest of the British-trained possibles and Pipe's father Martin is one of the few non-Irish trainers to have won this race, with Liberman in 2003.

Pylonthepressure
5 b g; Trainer Willie Mulins
Bumper form 11, best RPR 138
Left-handed 1, best RPR 138
Right-handed 1, best RPR 121

Easy winner of sole point and both bumpers, first of all in a 14-runner contest at Thurles and then when making all to beat previous good winner Space Cadet (RPR 132) by eight and a half lengths at Naas, the pair 19 lengths clear. The RPR of 138 he earned is the highest figure going into the race, but it was achieved in soft ground over 2m3f. Willie Mullins called it a "huge performance" from a "real racehorse", so he's clearly held in high regard.

Supasundae
5 b g; Trainer Andrew Balding
Bumper form 11, best RPR 129
Left-handed 1, best RPR 105
Right-handed 1, best RPR 129

Won 13-runner Wetherby bumnper on debut for Tim Fitzgerald last March and subsequently sold out of the yard to join Andrew Balding, for whom he turned in a massively improved performance to score at Ascot in a Listed contest in December by two and a quarter lengths from an Alan King-trained favourite. The 13-length third had recorded an RPR of 120 when easily winning at Cork for Willie Mullins the time before, while the fourth won a bumper next time and the fifth a hurdle, earning an RPR of 130. Very well bred by Galileo out of a half-sister to Nathaniel and Barry Geraghty was reportedly pretty impressed.

Stone Hard
5 b g; Trainer Willie Mullins
Bumper form 11 (right-handed), best RPR 132

Described as a real big chasing type with a high cruising speed, he won a point for Gordon Elliott, when reportedly one of the best he had, and has demonstrated plenty of ability for Willie Mullins in two bumpers. An easy winner at odds-on on his debut at Fairyhouse, he then trounced four rivals by 14 lengths and more (only market rival was Mullins-trained Rio Treasure, who had been third to Supasundae previously) at Gowran. Yet another powerful string for a yard set to be mob-handed.

Balko Des Flos
4 ch g; Trainer Willie Mullins
Bumper form (left-handed) 1, best RPR 122

Strong staying display on Leopardstown debut in January when winning by three lengths and 11, but hard to know what the form is worth as only the well-beaten seventh had run before and he could not have run to his previous form as he was beaten 99 lengths. That performance was enough to qualify him for Cheltenham according to trainer.

Bellshill
5 b g; Trainer Willie Mullins
Bumper form 12, best RPR 117
Left-handed 2, best RPR 117
Right-handed 1, best RPR 116

Any winner of the Champion Bumper coming off a reverse last time out would be unusual, but this one was a fair one-length second to last year's fifth Vigil at Leopardstown over Christmas and is entitled to be considered yet another possible for Willie Mullins.

See The World
5 b g; Trainer Emma Lavelle
Bumper form (right-handed) 1, best RPR 122

Debut success came against a bunch of largely untested rivals but the fact he won at all was astonishing. After turning into the straight apparently cantering, he hung badly left and virtually pulled himself up, dropping back to at least 20 lengths fourth with just two furlongs to run. However, Aidan Coleman eventually gathered him up and he flew home to win by four and a half lengths eased down. If the horses he beat aren't useless, he's very good.

Wait For Me
5 b g; Trainer Philip Hobbs
Bumper form (right-handed) 1, best RPR 125

Lots to like about the way he won what is often a decent bumper at Ascot in February, particularly because he did so on his debut. The only other horse to win that bumper first time on a racecourse was Sprinter Sacre, so he has some act to follow. He had apparently already 'won' a couple of schooling bumpers in Ireland, so clearly knew his job, but he was always cruising and fairly thumped a field containing six previous winners. Will be of major interest for one of the few British trainers to have won the race, but he is seen as a long-term prospect and connections were in no rush to confirm him for Cheltenham.

OTHERS TO CONSIDER

Bookies have understandably concentrated on Willie Mullins, who has seven of the first ten in the betting and plenty more possibles. Of the other Irish trainers Gordon Elliott could easily have **Space Cadet** fitter than when second to Pylonthepressure, while his **General Principle** looks very promising following a 22-length win at Punchestown in early February. Alan King's **Yanworth** is probably worth another chance after his second to Supasundae as he looked pretty useful the time before, while **Wishfull Dreaming** is another nice sort for Philip Hobbs, although he will have to improve a fair bit on his two starts to date.

Champion Bumper results and trends

	FORM	WINNER	AGE & WGT	Adj RPR	SP	TRAINER	B.Runs	BEST RPR LAST 12 MONTHS (RUNS SINCE)
14	3/2-1	Silver Concorde D	6 11-5	132^{-15}	16-1	D Weld (IRE)	$3^{(22G)}$	won Leopardstown bumper (2m) (0)
13	1	Briar Hill D	5 11-5	117^{-27}	25-1	W Mullins (IRE)	$1^{(23GS)}$	won Thurles bumper (2m) (0)
12	21	Champagne Fever D	5 11-5	144^{-1}	16-1	W Mullins (IRE)	$2^{(20G)}$	won Fairyhouse bumper (2m) (0)
11	21	Cheltenian D	5 11-5	126^{-13}	14-1	P Hobbs	$2^{(24G)}$	won Kempton cl 5 mdn bumper (2m) (0)
10	1	Cue Card	4 10-12	126^{-15}	40-1	C Tizzard	$1^{(24G)}$	won Fontwell class 6 bumper (1m6f) (0)
09	2-11	Dunguib D	6 11-5	147^{T}	9-2	P Fenton (IRE)	$3^{(24GS)}$	won Navan Gd2 bumper (2m) (0)
08	1	Cousin Vinny	5 11-5	118^{-23}	12-1	W Mullins (IRE)	$1^{(23GS)}$	won Punchestown bumper (2m) (0)
07	111	Cork All Star CD	5 11-5	145^{T}	11-2	J Harrington (IRE)	$3^{(24GS)}$	won Cheltenham Lstd bumper (2m½f) (0)
06	2131	Hairy Molly	6 11-5	126^{-9}	33-1	J Crowley (IRE)	$4^{(23G)}$	won Naas bumper (2m3f) (0)
05	011	Missed That D	6 11-5	135^{-14}	7-2f	W Mullins (IRE)	$3^{(24G)}$	won Naas bumper (2m) (0)

WINS-RUNS: 4yo 1-42, 5yo 5-137, 6yo 4-52 **FAVOURITES:** -£5.50

TRAINERS IN THIS RACE (w-pl-r): Willie Mullins 4-2-33, Dermot Weld 1-1-6, Philip Hobbs 1-0-9, Alan King 0-0-2, David Pipe 0-0-9, Donald McCain 0-0-3

FATE OF FAVOURITES: 1003306222 **POSITION OF WINNER IN MARKET:** 1025206006

Key trends

🐎Won last time out, 10/10

🐎Aged five or six, 9/10

🐎Won a bumper with at least 13 runners, 7/10

🐎Adjusted RPR of at least 126, 8/10 (both exceptions were once-raced winners trained by Willie Mullins)

🐎Off the track for at least 33 days, 8/10 (three not seen since Christmas or earlier)

🐎Won a bumper worth at least 4k (pounds or euros) to the winner, 7/10

🐎Bred in Ireland, 6/10

Others factors

🐎Cue Card in 2010 is the only winning four-year-old since Dato Star in 1995

🐎Ireland has won eight of the last ten and 17 of the 22 ever run

🐎Willie Mullins has the best record with eight victories (four in the last ten years) but is often mob-handed. On four of the occasions he has won it, he saddled just one runner. On the other four, the winner traded at a bigger price than at least one stablemate

🐎The 22 winners have been sired by 22 different stallions. Those successful so far are Montelimar, Where To Dance, Strong Gale, Accordion, Welsh Term, Florida Son, Glacial Storm, Mister Lord, River Falls, Broken Hearted, Teenoso, Flemensfirth, Overbury, Shernazar, Fasliyev, Bob Back, Presenting, King's Theatre, Astarabad, Stowaway, Shantou and Dansili

Notes

Thursday,
March 12
(New Course)
JLT Novices' Chase
Pertemps Network Final Handicap Hurdle
Ryanair Chase
Ladbrokes World Hurdle
Brown Advisory & Merriebelle Stable Plate
Fulke Walwyn Kim Muir Handicap Chase

1.30 JLT Novices' Chase
2m4f — Grade 1 — £120,000

C4/RUK

This race is always caught in the middle between the shorter Arkle and the longer RSA, but it is a Grade 1 in its own right and far from a consolation prize – last year's three-way battle between Taquin Du Seuil, Uxizandre and Double Ross was one of the finishes of the festival. Taquin Du Seuil was the first British-trained winner (in its first year as a Grade 1), with the three runnings as a Grade 2 all going to Ireland. The top stables are likely to be strongly represented, with the market pointing to Vautour and Valseur Lido as the main hopes for Willie Mullins (other entries include Un De Sceaux, Don Poli and Gitane Du Berlais) and the Paul Nicholls-trained Ptit Zig long earmarked for this contest, having won the Grade 2 novice chase over 2m5f at Cheltenham on New Year's Day in which Taquin Du Seuil was second the year before. The Noel Meade-trained Apache Stronghold, a Grade 1 winner from Valseur Lido at Leopardstown in February, is another leading contender.

Vautour

6 b g; Trainer Willie Mullins
Chase form 121, best RPR 153
Left-handed 121, best RPR 153
Cheltenham form (hurdles) 1, best RPR 158
At the festival 11 Mar 2014: made most, quickened between last 2, big jump last, ran on well to draw clear run-in, impressive, won Supreme Novices' Hurdle by six lengths from Josses Hill

Top-class novice hurdler last term who had an unbeaten first campaign for Willie Mullins, culminating in an impressive Supreme victory. Unsurprisingly put at the head of the ante-post lists for several festival races following that, including the Champion Hurdle, but connections decided on a chase campaign and he has looked very good in two of his three starts in the new discipline. He made all the running on his debut at Navan in November to thrash Clarcam (received 12lb in weight for age) by eight lengths, but then made a bad mistake five out against the same horse next time in a Grade 1 at Leopardstown and finished a rather tame 17-length second. That was surely not his form, though, and he was back on track at Leopardstown upped to 2m3f in January, when he had comfortably taken the measure of his only serious rival – the 140-rated Real Steel – when that one fell at the last. In pure form terms he has not achieved as much as some of his potential rivals, most notably Ptit Zig, but decent ground at Cheltenham brought out the best in him last year and there is doubtless more to come. He was only workmanlike on his one run at 2m4f over hurdles, but that did come after Cheltenham.

Ptit Zig

6 b g; Trainer Paul Nicholls
Chase form 1111F, best RPR 165
Left-handed 11, best RPR 165
Right-handed 11F, best RPR 160
Cheltenham form (all) 361, best RPR 165
At the festival 13 Mar 2013: in touch, hit 4th, headway 3 out, went 2nd well before last, no impression on winner and stayed on same pace for 3rd after last, finished third, beaten six and a quarter lengths by Flaxen Flare in Fred Winter Juvenile Handicap Hurdle
11 Mar 2014: hit 1st, in touch, blundered 4 out, weakened before 2 out, finished sixth, beaten 14 lengths by Jezki in Champion Hurdle

Was nominated as a horse with a future over fences by Paul Nicholls after his very first British hurdles start at Ludlow in February 2013, but for some reason he has taken people by surprise with his progress. Finished that juvenile season with a mark of 134 after running third in the Fred Winter and ended the last campaign on 157, although his only victory came in France. Fences have been the making of him, just as Nicholls said, and he made a big impression by winning his first four chase starts. The first two came at very short odds in small fields, but the change of gear he showed in the straight to pulverise

Josses Hill at Ascot in December stamped him as a top-class performer. So did his next performance when he slammed Champagne West by six lengths at Cheltenham and, while his trainer said he didn't think he was quite at his best, that represented the single best piece of novice chase form in Britain this season until Coneygree rocked up at Newbury in the Denman Chase. An RPR of 165 is some 12lb superior to what Vautour has yet achieved, is very high for a novice at any stage of the season, and he will be very hard to beat if reproducing it, although he blotted his copybook when falling as favourite for the Grade 1 Ascot Chase. He had jumped beautifully until clipping the top of the ninth in a race yet to develop, but going into the festival on the back of a fall is not ideal and it remains to be seen whether it has affected his confidence. If not, he's still the one to beat. Has all three novice chase options and is clearly not short of pace, but hard to see him heading to the Arkle unless the ground comes up very testing.

Apache Stronghold

7 b g; Trainer Noel Meade
Chase form 1221, best RPR 155
Left-handed 21, best RPR 155
Right-handed 12, best RPR 151

Useful novice over hurdles last season who swerved Cheltenham, but ran second to Vautour in the season-ending Grade 1 at Punchestown in May. Chase campaign has seen steady improvement, an opening win being followed by defeats at the hands of Mullins big guns Valseur Lido and Don Poli, the latter at 3m, a trip over which he seemed to get outstayed. Had eight lengths to find with Valseur Lido on Fairyhouse form when lining up for the Grade 1 Flogas Novice Chase at Leopardstown's trials meeting in February, but did not go unbacked and was brought with a challenge at the last to beat the favourite by half a length. There were positives and negatives to take from that performance, as he showed real tenacity but his jumping was not all that fluent. That had also proved his weakness against Don Poli the time before, but he proved with good leaps at the last two that he can do it under pressure. Will need to keep mistakes to a minimum at Cheltenham.

Valseur Lido

6 b g; Trainer Willie Mullins
Chase form 112, best RPR 158
Left-handed 2, best RPR 154
Right-handed 11, best RPR 158
Cheltenham form (hurdles) 0, best RPR 145
At the festival 11 Mar 2014: tracked leaders, niggled along approaching 2 out, outpaced between last 2, checked slightly after last, kept on run-in, finished tenth, beaten 11 and a half lengths by Vautour in Supreme Novices' Hurdle

Decent novice hurdler without matching the level of some of his more illustrious stablemates, although he was a creditable second to Faugheen in a Grade 1 at Punchestown in April. Already considerably better as a chaser, taking the step up to 2m4f in his stride when hammering Champagne James by 11 lengths at Punchestown in November. He then confirmed himself as potentially top class when thumping Apache Stronghold by eight lengths in the Grade 1 Drinmore Novice Chase at Fairyhouse just a couple of weeks later and was having his first run for a couple of months when just inched out of it by the same horse in the Grade 1 Flogas Novice Chase at Leopardstown in February. There will probably be more to come at Cheltenham and it might have been a risky move by bookmakers to push him out to 10-1 while his conqueror is a fair bit shorter. The likely pace in the JLT will surely test the jumping of all protagonists and this is where Valseur Lido scores highly.

Gilgamboa

7 b g; Trainer Enda Bolger
Chase form 1132, best RPR 156
Left-handed 132, best RPR 156
Right-handed 1, best RPR 156
Cheltenham form (hurdles) 0, best RPR 143
At the festival 11 Mar 2014: in touch, not fluent 4th, shaken up when tracking leaders about 2 lengths off the pace when blundered 2 out, soon weakened, finished 13th, beaten 16 lengths by Vautour in Supreme Novices' Hurdle

Useful novice hurdler who went down the handicap route early on and took the valuable Boylesports Hurdle at Leopardstown in January 2014 off a mark of 128. Was sent off at just 9-1 for the Supreme following that but proved out of his depth. Better as a chaser already, though, and following a cosy 2m victory from Blood Cotil at Navan in November, he was an impressive winner of a 2m3½f

Grade 2 at Limerick over Christmas. Proved no match for Un De Sceaux back at 2m1f in the Irish Arkle in January, after which connections said they were unlikely to take him on again, which makes this contest his most likely port of call. He surely won't be asked to try 2m again following a surprising odds-on defeat by 25-1 chance Rawnaq in the Flyingbolt at Navan in February, if he goes anywhere at all. The winner does have some decent hurdles form to his name (third in the 2013 Greatwood) and was getting 6lb, so it wasn't a complete disaster, but Gilgamboa's jumping was laboured and it was disappointing to see him run out of it after taking it up at the last. Perhaps better ground will help his jumping but most of his racing has been on a very soft surface and he needs to prove he can handle faster conditions.

Gitane Du Berlais

5 b m; Trainer Willie Mullins
Chase form (right-handed) 11, best RPR 153

Won a Grade 3 mares' novice hurdle last season without suggesting she was a superstar but has quickly built into a much better chaser. Jumping was a bit sticky at the end of her debut in a weak mares' beginners' chase at Limerick, although the downhill nature of the last fence makes it a tricky one, and she was much better at Sandown in the Grade 1 Scilly Isles in January, when she was always in control and slammed Irish Saint by eight lengths. She was getting 11lb in weight-for-age and sex allowances and that will be down to 8lb for this, but even so it puts her in the right ballpark if she travels over. She is another who has done all her racing on soft or heavy ground, though, and she does handle it particularly well, so it remains to be seen what a faster surface will mean to her.

Vroum Vroum Mag

6 b m; Trainer Willie Mullins
Chase form (right-handed) 111, best RPR 142

Mare who joined Willie Mullins only this season and was sent straight over fences, winning all three starts with the minimum of fuss. All successes came in mares' races, which are notoriously weak, so it's hard to rate the form highly, but she appeared to have a few firms running scared as she was as low as 12-1 fifth favourite in places with some firms. Hard to believe there aren't horses with stronger form claims, though.

OTHERS TO CONSIDER

It's at least 25-1 bar those featured, but that still brings in some decent sorts, including **God's Own**, who was nearly favourite for the Champion Chase at one point before losing the plot. If he can recover his form on better ground he could go well at a price, although trainer Tom George is adamant he goes better right-handed. **Splash Of Ginge**, a big handicap chase winner at the course on New Year's Day, seems to have two ways of running but is quite decent when he's in the right mood, as a Betfair Hurdle success would suggest. The John Ferguson-trained **Three Kingdoms**, whose form ties him in with Arkle second favourite Vibrato Valtat, would also be a player, with Tony McCoy saying he needed stepping up in trip after just catching Solar Impulse over 2m½f at Doncaster. Connections are reportedly still considering the Arkle or swerving Cheltenham and going straight to Aintree, though. He'd surely be shorter than 33-1 otherwise. Paul Nicholls' **Irish Saint** is useful but his record suggests he wants soft ground.

JLT Novices' Chase results

	FORM	WINNER	AGE & WGT	Adj RPR	SP	TRAINER	C.Runs	BEST RPR LAST 12 MONTHS (RUNS SINCE)
14	11321	**Taquin Du Seuil** C, D	7 11-4	167^{-6}	7-1	J O'Neill	5$^{(12G)}$	won Haydock Gd2 nov ch (2m5f) (0)
13	21241	**Beneffcient** D	7 11-4	161^{-8}	20-1	A Martin (IRE)	5$^{(13GS)}$	won Leop Gd1 Arkle nov ch (2m1f) (0)
12	1-111	**Sir Des Champs** C, D	6 11-4	161^{-8}	3-1	W Mullins (IRE)	3$^{(10G)}$	won Limerick Gd2 nov ch (2m3½f) (1)
11	4-122	**Noble Prince** D	7 11-4	164^{-6}	4-1	P Nolan (IRE)	3$^{(11G)}$	2nd Leop Gd1 Arkle nov ch (2m1f) (0)

WINS-RUNS: 5yo 0-3, 6yo 1-14, 7yo 3-19, 8yo 0-7, 9yo 0-3 **FAVOURITES:** -£4.00

TRAINERS IN THIS RACE (w-pl-r): Tony Martin 1-0-1, Willie Mullins 1-0-7, Alan King 0-1-1, Colin Tizzard 0-0-1, Henry de Bromhead 0-1-2, Nicky Henderson 0-0-6, Nigel Twiston-Davies 0-2-3, Noel Meade 0-0-1, Paul Nicholls 0-0-4, Philip Hobbs 0-1-2, Tom George 0-0-1

FATE OF FAVOURITES: 2024 **POSITION OF WINNER IN MARKET:** 2274

This lacks the quality of some of the other festival handicaps and, as a big-field 3m handicap hurdle, has a specialist element – dual winner Buena Vista had previously finished second and fifth and Creon, the 2004 winner, had been sixth the year before.

Good recent form has been less important in recent years, with four of the past ten winners having failed to make the first four on their previous outing, but over the longer term last-time-out winners have a strong record (ten winners in the past 19 years).

Favourites have a poor record and Fingal Bay last year became only the second market leader to have won in the past 17 runnings (11 of the last 13 winners started at double-figure odds – the exceptions being two successful favourites).

The bottom weight tends to run off a mark around the mid-130s nowadays and the best place to find the winner is from there up to 144. Last year, however, Fingal Bay ran off 148 and had top weight of 11st 12lb, with the first seven all rated 140-plus (that reflects the upward creep across the board in festival handicaps).

Pertemps Final results and trends

	FORM	WINNER	AGE & WGT	OR	SP	TRAINER	H.Runs	BEST RPR LAST 12 MONTHS (RUNS SINCE)
14	120-1	Fingal Bay C, D	8 11-12	148^T	9-2f	P Hobbs	6$^{(23G)}$	won Exeter class 2 hcap hdl (2m7½f) (0)
13	-2222	Holywell	6 11-4	140^{-5}	25-1	J O'Neill	6$^{(24GS)}$	2nd Warwick class 2 hcap hdl (3m1f) (0)
12	5P504	Cape Tribulation D	8 10-11	142^{-3}	14-1	M Jefferson	10$^{(24G)}$	5th Haydock Gd3 hcap hdl (3m) (1)
11	28700	Buena Vista CD	10 10-3	138^{-4}	20-1	D Pipe	29$^{(23G)}$	won Pertemps Final (3m) (6)
10	-8508	Buena Vista	9 10-1	133^{-1}	16-1	D Pipe	22$^{(24G)}$	5th Haydock Listed hcap hdl (3m1f) (2)
09	26211	Kayf Aramis D	7 10-5	129^{-7}	16-1	V Williams	9$^{(22GS)}$	won Warwick class 3 nov hdl (3m1f) (0)
08	-1271	Ballyfitz D	8 10-8	132^{-3}	18-1	N Twiston-Davies	6$^{(24GS)}$	won Haydock class 2 hcap hdl (3m) (0)
07	2-2F0	Oscar Park	8 10-9	140^T	14-1	D Arbuthnot	9$^{(24GS)}$	2nd Newbury class 2 hcap hdl (3m½f) (2)
06	58505	Kadoun D	9 11-7	142^{-2}	50-1	M O'Brien (IRE)	25$^{(24G)}$	8th Fairyhouse hcap hdl (2m) (2)
05	21102	Oulart D	6 10-2	121^{-11}	10-1	D Hughes (IRE)	6$^{(22G)}$	won Leopardstown hcap hdl (3m) (2)

WINS-RUNS: 5yo 0-20, 6yo 2-51, 7yo 1-56, 8yo 4-51, 9yo 2-22, 10yo 1-16, 11yo 0-15, 12yo 0-1, 13yo 0-2 **FAVOURITES:** -£4.50

FATE OF FAVOURITES: 0002000001 **POSITION OF WINNER IN MARKET:** 5070059601

Key trends

🐎 Aged six to nine, nine winners in last ten runnings

🐎 Winning form between 2m4f and 2m6f, 9/10

🐎 Carried no more than 11st 4lb, 8/10

🐎 Off track between 20 and 48 days, 8/10

🐎 Won a Class 3 or higher, 8/10

🐎 Officially rated 129 to 142, 8/10

🐎 Won over at least 3m, 7/10

🐎 Six to ten runs over hurdles, 7/10 (exceptions 22-plus)

Other factors

🐎 Creon in 2004 was the last winner from out of the handicap (2lb wrong)

🐎 Five winners had run at the festival before, including a dual winner (Buena Vista) who recorded a top-two finish in this race the previous year

🐎 Irish winners had all finished unplaced in the Leopardstown qualifier

🐎 Two winners were novices

🐎 Eight winners started 14-1 or bigger

🐎 Pragada in 1988 is the only winning five-year-old in the race's 40-year history, while Buena Vista in 2011 was the first horse aged older than nine to oblige since 1981

2.40 Ryanair Chase
2m5f   Grade 1   £300,000

C4/RUK

With last year's winner Dynaste ruled out for the rest of the season, the door is open for an up-and-coming chaser to make the grade here. Chief among that group is the Gordon Elliott-trained Don Cossack, whose second season over fences has brought a four-timer in Graded contests, including an impressive victory over Boston Bob in the Grade 1 John Durkan at Punchestown in December. Cue Card, the 2013 winner, will drop back in trip, having been given time to recover from an injury sustained in the King George at Christmas (and not even entered in the Gold Cup). Ascot Chase winner Balder Succes is progressive at the trip and, in an open-looking contest, others likely to come here in preference to other targets include Johns Spirit (trained by Jonjo O'Neill), Ma Filleule (Nicky Henderson) and Ballycasey (Willie Mullins).

Don Cossack
8 br g; Trainer Gordon Elliott
Chase form 1212F241111, best RPR 169
Left-handed 2F2, best RPR 155
Right-handed 12141111, best RPR 169
Cheltenham form F
At the festival 12 Mar 2014: in touch headway 9th, travelling okay in behind leaders when fell 14th in RSA Chase won by O'Faolains Boy

Has always threatened to be top class since his days in bumpers but has taken time to rise through the ranks. He did win a Grade 1 chase as a novice before being put in his place in the spring upped to 3m, but this is the season he has come of age, winning all four starts and showing improved RPRs every time. After an easy success in a 2m7f Punchestown Grade 3, he dropped back to 2m4f and made mincemeat of the 159-rated Wonderful Charm in the Grade 2 Powers Irish Whiskey Chase at Down Royal, cutting out all the running. Next time at Punchestown in the Grade 1 John Durkan Memorial he was held up behind the leaders and brought through after the last to beat Boston Bob. His latest run was his best yet as he looked to have taken Champagne Fever's measure in the Grade 2 Kinloch Brae at Thurles before that one fell at the last. In pure form terms he is a bit behind the best of the entries a he has yet to burst through the 170 RPR barrier, but that is surely coming and he acts on any ground. Has Arkle and Gold Cup entries but it will be amazing if he goes anywhere else considering his owner is the race sponsor and has other Gold Cup contenders.

Cue Card
9 b g; Trainer Colin Tizzard
Chase form 1U21215112312445, best RPR 178
Left-handed 1U2121214, best RPR 178
Right-handed 1513245, best RPR 175
Cheltenham form (all) 1124U21, best RPR 176
At the festival 17 Mar 2010: took keen hold, held up well in rear, scythed through field from 5f out, tracked leader over 2f out and still cruising, led over 1f out, hung left briefly but romped clear, won Champion Bumper by eight lengths from Al Ferof
15 Mar 2011: took keen hold, held up in midfield, progress before 3 out, joined leader 2 out, ridden soon after, hanging and not quicken before last, faded, finished fourth, beaten six and a half lengths by Al Ferof in Supreme Novices' Hurdle
13 Mar 2012: led until mistake and headed 9th, chased winner from 4 out, stayed on well to try and close on winner after 2 out and 4 lengths down soon after, readily outpaced from last but stayed on well for clear 2nd, beaten seven lengths by Sprinter Sacre in Racing Post Arkle Chase
14 Mar 2013: made all, not fluent 3rd, reached for 8th, asserted approaching last, soon clear, ran on well and in command after, won Ryanair Chase by nine lengths from First Lieutenant

Brilliant campaigner for Colin Tizzard for several years, having won the Champion Bumper in 2010 and Ryanair in 2013 and finished fourth in a Supreme Novices' Hurdle and second in an Arkle in between. Looked better than ever at the beginning of last season when winning the Betfair Chase with seemingly a bit in hand, but it all went badly wrong afterwards. You can't say he didn't put up a top-class effort when he was second in the first of Silviniaco Conti's King Georges, but he'd beaten that one at Haydock and, having cantered into the straight with a clear advantage at Kempton, he traded at 1-10 in running but faltered badly between the last two and was passed before the last. It was hard to say he didn't stay given he lost no further ground in the last 100 yards and he was reported on target for the Gold Cup until a pelvic injury ruled him out for the season. He came back this term and followed a similar route, running in the Haldon Gold Cup before trying to win the Betfair Chase again, but each time he ran nearly 10lb below his efforts of 12 months earlier, as he did when only fifth in the King George in December, when he returned home with a cut. Connections now say he doesn't stay 3m, hence this attempt to win a second Ryanair, but while he is the clear pick on his old form it has to be a worry that since returning from injury he has not come close to matching it. The hope is better ground and Cheltenham, where he has such a fantastic record, will spark a revival.

Champagne Fever

7 gr g; Trainer Willie Mullins
Chase form 132614F1, best RPR 167
Left-handed 32, best RPR 161
Right-handed 1164F1, best RPR 167
Cheltenham form (all) 112, best RPR 164
At the festival 14 Mar 2012: prominent, led after 1f, made rest, ridden when pressed over 1f out, kept on well and in control towards finish, won Champion Bumper by a length and a quarter from New Year's Eve 12 Mar 2013: led, ridden and headed narrowly last, rallied gamely to regain lead final 110yds, soon edged right, stayed on well towards finish, won Supreme Novices' Hurdle by half a length from My Tent Or Yours 11 Mar 2014: led after 1st, pushed along approaching 2 out, ridden approaching last, hard pressed final 110yds, kept on gamely, headed last stride, finished second, beaten a head by Western Warhorse in Racing Post Arkle

Big player if he runs, but also in the Champion Chase and dealt with in more detail in Wednesday's section.

Johns Spirit (pictured, left)

8 b g; Trainer Jonjo O'Neill
Chase form 5812673311540126, best RPR 163
Left-handed 867331154012, best RPR 162
Right-handed 5126, best RPR 163
Cheltenham form 67115412, best RPR 162
At the festival 12 Mar 2013: held up, mistake 7th, headway 11th, 6th and in touch when blundered badly 4 out, tried to rally next, no impression on leaders after, finished seventh, beaten 16 and a half lengths by Rajdhani Express in Rewards4Racing Novices'

Handicap Chase
13 Mar 2014: in rear, hit 9th, headway approaching
3 out, chased leaders under pressure 2 out, one pace
approaching last, finished fourth, beaten 15 and a half
lengths by Ballynagour in Byrne Group Plate

Really good handicapper for Jonjo O'Neill over the last couple of seasons, winning the Paddy Power Gold Cup in 2013 and coming within a head of doing so again off a 17lb higher mark on ground softer than he is supposed to like in November. After that career-best effort, which earned him a Racing Post Rating of 162 (just 4lb shy of Don Cossack's best) he was upped in trip and grade to run in the King George at Kempton and he travelled well for a long way before appearing not to stay and dropping back to sixth, although his RPR (163) suggests he ran right up to form. His Paddy Power second took his form figures on the Old Course at Cheltenham to 71112 compared to 654 on the New Course, over which this race is run and where he has yet to get within 14 lengths of a winner, so he does need to prove his effectiveness. However, on RPRs his best form is now at Kempton, so he is no one-trick pony and might simply be improving. Other Paddy Power winners Our Vic and Imperial Commander have come on to land this race and he's one to consider seriously.

Balder Succes
7 b g; Trainer Alan King
Chase form 1F15111324211, best RPR 169
Left-handed 1F111, best RPR 163
Right-handed 51324211, best RPR 169
Cheltenham form (all) FUF, best RPR 151
At the festival 16 Mar 2012: held up, headway into midfield 3rd, racing on outer when fell 4th in Triumph Hurdle won by Countrywide Flame
12 Mar 2013: in rear, hit 4th, still behind when hampered and unseated rider 4 out in Champion Hurdle won by Hurricane Fly

Decent performer with a good win record (12-28, 7-13 over fences) and seemingly still improving. Began the campaign as Alan King's No. 1 contender for the Champion Chase but came up short when joint-favourite for the Tingle Creek at Sandown and again when 11-10 to beat Special Tiara in the Desert Orchid at Kempton over Christmas. The step up to 2m4½f did the trick back at Kempton next time, though, as he thumped Fox Appeal (good handicap second off 149 next time) by ten lengths in a conditions chase, albeit he was entitled to win at the weights. He subsequently turned in a career-best to win the Grade 1 Ascot Chase in February, jumping well to beat Ma Filleule by just over three lengths. That confirmed the Ryanair as his best chance of festival success, although a major worry is that he has always been considered better on flat tracks and connections swerved last season's Racing Post Arkle to concentrate on Aintree, where he won. He certainly hasn't had much luck at Cheltenham as he fell in the Triumph Hurdle, unseated his rider when out of his depth in the Champion Hurdle and fell two out in his sole novice chase outing when going like the winner. That aside, he goes there with very strong claims.

Ma Filleule

7 gr m; Trainer Nicky Henderson
Chase form 111P5P121532, best RPR 164
Left-handed 111P5P1213, best RPR 164
Right-handed 152, best RPR 158
Cheltenham form (all) 02P2, best RPR 157
At the festival 15 Mar 2013: bumped 1st, chased leaders, beaten when hit 2 out, finished 13th, beaten 82 lengths by Salubrious in Martin Pipe Handicap Hurdle
11 Mar 2014: in touch, took closer order approaching 9th, challenging when blundered 3 out, rider lost iron for a spell, led approaching 2 out, ridden after last, headed final 110yds, outpaced by winner towards finish, finished second, beaten one and a quarter lengths by Holywell in Baylis & Harding Affordable Luxury Handicap Chase

Ex-French mare who was pulled up on her first chase start for Nicky Henderson last season but then made huge progress, winning at Kempton over Christmas, running second to Holywell at Cheltenham and romping away with the Topham Chase at Aintree. Handicap mark shot up from an opening 142 to 162 and she was being talked about as a lively outsider for the Gold Cup before embarking on her second campaign in Britain. That talk has died down, though, as she ran no sort of race on her return in the Grade 1 JNwine.com Champion Chase at Down Royal in November, when beaten 65 lengths into fifth by Road To Riches. That clearly wasn't her form and she was much better next time at Aintree, even though a beaten favourite when third of four to Sam Winner. A 3m winner in the past, she travelled very well that day but appeared to get outstayed in better company, and a good second in the 2m5½f Ascot Chase in February

confirmed this is the right race for her. Balder Succes beat her by just over three lengths that day, but it was her first run for a couple of months and should have teed her up nicely for Cheltenham. Jumping is her strength and, unlike her conqueror, she has no problems with the track.

Menorah

10 b g; Trainer Philip Hobbs
Chase form U11F314313P22P051128, best RPR 174
Left-handed F313P220512, best RPR 174
Right-handed U11431P18, best RPR 172
Cheltenham form (all) 111543P20, best RPR 172
At the festival 16 Mar 2010: tracked leaders, driven to challenge and went left 2 out, led soon after, wandered under pressure approaching last, hard ridden run-in, held on all out, won Supreme Novices' Hurdle by a head from Get Me Out Of Here
15 Mar 2011: chased leaders, hit 4 out, ridden to stay right there 2 out, one pace when hit last, weakened run-in, finished fifth, beaten nine and a half lengths by Hurricane Fly in Champion Hurdle
13 Mar 2012: in touch, headway to track leading duo after 4 out, ridden and hit 3 out, 7 lengths 3rd and ridden when blundered and weakened 2 out, finished third, beaten 29 lengths by Sprinter Sacre in Racing Post Arkle Chase
14 Mar 2013: in rear, niggled along before 3rd, never looked happy, lost touch 11th, tailed off when pulled up before 13th in Ryanair Chase won by Cue Card
13 Mar 2014: in touch to 10th, weakened 12th, finished 10th, beaten 71 lengths by Dynaste in Ryanair Chase

A real enigma in recent seasons but undoubtedly a top-class performer when on song, as he proved when a comfortable winner of the Grade 2 Charlie Hall Chase on his return at Wetherby, which he followed with a good second to Silviniaco Conti in the Betfair Chase at Haydock. Turned in one of his moody displays last time out, though, never travelling from an early stage and finishing a well-beaten eighth in the King George. It's hard to know what to expect of him this year – although he clearly handles Cheltenham well, having won a Supreme Novices' Hurdle, a Greatwood and run right up to his chase best off a massive weight in a handicap, he seems to have taken a real dislike to this race. He didn't appear to want to know after a couple of fences when pulled up two years ago and it was a similar story last March when he dropped right out just after halfway and completed in his own time. On his best behaviour, though, he is clearly capable of winning.

Taquin Du Seuil

8 b g; Trainer Jonjo O'Neill
Chase form 11321132P4, best RPR 164
Left-handed 1121132P4, best RPR 164
Right-handed 3, best RPR 152
Cheltenham form (all) 6121, best RPR 164
At the festival 13 Mar 2013: chased leaders from 3rd, went 2nd briefly 2 out, weakened under pressure before last, finished sixth, beaten 17 lengths by The New One in Neptune Investment Management Novices' Hurdle 13 Mar 2014: held up in rear, jumped slowly 4th and 12th, headway to track leaders after 4 out, driven to dispute close 2nd 2 out, challenged last and stayed upsides until led under pressure final 75yds, stayed on well, won JLT Novices' Chase by three-quarters of a length from Uxizandre

Grade 1 novice hurdle winner, having taken a heavy-ground Challow at Newbury in 2012, and had an excellent first campaign over fences last term, culminating in victory at the festival, when he proved good ground holds no fears for him. Jumping is not always his strong suit and, while it didn't stop him in the JLT, it hasn't really helped him this term. Put disappointing Newton Abbot return behind him when second in the Charlie Hall at Wetherby, finishing strongly for a four-length second to Menorah and seemingly proving his stamina for 3m-plus in the process. However, it subsequently transpired that Wetherby's distances have been wrong for several years and his next two starts were far from conclusive. Can probably be forgiven a pulled-up effort in the Betfair Chase when Jonjo O'Neill's horses were seemingly out of form but, having moved up to challenge in the home straight in Newbury's Denman Chase, he was left behind from three out and was a 15-length fourth to Coneygree with a couple of fringe Gold Cup contenders also ahead of him. It's possible he needed that first run since November, but the Ryanair now looks the obvious target. Still needs to prove he's better than as a novice, but O'Neill will doubtless have him spot on for the big day.

Ballycasey

8 gr g; Trainer Willie Mullins
Chase form 114F2173, best RPR 156
Left-handed 1147, best RPR 156
Right-handed F213, best RPR 156
Cheltenham form 4, best RPR 154
At the festival 12 Mar 2014: chased leaders, led 3 out, soon ridden, headed approaching 2 out, no extra last, one pace into 4th final 110yds, finished fourth, beaten eight and a half lengths by O'Faolains Boy in RSA Chase

Relatively lightly raced grey who has won six of his 12 starts under rules but has arguably always had a bigger reputation than his performances have merited. He did beat the subsequently massively improved Don Cossack in a three-runner Grade 1 novice chase at Leopardstown last February but then clearly didn't stay when sent off joint-favourite for the RSA Chase, in which he finished a one-paced fourth. Fell when looking likely to land the weakly contested Powers Gold Cup a month later and was then run out of the Champion Novice Chase by Carlingford Lough over 3m1f at Punchestown. Didn't have much to beat on his return this season at Gowran but was then chosen by Ruby Walsh for the Grade 1 Paddy Power Dial-A-Bet Chase at Leopardstown, for which he was made just 5-2. He couldn't live with stablemate Twinlight or most of the others, though, as he finished only seventh of nine. This 2m5f trip is probably his ideal, but a lifetime best RPR of 156 suggests he has the best part of a stone to find to be a serious contender and he was beaten more than 25 lengths by Balder Succes in the Ascot Chase. At least his position in the betting is now more in keeping with his form.

OTHERS TO CONSIDER

It's always hard to second-guess the final line-up of this race, but it seems apparent **Hidden Cyclone** will be heading for the Champion Chase and Djakadam the Gold Cup. **Uxizandre**, who ran better than he had in Ireland in December but still looked booked for a disappointing second to Mr Mole in the Game Spirit before unseating at the last, could go back up in trip again, but his normally sure-footed jumping has deserted him lately. **Eduard** swerved Cheltenham last year but proved himself a top novice at Ayr last spring and has improved this term. He hasn't run since an excellent second in the Peterborough Chase at Huntingdon and might be dependent on give in the ground, but if he turns up he is entitled to run a big race, as is Huntindgon winner **Wishfull Thinking**. If you ignore his pulled-up King George effort he has been in the form of his life this season and despite his age remains high class. **Wonderful Charm** goes well fresh but not yet at Cheltenham.

	FORM	WINNER	AGE & WGT	Adj RPR	SP	TRAINER	C.Runs	BEST RPR LAST 12 MONTHS (RUNS SINCE)
14	21-25	**Dynaste** C, D, BF	8 11-10	179^T	3-1f	D Pipe	7$^{(11G)}$	2nd Gd1 Betfair Chase (3m1f) **(1)**
13	2-151	**Cue Card** C, D	7 11-10	174^{-2}	7-2	C Tizzard	8$^{(8GS)}$	won Gd1 Ascot Chase (2m5½f) **(0)**
12	121-1	**Riverside Theatre** D	8 11-10	176^T	7-2f	N Henderson	8$^{(12G)}$	won Gd1 Ascot Chase (2m5½f) **(0)**
11	1-4FP	**Albertas Run** CD	10 11-10	176^{-1}	6-1	J O'Neill	22$^{(11G)}$	won Gd1 Melling Chase (2m4f) **(3)**
10	P1362	**Albertas Run** C, D	9 11-10	171^{-3}	14-1	J O'Neill	17$^{(13G)}$	won Ascot Gd2 chase (2m3f) **(3)**
09	14-16	**Imperial Commander** C, D	8 11-10	165^{-19}	6-1	N Twiston-Davies	5$^{(10GS)}$	won Paddy Power Gold Cup (2m4½f) **(1)**
08	23-22	**Our Vic** CD, BF	10 11-10	176^{-2}	4-1	D Pipe	17$^{(9GS)}$	2nd Gd1 King George VI Chase (3m) **(1)**
07	-1F31	**Taranis** CD	6 11-0	169^{-13}	9-2	P Nicholls	7$^{(9GS)}$	3rd Gd3 Boylesports Gold Cup (2m5f) **(0)**
06	-4B13	**Fondmort** CD	10 11-0	179^T	10-3jf	N Henderson	27$^{(11G)}$	won Cheltenham Listed hcap ch (2m5f) **(1)**
05	2-222	**Thisthatandtother** C, BF	9 11-3	173^{-3}	9-2	P Nicholls	11$^{(12G)}$	2nd Paddy Power Gold Cup (2m4½f) **(2)**

WINS-RUNS: 6yo 1-5, 7yo 1-11, 8yo 3-30, 9yo 2-32, 10yo 3-17, 11yo 0-7, 12yo 0-3, 13yo 0-1 **FAVOURITES:** £0.67

TRAINERS IN THIS RACE (w-pl-r): David Pipe 2-1-5, Jonjo O'Neill 2-1-4, Nicky Henderson 2-2-12, Paul Nicholls 2-2-14, Colin Tizzard 1-0-2, Nigel Twiston-Davies 1-0-2, Tony Martin 0-0-1, Alan King 0-2-4, John Joseph Hanlon 0-1-1, Mouse Morris 0-1-2, Nicky Richards 0-0-2, Noel Meade 0-0-1, Philip Hobbs 0-1-5, Tom George 0-0-1, Willie Mullins 0-1-6

FATE OF FAVOURITES: P145224121 **POSITION OF WINNER IN MARKET:** 2132282121

Key trends

🐎Adjusted RPR of at least 165, 10/10

🐎Officially rated at least 152, 10/10

🐎Course winner, 9/10

🐎From the first three in the market, 9/10

🐎No more than four runs since October, 9/10

🐎At least seven runs over fences, 9/10

🐎Top-three finish last time out, 7/10

Other factors

🐎Four of the seven beaten favourites had won a Grade 1 chase last time out

🐎Five winners had recorded a top-four finish in a Grade 1 or 2 chase over 3m-plus – the other five achieved that subsequently

🐎The five winners between 2005 and 2009 had either won or been placed in a Paddy Power or December Gold Cup but none of the last five had run in either contest

Notes

3.20 Ladbrokes World Hurdle — C4/RUK
3m Grade 1 £300,000

More Of That's impressive victory last year at the age of six seemed to set him up as the new dominant force in the staying division but he made a lacklustre reappearance at Newbury in late November and then was reported to have broken a blood vessel on the gallops in the second week of February, making him "an unlikely runner at Cheltenham" according to trainer Jonjo O'Neill. With last year's runner-up Annie Power seemingly set to go for the Mares' Hurdle (now also Grade 1), this race is wide open. Paul Nicholls, having retired four-time winner Big Buck's, is set to run Saphir Du Rheu in the same colours and last year's fourth Zarkandar, while 2012 Champion Hurdle winner Rock On Ruby goes up against his old stable under the tutelage of Nicholls' former assistant Harry Fry. There would be no more popular or emotive winner than Lieutenant Colonel, trained by Sandra Hughes since the death of her father Dessie in November.

More Of That
7 b g; Trainer Jonjo O'Neill
Hurdles form 111113, best RPR 172
Left-handed 11113, best RPR 172
Right-handed 1, best RPR 128
Cheltenham form 11, best RPR 172
At the festival 13 Mar 2014: held up, headway approaching 2 out, soon tracked leaders, disputed lead before last where took narrow advantage, ridden run-in, stayed on well and in command final 75yds, won World Hurdle by one and a half lengths from Annie Power

Title defence in the balance for last year's impressive winner after he broke a blood vessel during a gallop at Jackdaws Castle in mid-February, after which Jonjo O'Neill said he would have to be considered an unlikely runner. That would be a shame as he was one of the stars of last season, going through the campaign unbeaten and improving from a handicap mark of 130 to 169 for his commanding festival success from star mare Annie Power. Things have not looked good for a while, though, as he was a big drifter on his seasonal return in the Grade 2 Long Distance Hurdle at Newbury in December and weakened rapidly on the run-in to finished 25 lengths third to Medinas and Cole Harden. That was at a time when O'Neill's horses were running poorly, but this latest setback has to be even more worrying.

Annie Power
7 b g; Trainer Willie Mullins
Hurdles form 111111121, best RPR 164
Left-handed 1112, best RPR 164
Right-handed 11111, best RPR 161
Cheltenham form 12, best RPR 164
At the festival 13 Mar 2014: held up racing with zest, switched right and headway approaching 2 out, big effort to challenge and draw level before last where headed narrowly, ridden run-in, not quicken and held final 75yds, finished second, beaten one and a half lengths by More Of That in World Hurdle

Terrific mare whose unbeaten run came to an end only in last season's World Hurdle, when she was beaten by More Of That but finished five lengths clear of the rest of the field. She subsequently won a Grade 1 mares' race at Punchestown at odds of 1-6 and looked

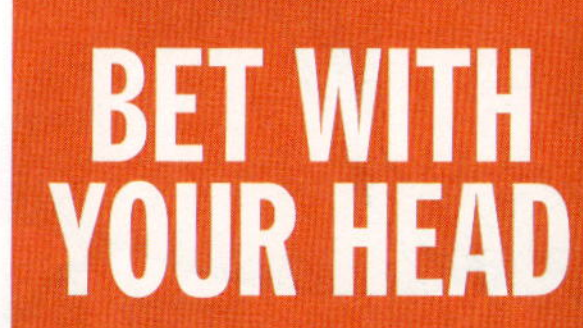

Get the most important information, tips and predictions to help you make a swift and savvy bet on the racing from Cheltenham.

Please gamble responsibly. 18+ www.gambleaware.co.uk

booked for another excellent campaign this season until found to be lame on the day of her intended comeback at Fairyhouse. She is reportedly over that now and goes straight to Cheltenham but because of her absence the intended target is said to be the Mares' Hurdle, for which she will be a short-priced favourite. Connections could be tempted if More Of That is confirmed a non-runner (she is favourite in some lists) but she cannot be backed with any firm not offering the non-runner no bet concession.

Saphir Du Rheu

6 gr g; Trainer Paul Nicholls
Hurdles form 33105411141, best RPR 162
Left-handed 3304141, best RPR 162
Right-handed 1511, best RPR 158
Cheltenham form 0, best RPR 104
At the festival 13 Mar 2013: hit 3rd in mid-division, behind from 4 out, finished 20th, beaten 55 lengths by Flaxen Flare in Fred Winter Juvenile Handicap Hurdle

Had a terrific second season over hurdles last term, running up a hat-trick of wins which included the Lanzarote and Welsh Champion Hurdle, in the latter giving 11lb (not including jockey's claim) and a head beating to subsequent Coral Cup winner Whisper.

However, he missed Cheltenham after flopping at odds of 2-5 in Fontwell's National Spirit Hurdle, a third race on atrocious ground in the space of six weeks evidently having taken its toll. Seen as a future Gold Cup horse by Paul Nicholls and his novice chase campaign was eagerly anticipated, but it went wrong straight away when he unseated on his debut in a race won by Coneygree. He got it right over Exeter's soft fences but then fell in the Grade 1 Feltham and, while Nicholls was originally keen to press on over fences, the decision was finally made to revert to hurdles in the hope that he could emulate owner Andy Stewart's Big Buck's, who became arguably the best staying hurdler ever following his failed chase career. Back over hurdles, Saphir Du Rheu immediately stamped himself as a worthy contender when getting up on the line to beat Reve De Sivola in the Grade 2 Cleeve on Trials Day. In pure form terms that needs improving upon as he was getting 4lb and Cheltenham doesn't suit the runner-up, who is far better at Ascot, but it was a good start. Does seem to handle really deep ground well, though, and was tailed off on his only previous appearance at the festival when joint-favourite for the Fred Winter.

Zarkandar (below, right)

8 b g; Trainer Paul Nicholls
Hurdles form 11115F111412222446312,
best RPR 165
Left-handed 1115F14122446312, best RPR 165
Right-handed 11122, best RPR 164
Cheltenham form 1514224, best RPR 165
At the festival 18 Mar 2011: in touch, closed 2 out,
led approaching last, ran on well run-in, always in
control, won Triumph Hurdle by two and a quarter
lengths from Unaccompanied
13 Mar 2012: in touch, ridden after 3 out and soon
outpaced, rallied but only 7th approaching last, stayed
on strongly closing stages to take 5th last strides,
beaten six and three-quarter lengths by Rock On Ruby
in Champion Hurdle
12 Mar 2013: tracked leader, driven from 3 out,
outpaced into 4th approaching last, weakened closing
stages, finished fourth, beaten six and three-quarter
lengths by Hurricane Fly in Champion Hurdle
13 Mar 2014: held up in rear, mistake 4th, carried
right slightly approaching 2 out, ridden and headway
to go 4th approaching last, kept on run-in but unable
to challenge

Really tough and consistent performer who
won the 2011 Triumph Hurdle and finished
in the first five in the next two Champion
Hurdles, but has lost a bit of his speed as he has
got older. He remains high class at staying trips
and seems at least as good as ever this season,
having beaten star French hurdler Gemix in
a Grade 1 at Auteuil in November and
then run second in the Grade 1 Long
Walk Hurdle, where Reve De Sivola

won for the third year on the trot. That was a
race Zarkandar really should have won as he
appeared to be going much the best having hit
the front two out, but he idled in front and the
famously game Reve De Sivola outbattled him.
Sam Twiston-Davies blamed himself for going
too soon and if he rides this time (he may be on
Saphir Du Rheu anyway and Noel Fehily rides
a lot of Zarkandar's owners' horses) you can
bet he will play it a bit later. Fourth last season
when Nicholls thought some of his festival
runners were under the weather, so could
easily improve on that.

Rock On Ruby

10 b g; Trainer Harry Fry
Hurdles form 12231213312322311, best RPR 171
Left-handed 1223113312211, best RPR 171
Right-handed 2323, best RPR 166
Cheltenham form (hurdles) 2213211, best RPR 171
At the festival 16 Mar 2011: in touch, good headway
to chase leaders 2 out, ridden and 1 length down when
left with 2 lengths lead last, stayed on well under
pressure, caught last stride, finished second, beaten a
short head by First Lieutenant in Neptune Investment
Management Novices' Hurdle
13 Mar 2012: tracked leaders in 3rd, went 2nd before
3 out, challenged 2 out, led soon after and driven to
assert, kept on under pressure run-in, won going away
by three and three-quarter lengths from Overturn in
Champion Hurdle
12 Mar 2013: led and raced keenly, driven
and hit 2 out, headed soon after,
stayed on run-in but no

impression on winner, finished second, beaten two and a half lengths by Hurricane Fly in Champion Hurdle 11 Mar 2014: tracking leaders when blundered badly 3rd and rider lost whip, stayed in touch but never jumping with any real fluency after, hit 5th, behind when blundered 9th, no chance when hit 4 out, finished eighth, beaten 52 lengths in Racing Post Arkle Chase won by Western Warhorse

Top-class and teak-tough ten-year-old whose exceptional Cheltenham Festival record was spoiled only when he went novice chasing last season and finished tailed off in the Racing Post Arkle. That was the first time in four festival appearances he'd finished out of the first two and he had his day in the sun when winning the 2012 Champion Hurdle and was a brave second from the front the following year. He was always seen as a staying two-miler and once it was decided he was not going to make a chaser the obvious plan was a step up in trip as he has undoubtedly lost a bit of his speed. Whether he will have the stamina for 3m is the question, though, as he only broke the ice over 2m4f this season when bagging a pair of Cheltenham wins. The form he produced for both of those successes is some way below his best at 2m and he needs to find at least 10lb on it when going into unknown territory. Trainer Harry Fry said he didn't want to find out about his stamina until the festival, which is why he missed the Cleeve, but that suggests he must have some doubts in his mind. Easy to see him travelling well and looking menacing turning for home. Not so easy to see him winning, although there's no doubt he'll give his all.

Lieutenant Colonel

6 br g; Trainer Sandra Hughes
Hurdles form 21261311, best RPR 159
Left-handed 261, best RPR, best RPR 157
Right-handed 12131, best RPR 159
Cheltenham form 6, best RPR 139
At the festival 12 Mar 2014: tracked leaders, well in touch from 3 out, not quicken after 2 out, edged left and weakened last, finished sixth, beaten 13 and a half lengths by Faugheen in Neptune Investment Management Novices' Hurdle

Fair novice hurdler last season when not disgraced in sixth in the Neptune, although was left behind from two out. Won a Grade 2 at Fairyhouse the following month before no match for Vautour at Punchestown and attention was quickly switched to fences for his first start of this season. However, although he gave notice that he has a future over fences, a couple of bad mistakes cost him victory at odds of 1-2 at Naas and he was put back over hurdles. He has progressed well, winning a pair of Grade 1s, the first over 2m4f and the second on his first attempt at 3m when staying on strongly to deny Jetson by three-quarters of a length. Has a fair profile, but the fact he hasn't yet broken through the 160 RPR barrier suggests he still has a lot more to find to win.

Un Temps Pour Tout (below)

6 b g; Trainer David Pipe
Hurdles form 3331133132133, best RPR 157
Left-handed 33311331323, best RPR 157
Right-handed 13, best RPR 156
Cheltenham form 3, best RPR 157

Decent novice hurdler in France and quickly improved on that form for David Pipe last season, running Zamdy Man to just under two lengths on his British debut at Haydock and then slamming the now much-improved Cole Harden by 16 lengths at Ascot. Was fancied for various different races at last season's festival but pulled up lame the week before and was forced to miss the gig, although it wasn't that serious as he was back out at Punchestown in early May, when finishing third of 25 in a valuable 2m4f handicap. He clearly had one or two further issues over the summer as he

didn't make the track until the Cleeve Hurdle in January, where he was heavily backed (7-4 favourite from an overnight 7-2) but could manage only third to Saphir Du Rheu and Reve De Sivola. That was still an excellent effort on his first run for eight months, though, and there's every reason to think this expensive purchase (£450,000) has more to come.

Whisper

7 b g; Trainer Nicky Henderson
Hurdles form 14141331211, best RPR 159
Left-handed 141131211, best RPR 159
Right-handed 43, best RPR 146
Cheltenham form 4131, best RPR 159
At the festival 12 Mar 2014: always in leading group, ridden to lead before last, hard pressed flat, just held on, won Coral Cup by a short head from Get Me Out Of Here

Had an excellent second campaign over hurdles last season, shrugging off a 6lb rise for a head defeat to Saphir Du Rheu at Ffos Las by winning the Coral Cup on his very next start. Stepped up to 3m for the Grade 1 Liverpool Hurdle at Aintree next time, he won by a length from At Fishers Cross with Zarkandar back in fourth. He was all set for a chase campaign this season, but having been beaten at 2-5 on his debut on New Year's Day (didn't jump badly by any means) those plans appear to have been shelved as his only festival entry is in the World Hurdle.

Beat That

7 b g; Trainer Nicky Henderson
Hurdles form 12116, best RPR 159
Left-handed 16, best RPR 159
Right-handed 121, best RPR 152
Cheltenham form 6, best RPR 133

Beaten favourite in two bumpers in first season but had an excellent novice hurdle campaign, winning three of his four starts. Began with a ten-length drubbing of the useful Champagne West at Ascot and was not disgraced when second to Killala Quay (subsequently fourth in the Neptune) in the Grade 2 Winter Novice Hurdle at Sandown on his next start. Swerved Cheltenham for Aintree and, having travelled well all the way, was an easy winner of the Grade 1 Sefton Novices' Hurdle there (Cole Harden beaten four lengths into second) on his first attempt at 3m. Followed up with a battling display to beat Don Poli in another Grade 1 at Punchestown. Belated return this season was not particularly promising, though, as he was far too keen early and finished a well-beaten 27-length sixth to Rock On Ruby over 2m4½f at Cheltenham. Said to be still on target, but hard to know what to expect.

OTHERS TO CONSIDER

This will be very open if Jonjo O'Neill can't get More Of That back to his best and a big field is probably guaranteed. Nicky Henderson already has a couple of contenders and **Blue Fashion**, last seen when running second to Faugheen at Ascot in November, is another who could make the field. Almost certain to line up is **Reve De Sivola**, although he doesn't really have the pace on good ground around Cheltenham. Potential Irish raiders include **Dedigout**, who has now won his last two, although that might have been different if Briar Hill had stood up at the last in the Boyne Hurdle at Navan in February. That was a big return to form from the latter, but he did take a heavy fall. **Jetson** is a bit old for this but closely matched with Lieutenant Colonel and twice the price, while **Monksland**, who returned from two years off at Leopardstown in December and has run well again since, looks likely to travel. **At Fishers Cross**, third last year and a previous winner of the Albert Bartlett, has disappointed all season and his tame defeat at Haydock in February surely now makes him an unlikely starter.

World Hurdle results and trends

	FORM	WINNER	AGE & WGT	Adj RPR	SP	TRAINER	H.Runs	BEST RPR LAST 12 MONTHS (RUNS SINCE)
14	1-111	**More Of That** C	6 11-10	165^{-14}	15-2	J O'Neill	4$^{(10G)}$	won Gd2 Relkeel Hdl (2m4½f) (0)
13	22/21	**Solwhit**	9 11-10	169^{-5}	17-2	C Byrnes (IRE)	20$^{(13GS)}$	2nd Punchestown Hurdle (2m4f) (1)
12	1-111	**Big Buck's** CD	9 11-10	182^{T}	5-6F	P Nicholls	28$^{(11G)}$	won Gd1 Liverpool Hurdle (3m½f) (3)
11	11-11	**Big Buck's** CD	8 11-10	180^{T}	10-11F	P Nicholls	23$^{(13G)}$	won Gd1 World Hurdle (3m) (3)
10	11-11	**Big Buck's** CD	7 11-10	180^{T}	5-6F	P Nicholls	19$^{(14G)}$	won Gd1 Liverpool Hurdle (3m½f) (2)
09	1-U11	**Big Buck's** CD	6 11-10	170^{-7}	6-1	P Nicholls	15$^{(14GS)}$	won Gd2 Cleeve Hurdle (3m) (0)
08	13-11	**Inglis Drever** C, D	9 11-10	174^{T}	11-8F	H Johnson	20$^{(17GS)}$	won Newb Gd2 Long Dist Hdl (3m½f) (1)
07	1F-12	**Inglis Drever** CD	8 11-10	171^{-2}	5-1	H Johnson	16$^{(14GS)}$	2nd Gd2 Cleeve Hurdle (3m) (0)
06	2-211	**My Way De Solzen** D	6 11-10	161^{-8}	8-1	A King	10$^{(20G)}$	won Gd1 Long Walk Hurdle (3m) (1)
05	-2211	**Inglis Drever**	6 11-10	166^{-14}	5-1	Howard Johnson	9$^{(12G)}$	won Gd2 Kingwell Hurdle (2m) (0)

WINS-RUNS: 5yo 0-7, 6yo 4-31, 7yo 1-37, 8yo 2-28, 9yo 3-20, 10yo 0-8, 11yo 0-6, 13yo 0-1 **FAVOURITES:** -£2.05

TRAINERS IN THIS RACE (w-pl-r): Paul Nicholls 4-1-13, Jonjo O'Neill 1-0-9, Tony Martin 0-0-1, David Pipe 0-1-6, Edward O'Grady 0-0-1, Mouse Morris 0-0-2, Nick Williams 0-0-2, Nicky Henderson 0-1-9, Nigel Twiston-Davies 0-0-3, Noel Meade 0-0-1, Philip Hobbs 0-0-2, Rebecca Curtis 0-1-1, Willie Mullins 0-3-15

FATE OF FAVOURITES: 23F14111P2 **POSITION OF WINNER IN MARKET:** 3431311143

Key trends

🐎Aged six to nine, 10/10

🐎Top-two finish last time out, 10/10

🐎Ran no more than four times since August, 10/10

🐎Not out of the first two all hurdle starts that season, 9/10

🐎Adjusted RPR of at least 165, 9/10

🐎Previously ran at the festival, 9/10

🐎Ran between nine and 20 times over hurdles, 7/10

🐎Won a Graded hurdle over at least 3m, 7/10

Other factors

🐎Four of the last five winners aged nine or older were previous winners of the race (Solwhit in 2012 the exception)

🐎A five-year-old has never won. However, three of the six to have run in the past ten seasons were placed

🐎Six winners had finished first or second in this race before

🐎Four of the five Irish winners since the mid-1980s prepped in the Boyne Hurdle at Navan (the other, Solwhit in 2013, prepped in the Grade 3 Limestone Lad at Navan)

🐎The record of Cleeve Hurdle winners is 843117214. The winners were Inglis Drever (2008) and Big Buck's (2009 and 2012)

🐎Aside from Inglis Drever and Big Buck's, the other three winners (My Way De Solzen, Solwhit and More Of That) were established performers over shorter trips, with all three having won a Grade 2 or 3 hurdle over 2m3f-2m4f last time out

Notes

4.00 Brown Advisory & Merriebelle Plate   C4/RUK

2m5f handicap chase   Grade 3   £90,000

Overall this race (established in 1951 and traditionally known as the Mildmay of Flete) has been the biggest graveyard for favourites at the festival with just four winning. The only two successful favourites in recent years both came from the Pipe stable – Majadou (trained by Martin) in 1999 and Salut Flo (trained by David) in 2012. Apart from that pair, only one other winner in the past 16 runnings has gone off shorter than 12-1.

Last year Pipe had his third winner in five years when Ballynagour (12-1) drew clear of 5-1 favourite Colour Squadron. That means the Pipe stable has won the race a remarkable seven times in the past 17 runnings.

Some of the bigger stables struggle to get runners at the lower end of the handicap and Paul Nicholls has not won in 23 attempts (second and fourth are his best showings). Nicky Henderson has been more successful, with two winners and a third from his last 13 runners that have been in the ideal ratings band (128-140).

Another trainer to note is Venetia Williams, who has form figures of 221PP17F0100 since 2005 with runners in the ideal ratings band and often at big odds. There has been a single Irish-trained winner in the race's long history.

Brown Advisory & Merriebelle Stable Plate results and trends

	FORM	WINNER	AGE & WGT	OR	SP	TRAINER	C.Runs	BEST RPR LAST 12 MONTHS (RUNS SINCE)
14	P18-P	**Ballynagour** D	8 10-9	140^{-1}	12-1	D Pipe	8$^{(23G)}$	8th Cheltenham Gd3 hcap ch (2m5f) (1)
13	4P61P	**Carrickboy**	9 10-5	136^{-13}	50-1	V Williams	16$^{(22GS)}$	won Chepstow class 2 hcap ch (2m3½f) (1)
12	112/0	**Salut Flo**	7 10-10	137^{-5}	9-2f	D Pipe	6$^{(22G)}$	12th Atlantic4 Gold Cup hcap ch (2m5f) (0)
11	152F1	**Holmwood Legend** (5x) D	10 10-6	130^{-5}	25-1	P Rodford	12$^{(20G)}$	won Sandown class 3 hcap ch (2m4½f) (0)
10	-3144	**Great Endeavour** D	6 10-1	135^{-11}	18-1	D Pipe	3$^{(24G)}$	4th Fontwell class 3 nov ch (2m6f) (1)
09	20272	**Something Wells**	8 10-7	139^{-1}	33-1	V Williams	10$^{(23GS)}$	2nd Ascot class 2 hcap ch (2m5½f) (2)
08	547U5	**Mister McGoldrick** D	11 11-7	145^{-6}	66-1	S Smith	33$^{(22GS)}$	4th Wetherby class 2 hcap ch (2m½f) (2)
07	6-134	**Idole First** C, D	8 10-7	136^{T}	12-1	V Williams	8$^{(23GS)}$	won Kempton class 3 hcap ch (2m4½f) (2)
06	0-433	**Non So**	8 11-3	137^{T}	14-1	N Henderson	10$^{(24G)}$	3rd Wetherby class 2 hcap ch (2m4½f) (0)
05	-2384	**Liberthine**	6 10-1	128^{-6}	25-1	N Henderson	6$^{(22G)}$	3rd Kempton class 2 hcap ch (2m4½f) (2)

WINS-RUNS: 5yo 0-4, 6yo 2-21, 7yo 1-37, 8yo 4-65, 9yo 1-43, 10yo 1-32, 11yo 1-18, 12yo 0-2, 13yo 0-3 **FAVOURITES:** -£4.50

FATE OF FAVOURITES: 4F0F223102 **POSITION OF WINNER IN MARKET:** 0650000106

Key trends

🐎 Won a Class 3 or higher, 10/10

🐎 Won between 2m3f and 2m5f, 9/10

🐎 Ran between three and 16 times over fences, 9/10

🐎 Officially rated 128 to 140, 9/10

🐎 Ran within the last 42 days, 8/10

🐎 Carried no more than 10st 10lb, 8/10

🐎 Top-five finish last time out, 7/10 (last three winners the exceptions)

🐎 Ran at a previous festival, 7/10

Other factors

🐎 None of the last ten winners had figured prominently in one of the big 2m4f handicaps run at Cheltenham earlier in the season

🐎 The two novices to win were rated 133 and 135

🐎 Ireland has not won this since Double-U-Again in 1982

🐎 Salut Flo in 2012 was the first winning favourite since Majadou (1999), who was also the last winner before him to be sent off at shorter than 12-1 (both trained by the Pipe stable)

🐎 The last three winners were well beaten on their last start (two pulled up, one unplaced). Two were trained by David Pipe and had not run since the turn of the year

<h2>4.40 Fulke Walwyn Kim Muir Handicap Chase   RUK</h2>

3m2f   Amateur riders   £60,000

This is a highlight of the season for amateur riders and the best jockeys are in big demand – the non-claiming amateurs Jamie Codd, Richard Harding and the now retired Richard Burton have each had two victories in the past ten runnings, while last year's race went to Robbie McNamara (on Spring Heeled), who has since turned professional.

With little between most of the runners nowadays (last year's lowest-rated was 131), the higher-rated runners have started to do well. The topweight won in 2009 and 2010, Junior was successful under 11st 6lb in 2011, the first four came from the highest four marks in the handicap in 2012, the 2013 joint-top-rated was beaten a head and last year's first three were all at the higher end (140-144) – five of the past six winners account for all but one of the best weight-carrying performances in the past 30 years.

A number of shrewd trainers target this race and their runners merit respect. Seven of the past 13 winners have come from the Pipe stable, Nicky Henderson and Donald McCain. David Pipe, whose father Martin won this race on three occasions, had the first two in 2011. Henderson has had three successes, including a couple of 1-2s, while McCain has had two winners and a runner-up. In contrast, Paul Nicholls has had one placed horse from 16 runners.

Spring Heeled last year became the first Irish-trained winner since Greasepaint in 1983. He was the second novice to win in successive years, although only the fifth to do so since Glyde Court in 1985, which is the lowest return for any long-standing festival handicap.

This can often be a plot race and punters should give consideration to runners with a light preparation and who may not have shown good recent form, with nine of the past 12 winners unplaced last time out.

Eight- and nine-year-olds have done best in recent years, accounting for 15 of the past 21 winners from around half the total runners.

Kim Muir Handicap Chase results and trends

	FORM	WINNER	AGE & WGT	OR	SP	TRAINER	C.Runs	BEST RPR LAST 12 MONTHS (RUNS SINCE)
14	13280	Spring Heeled (2ow)	7 11-8	140-5	12-1	J Culloty (IRE)	10(23G)	2nd Limerick hcap ch (3m) (2)
13	34136	Same Difference	7 11-0	137-2	16-1	N Twiston-Davies	6(24GS)	3rd Newbury class 2 nov ch (3m) (1)
12	-37P9	Sunnyhillboy C	9 11-11	142-1	13-2f	J O'Neill	11(23G)	3rd Irish Grand National (3m5f) (3)
11	31-32	Junior	8 11-6	134-4	10-3f	D Pipe	6(24G)	3rd Cheltenham Gd3 hcap ch (3m3½f) (0)
10	0-311	Ballabriggs D	9 11-12	140T	9-1	D McCain	10(24G)	won Ayr class 2 hcap ch (3m1f) (0)
09	14339	Character Building D	9 11-12	139-10	16-1	J Quinn	10(24GS)	3rd Cheltenham cl 2 hcap ch (3m2½f) (1)
08	1-43P	High Chimes	9 10-10	127-7	14-1	E Williams	7(24GS)	3rd Haydock class 2 hcap ch (3m) (1)
07	36120	Cloudy Lane D, BF	7 10-11	124T	15-2f	D McCain	5(24GS)	2nd Newcastle class 3 nov ch (3m) (1)
06	3621P	You're Special C, BF	9 10-12	125-6	33-1	F Murphy	18(21G)	won Doncaster class 2 hcap ch (3m2f) (1)
05	31522	Juveigneur	8 11-7	128-6	12-1	N Henderson	19(24G)	2nd Newbury class 3 hcap ch (3m) (0)

WINS-RUNS: 6yo 0-17, 7yo 3-48, 8yo 2-60, 9yo 5-48, 10yo 0-29, 11yo 0-16, 12yo 0-11, 13yo 0-6 **FAVOURITES:** £10.33

FATE OF FAVOURITES: 001U031120 **POSITION OF WINNER IN MARKET:** 5018531106

Key trends

🐎 Rated within 7lb of RPR top-rated, 10/10

🐎 Ran over at least 3m last time out, 10/10

🐎 Officially rated 124 to 142, 10/10

🐎 Aged seven to nine, 10/10

🐎 Won over at least 3m, 8/10

🐎 Finished in first three in either or both of last two starts, 8/10

🐎 Won a handicap chase, 7/10

Other factors

🐎 Last year Spring Heeled became the first winner for Ireland since Greasepaint in 1983

🐎 Four winners had run at a previous festival

🐎 Four winners had run within the past 33 days, the other six had been off for at least 58

🐎 None of the last eight winners had run more than 11 times over fences

Friday, March 13 (New Course)

- JCB Triumph Hurdle
- Vincent O'Brien County Handicap Hurdle
- Albert Bartlett Novices' Hurdle
- Betfred Cheltenham Gold Cup
- Foxhunter Chase
- Martin Pipe Conditional Jockeys' Handicap Hurdle
- Johnny Henderson Grand Annual Chase

1.30 JCB Triumph Hurdle — C4/RUK
2m1f *Grade 1* *£120,000*

Many will be waiting until this race for their banker of the meeting as Peace And Co bids to justify his short odds and tall reputation with victory for trainer Nicky Henderson, who has already won the Triumph a record five times. The French import could not have been more impressive in his two British runs, winning a pair of Grade 2s in clear-cut style and recording a Racing Post Rating of 145 each time. Henderson has strong back-up in Hargam, who has beaten the same two horses that finished runner-up to Peace And Co but by lesser margins, as well as Top Notch (in the same ownership as Peace And Co). One of the horses beaten into second by both Peace And Co and Hargam is the Alan King-trained Karezak, who has ground to make up but is far from out of the reckoning. Willie Mullins, as in the other Grade 1 events, will be a threat, with his chief hopes appearing to be Petite Parisienne and Kalkir (first and second in the Grade 1 Spring Juvenile Hurdle, which featured the Triumph winner in each of the past three years).

Peace And Co
4 b g; Trainer Nicky Henderson
Hurdles form (all left-handed) 111, best RPR 145
Cheltenham form 1, best RPR 145

Won sole hurdle in France in June and was the subject of plenty of gossip before his British debut for Nicky Henderson in a Grade 2 at Doncaster in December. All the rumours of him burning up the gallops were apparently true as he made mincemeat of dual winner Starchitect, scoring by 19 lengths with another 13 back to the third. He maintained his unbeaten record in the Triumph Hurdle Trial at Cheltenham in January, although it was an unsatisfactory race run at a crawl early on. The horse he beat there, Karezak, had been beaten much more easily by Bristol De Mai at Chepstow, but it was a muddling race and Peace And Co did himself no favours by pulling really hard early. If he has a flaw it is the fact he can be very fresh and seems highly strung.

He raced in earplugs at Cheltenham but that didn't stop him and Barry Geraghty won't want him to lose too much energy getting down to the start in front of the packed stands. Other than that he's a good trends fit, but his best RPR of 145 is at odds with an official rating of 155 and he looks fairly stingy at 2-1 ante-post.

Hargam
4 gr g; Trainer Nicky Henderson
Hurdles form 211, best RPR 142
Left-handed 21, best RPR 135
Right-handed 1, best RPR 142
Cheltenham form 21, best RPR 135

Gives Nicky Henderson the first two in the betting and has similar formlines to Peace And Co, having beaten both Karezak and Starchitect in separate races. Hard to say his form is quite as good, as Karezak was giving him weight at Cheltenham compared to the other way round with Peace And Co, and he only beat Starchitect by six lengths at Musselburgh

MEMBERS' CLUB
Your Cheltenham Services

RPR

RACINGPOST.com/membersclub
Your Cheltenham guide

rather than 19. However, he has the advantage of having proved himself on good ground and he did win as he liked last time.

Petite Parisienne
4 gr f; Trainer Willie Mullins
Hurdles form 21, best RPR 136
Left-handed 1, best RPR 136
Right-handed 2, best RPR 122

Winner of a small Flat contest in the French provinces, but that was enough to see her bought for €135,000 and sent to Willie Mullins, for whom she now seems his first string. Made odds-on favourite for her debut at Punchestown in December but raced keenly and arguably gave runaway leader too much of an advantage and was beaten just under three lengths. However, a hot pace in the Grade 1 Spring Juvenile Hurdle at Leopardstown in February gave her the platform to show what she could do and she travelled strongly before picking it up at the last and stayed on strongly to win by a length and three-quarters from favourite and stablemate Kalkir, despite jockey Bryan Cooper putting up 1lb overweight. That was a second short-priced defeat on the spin for the favourite, but it wasn't as bad a race as some seemed to think immediately afterwards and she's entitled to be considered a player with the 7lb mares' allowance. The Spring has produced the winner of the last three Triumph Hurdles.

Kalkir (right)
4 gr g; Trainer Willie Mullins
Hurdles form 4122, best RPR 144
Left-handed 422, best RPR 144
Right-handed 1, best RPR 135

Enjoyed brief spell at the head of the Triumph market following sparkling debut for Willie Mullins when winning a Grade 3 at Fairyhouse by eight lengths but has found things tougher upped further in class on his last two starts, getting rolled over at short prices both times. It's possible a steady gallop was to blame for his defeat to Fiscal Focus (improved form anyway) at Leopardstown over Christmas, but that excuse wasn't available when he finished just under two lengths second to stablemate Petite Parisienne in the Spring Juvenile Hurdle. Ruby Walsh went for home a long way out there in the hope of making use of his stamina, but he

couldn't fend off the filly. However, he's not without a shout of turning the form around if he is played later over Cheltenham's stiffer 2m1f (two of the last three Triumph winners were beaten in the Spring).

Top Notch
4 b g; Trainer Nicky Henderson
Hurdles form 11111, best RPR 141
Left-handed 1111, best RPR 141
Right-handed 1, best RPR 137

Yet another Nicky Henderson-trained juvenile, which means between them he and Willie Mullins have the first five in the betting. This one was fairly impressive at Newbury under a big penalty for his two French successes on his British debut in December, but then had to work a lot harder to beat Golden Doyen at odds of 30-100 at Ascot in January. Didn't have anything to beat when an easy winner at odds of 2-13 at Haydock but impressed with his jumping and, despite being in the same ownership as the favourite, he is reportedly an intended runner.

Karezak
4 b g; Trainer Alan King
Hurdles form (left-handed) 12222, best RPR 137
Cheltenham form 22, best RPR 137

One of the more experienced contenders, having run five times over hurdles. Was a fairly talented maiden on the Flat, although seemed to have a penchant for finishing second, which he did five times on the spin once moved up to middle distances. Broke his duck over hurdles at the first time of asking, when beating Golden Doyen Chepstow, but has since reverted to type by finishing second four times in a row. However, he doesn't give the impression he's not trying and he has been fairly close to the front two in the betting in two of them. Looks tough and his best run by far on the Flat came on fast ground, so no surprise if he shows improved form given a dry week.

Fiscal Focus
4 b g; Trainer Desmond McDonogh
Hurdles form (left-handed) 16, best RPR 144

Was sent off at 33-1 on his hurdles debut, which was big enough considering he was a high 80s horse on the Flat, and he belied

those odds with a two-length defeat of Kalkir. Whether that was a fluke is hard to gauge, not least because his next start came in the Irish Champion Hurdle against Hurricane Fly and Jezki and he was never going to have a prayer against those two. He raced too keenly and finished tailed off against the big guns but is certainly better than that and, while his win came on sticky ground and he was a heavy-ground winner on the Flat, his best run on the level came on a decent surface.

Bristol De Mai

4 gr g; Trainer Nigel Twiston-Davies
Hurdles form 113, best RPR 144
Left-handed 11, best RPR 144
Right-handed 3, best RPR 134

Won over hurdles in France and made a sparkling British debut in the Grade 1 Finale Juvenile Hurdle at Chepstow over Christmas, always travelling well and cruising clear of good yardstick Karezak for a six-length win. Well supported on the back of that in the Listed Contenders Hurdle at Sandown in January but could manage only a one-paced third, beaten eight and a half lengths, to proven handicapper Garde La Victoire and Supreme contender Jollyallan. Probably better than that and has proved he can travel well in a decent field, but needs to show he's as good on faster ground and is another in the same ownership as Peace And Co.

Pain Au Chocolat (below)

4 b g; Trainer Alan King
Hurdles form 2211, best RPR 129
Left-handed 21, best RPR 123
Right-handed 21, best RPR 129

Going the right way for Alan King and, after finishing second when odds-on for British debut, has won his last two. The first was a fairly run-of-the-mill novice hurdle at Plumpton, though, while the second came in a small-field four-year-old handicap off a mark of 136. Clearly has some talent but looks a fair way off the best of his generation on the evidence so far and a bit off-putting that King was sure the subsequently disappointing Chatez was his best juvenile.

Dicosimo

4 b g; Trainer Willie Mullins
Hurdles form F11, best RPR 136
Left-handed F1, best RPR 117
Right-handed 1, best RPR 136

Fell on French debut but made no mistake next time at Auteuil and subsequently joined Willie Mullins for Rich Ricci, owner of so many top-class performers. Ran out a seven-and-a-half-length winner from three previous scorers on his Irish debut at Gowran in January, but there are negatives. First, his jumping was awful at times (it was pretty foggy) and he seems to be all about stamina (trainer says he will keep on galloping), so a good-ground Triumph might not be his cup of tea.

OTHERS TO CONSIDER

Vercingetorix made a big impression on his debut in December and it's hard to believe he is as bad as he looked when dropping right out in the Spring Juvenile, but whether he will travel has to be open to doubt. **Golden Doyen** has a victory over Hargam to his name and made Top Notch work hard at Ascot, so is entitled to line up, while **Arabian Revolution** is beginning to get his act together after looking quirky on the Flat and might improve for better going. Bivouac, another Henderson runner, looked pretty useful when winning at Kempton over Christmas considering he gave the runner-up 10lb and an easy lead and took a fair bump from another rival at halfway, and he has to be better than in the Triumph Hurdle Trial in January (well-beaten fifth), although he might have the Fred Winter as an option. That could also be said of a lot of the other rags in the betting as Peace And Co seems to have a lot of people thinking he only has to turn up.

Triumph Hurdle results and trends

	FORM	WINNER	AGE & WGT	Adj RPR	SP	TRAINER	H.Runs	BEST RPR LAST 12 MONTHS (RUNS SINCE)
14	12	**Tiger Roll** D	4 11-0	150^{-2}	10-1	G Elliott (IRE)	2$^{(15G)}$	2nd Gd1 Leopardstown nov hdl (2m) (0)
13	111	**Our Conor**	4 11-0	160^{-3}	4-1	D Hughes (IRE)	3$^{(17GS)}$	won Gd1 Leopardstown nov hdl (2m) (0)
12	12123	**Countrywide Flame** D	4 11-0	151^{-6}	33-1	J Quinn	6$^{(20G)}$	2nd Gd1 Finale Hurdle (2m½f) (1)
11	1	**Zarkandar**	4 11-0	155^{-2}	13-2	P Nicholls	1$^{(23G)}$	won Gd2 Adonis Nov Hdl (2m) (0)
10	4211	**Soldatino** D	4 11-0	150^{-6}	6-1	N Henderson	2$^{(17G)}$	won Gd2 Adonis Nov Hdl (2m) (0)
09	11	**Zaynar** D	4 11-0	152^{-6}	11-2	N Henderson	2$^{(18GS)}$	won Newb class 4 nov hdl (2m½f) (1)
08	12	**Celestial Halo** D, BF	4 11-0	145^{-11}	5-1	P Nicholls	2$^{(14GS)}$	won Newb class 3 nov hdl (2m½f) (1)
07	12111	**Katchit** CD	4 11-0	150^{-10}	11-2	A King	6$^{(23GS)}$	2nd Wetherby Listed nov hdl (2m) (3)
06	811	**Detroit City** D	4 11-0	152^{-2}	7-2f	P Hobbs	3$^{(17G)}$	won Sandown class 3 nov hdl (2m½f) (0)
05	111	**Penzance** D	4 11-0	137^{-13}	9-1	A King	3$^{(23G)}$	won Gd2 Adonis Nov Hdl (2m) (0)

WINS-RUNS: 4yo 10-187 **FAVOURITES:** -£5.50

TRAINERS IN THIS RACE (w-pl-r): Alan King 2-4-12, Nicky Henderson 2-2-12, Paul Nicholls 2-2-15, Gordon Elliott 1-0-5, Philip Hobbs 1-2-4, Alan Fleming 0-0-1, Brian Ellison 0-0-2, Charlie Mann 0-1-1, Dermot Weld 0-2-3, David Pipe 0-0-4, Donald McCain 0-0-2, Evan Williams 0-1-3, John Ferguson 0-0-2, Jonjo O'Neill 0-0-1, Nigel Twiston-Davies 0-0-1, Noel Meade 0-0-3, Tim Vaughan 0-0-4, Tony Carroll 0-0-2, Venetia Williams 0-0-3, Willie Mullins 0-1-11, Warren Greatrex 0-0-1

FATE OF FAVOURITES: 3102244364 **POSITION OF WINNER IN MARKET:** 4122333026

Key trends

🐎 Last ran between 19 and 55 days ago, 10/10

🐎 Won at least 50 per cent of hurdle races, 10/10

🐎 Top-three finish last time out, 10/10 (seven won)

🐎 Adjusted RPR of at least 145, 9/10 (the last nine)

🐎 By Group 1-winning sire, 8/10

🐎 Ran two or three times over hurdles, 7/10

Other factors

🐎 Zarkandar is the only once-raced hurdler to win in the past 30 years

🐎 Four winners were undefeated over hurdles

🐎 Five had won Graded hurdle events (three had landed the Adonis at Kempton in February)

🐎 Of the six who raced on the Flat in Britain and Ireland, five had recorded an RPR of at least 86 (four of them had won over distances of 1m1f to 1m6f)

🐎 Since the introduction of the Fred Winter Hurdle in 2005, nine of the ten winners have had an SP of 10-1 or shorter

Notes

In recent years this race has been won by Ireland or one of the big British stables (Paul Nicholls, Martin Pipe, Philip Hobbs and Jonjo O'Neill have saddled the only home winners since 2000). Nicholls formerly had some success controlling the handicap, winning in 2004, 2006 and 2009, and even though that has become more difficult he was on the mark again last year with Lac Fontana.

Six of the last eight winners came from Ireland and four of them were trained by a Mullins. Willie Mullins had his first festival handicap victory in this race with Thousand Stars in 2010 and followed up in 2011 with Final Approach (he didn't have a runner in 2012 but was runner-up in the last two years).

Lac Fontana last year was the ninth winner in a row rated in the 130s and the tenth winner in the last 11 runnings to have been a first- or second-season hurdler – a key factor nowadays. Nine five-year-olds and three six-year-olds have won in the past 16 runnings.

In more than half a century only two winners have broken the effective ceiling weight of 11st 2lb – Blowing Wind carried 11st 8lb in 1998 and Spirit Leader 11st 7lb in 2003. What those two high-weight winners had in common was that they were coming off big handicap wins (the Imperial Cup for Blowing Wind and the Tote Gold Trophy for Spirit Leader).

The Betfair Hurdle and the BoyleSports Hurdle have been the key races in recent years – eight of the past 13 winners had run in one of those hot contests (as well as a runner-up and four thirds in the last four years).

Ten of the past 16 winners were in the first four in the market (Lac Fontana was 11-1 fifth favourite last year).

County Hurdle results and trends

FORM	WINNER	AGE & WGT	OR	SP	TRAINER	H.Runs	BEST RPR LAST 12 MONTHS (RUNS SINCE)
14	8-141	**Lac Fontana** CD	5 10-11	139^{-3}	11-1	P Nicholls	6$^{(28G)}$	won Chelt class 2 hcap hdl (2m1f) (0)
13	31923	**Ted Veale**	6 10-6	134^{-2}	10-1	A Martin (IRE)	5$^{(28G)}$	3rd Boylesports Hcap Hurdle (2m) (0)
12	10120	**Alderwood** D	8 11-1	139^{-3}	20-1	T Mullins (IRE)	12$^{(26G)}$	won Killarney hcap hdl (2m6f) (2)
11	13-51	**Final Approach**	5 10-12	139^{-8}	10-1	W Mullins (IRE)	4$^{(26G)}$	won MCR Hcap Hurdle (2m) (0)
10	40110	**Thousand Stars** D	6 10-5	134^{-5}	20-1	W Mullins (IRE)	14$^{(28G)}$	14th MCR Hcap Hurdle (2m) (0)
09	1349	**American Trilogy** D	5 11-0	135^{-7}	20-1	P Nicholls	4$^{(27GS)}$	3rd Cheltenham Gd2 nov hdl (2m½f) (2)
08	22233	**Silver Jaro** BF	5 10-13	132^{-11}	50-1	T Hogan (IRE)	10$^{(22GS)}$	3rd Pierse Hcap Hurdle (2m) (1)
07	-1713	**Pedrobob**	9 10-0	135^{-10}	12-1	A Mullins (IRE)	7$^{(28GS)}$	3rd Gd3 Tote Trophy Hcap Hdl (2m½f) (0)
06	U1131	**Desert Quest** (4x) D	6 10-10	131^{-4}	4-1jf	P Nicholls	8$^{(29G)}$	won Newbury class 3 hcap hdl (2m½f) (0)
05	60048	**Fontanesi** (5oh) D	5 10-0	128^{-2}	16-1	M Pipe	16$^{(30G)}$	2nd Aintree class 3 hcap hdl (2m½f) (9)

WINS-RUNS: 5yo 5-56, 6yo 3-77, 7yo 0-68, 8yo 1-36, 9yo 1-20, 10yo 0-11, 11yo 0-3, 12yo 0-1 **FAVOURITES:** -£7.50

FATE OF FAVOURITES: 010260000P **POSITION OF WINNER IN MARKET:** 8140704035

Key trends

- Achieved career-best RPR of at least 129 on a left-handed track, 10/10
- Officially rated 128 to 139, 10/10
- Carried no more than 11st 1lb, 10/10
- Ran between four and 14 times over hurdles, 9/10
- No previous festival form, 8/10
- Aged five or six, 8/10

Other factors

- There have been five winning novices since 1996 – all were rated no higher than 139
- Only one winner ran in the Betfair Hurdle (Pedrobob third in 2007). Four ran in the Boylesports Hurdle, finishing 3013
- Paul Nicholls has had four winners, two seconds and a fourth since 2004.
- Ireland has won six of the last eight runnings

2.40 Albert Bartlett Novices' Hurdle C4/RUK
3m *Grade 1* *£120,000*

Willie Mullins has won the Supreme, Neptune and Triumph but this Grade 1 novice hurdle has eluded him so far (he has had two beaten favourites and gone closest with a runner-up and two thirds). With 21 entries, he has his usual set of enviable options and the ante-post market has identified his main hope as Black Hercules (last year's Champion Bumper fourth and winner of both runs over hurdles before Christmas). Another leading Irish contender is the Gordon Elliott-trained No More Heroes, in the Gigginstown House Stud colours carried to victory by Very Wood last year. Dan Skelton has a decent chance of a first festival winner with Value At Risk, while other leading British hopes include Caracci Apache and Vyta Du Roc (both trained by Nicky Henderson), Blaklion (Nigel Twiston-Davies) and Thomas Brown (Harry Fry).

Black Hercules
6 b g; Trainer Willie Mullins
Hurdles form (right-handed) 11, best RPR 143
Cheltenham form (bumper) 4, best RPR 135
At the festival 12 Mar 2014: led at good pace, driven and headed over 1f out, one pace after, finished fourth, beaten three and three-quarter lengths by Silver Concorde in Champion Bumper

Fourth in last season's Champion Bumper but bred to make a stayer and, after winning a big-field but weak maiden hurdle over 2m on his debut in November, he was upped to 3m next time at Cork. He made all in a five-runner Grade 3 contest there, but the race could not have been much further removed from what he'll face at Cheltenham as it was run in a bog at a really slow pace with the winning time more than a minute outside standard. We know he handles Cheltenham and good ground given last season's bumper run and he has immense promise, although looks short enough considering a top Racing Post Rating of 143 puts him behind quite a few potential rivals. Largely fluent jumper.

No More Heroes
6 b g; Trainer Gordon Elliott
Hurdles form 4115, best RPR 150
Left-handed 15, best RPR 150
Right-handed 41, best RPR 130

Highly regarded Gigginstown-owned six-year-old who is actually in his second season as a novice hurdler as he was a really eyecatching fourth on his maiden hurdle debut in November 2013 before switching to bumpers.

Didn't take in Cheltenham last year but twice achieved an identical RPR to that awarded to Champion Bumper winner Silver Concorde, the first time when winning by 39 lengths at Leopardstown and then when beating Milsean over 2m3f at Naas. Was always likely to prove a stayer but, having won easily on his return over 2m6f, he dropped back to 2m4f at Navan and took the scalp of Shaneshill, showing plenty of pace to lead inside the final 100 yards and win going away. Was made favourite for this race after that but then could manage only fifth at Leopardstown in January, his trainer Gordon Elliott reporting that he scoped badly afterwards. Has a bit to prove now, including his ability to act on faster ground, but hard to believe he is not considerably better than his last run and will improve for 3m.

Value At Risk
6 b g; Trainer Dan Skelton
Hurdles form (left-handed) 12, best RPR 141
Cheltenham form (all) 02, best RPR 141
At the festival 12 Mar 2014: tracked leaders, troubled passage from over 5f out to over 3f out, weakened 2f out, finished 13th, beaten 16 and a half lengths by Silver Concorde in Champion Bumper

Good bumper horse who ran into traffic problems at last year's festival but proved he was better than his midfield finish when running a close third to the Cheltenham front two in the Grade 1 at Punchestown in April. Looked a horse of immense potential when slamming next-time-out winner Foryourinformation by 22 lengths on his

hurdles debut at Newbury in December, after which trainer Dan Skelton nominated the Neptune as his likely target for this season, with chasing as his long-term project. That all changed when he was surprisingly overhauled by Ordo Ab Chao in a Neptune trial in January, looking tapped for speed. Having raced in the front two for most of the way, he looked a sitting duck with plenty queueing up behind him turning form home, but to his credit he battled all the way and was gaining on the winner again at the line. Clearly staying is his forte and he looks certain to improve for a first run at 3m, while better ground will not be a hindrance to him.

Blaklion (left)

6 b g; Trainer Nigel Twiston-Davies
Hurdles form 112132, best RPR 147
Left-handed 12132, best RPR 147
Right-handed 1, best RPR 124
Cheltenham form 21, best RPR 147

Tough and classy performer who has been given plenty of experience and is up there with the best on the figures despite suffering defeat on three of his last four starts. Two of those reverses came against Parlour Games, who is one of the Neptune favourites and inbetween those he was an impressive 11-length winner of a Grade 2 over the Albert Bartlett course and distance, although none of his five victims has yet done much for the form. Given he stays so well it was surprising he was cut down by Caracci Apache at Doncaster in January, having led by four lengths at the last, but it's possible his heavy schedule had caught up with him. Despite his losses he will go in there with a fairly solid profile, not least because he has had two starts at Cheltenham and six of the last ten winners had at least the same.

Caracci Apache

5 b g; Trainer Nicky Henderson
Hurdles form 111, best RPR 146
Left-handed 11, best RPR 146
Right-handed 1, best RPR 132

Showed next to nothing in a couple of bumpers in the spring but it has been different since obstacle were put in the way and he has improved with every step up in trip. First two runs were in modest enough company, with success over 2m at Sandown followed by

another over 2m5f at Plumpton, but his latest win at Doncaster in the River Don put him in the picture. Although seemingly outpaced turning for home, he finished strongly despite wandering across the track and got up to beat Blaklion by a head. He won't want to get so far behind at the festival or wander around, but is only young and clearly has the stamina for the job.

Martello Tower

7 b g; Trainer Margaret Mullins
Hurdles form 411F12, best RPR 144
Left-handed 41F2, best RPR 144
Right-handed 11, best RPR 142

Lightly raced and improving seven-year-old who won a 3m Grade 3 at Cork in November and might have added a 2m4f Grade 2 at Navan later that month but for falling two out when he was bang in contention. He showed stamina to be his strong suit next time when rallying close home to beat Outlander in a three-runner heavy-ground Grade 3 at Limerick and, while no match for that one when second back at 2m4f at Leopardstown in January, Outlander is now one of the favourites for the Neptune on the back of his win. Clearly has talent and has won on decent ground as well as heavy.

Thomas Brown

6 b g; Trainer Harry Fry
Hurdles form 121, best RPR 144
Left-handed 21, best RPR 144
Right-handed 1, best RPR 130
Cheltenham form 1, best RPR 144

Strong stayer whose form ties in with some of the better British novices. November's debut saw him beat the strong-travelling but often weak-finishing Vago Collonges (third to Ordo Ab Chao and Value At Risk on Trials Day) over 2m5½f at Exeter and it was a muddling race in which he was beaten over 2m5f at Newbury later that month. The four-runner event turned into a sprint after an early crawl and he was beaten three lengths by Out Sam. That was a remarkably good race, though, with the winner going in again at Ascot and third-placed Tea For Two winning his next two (including the Lanzarote by 16 lengths off 134). Thomas Brown did his bit for the form as well, seeing off Robinsfirth (close fourth to Ordo Ab Chao on Trials Day) and Zeroeshadesofgrey (close third to Caracci Apache and Blaklion at Doncaster) at Cheltenham in January, after which trainer Harry Fry nominated this race. Has yet to try 3m but Fry says staying is his game and more of a worry is genuine fast ground given he's a son of Sir Harry Lewis, who gets plenty of mudlarks. Still, he won a point-to-point on good, so maybe it's not an issue.

Vyta Du Roc

6 gr g; Trainer Nicky Henderson
Hurdles form 5311112, best RPR 148
Left-handed 531112, best RPR 148
Right-handed 1, best RPR 146
Cheltenham form 1, best RPR 144

Tough and consistent since joining Nicky Henderson from France even if he has his own way of doing things. First two wins in low grade were straightforward enough, but when upped in the class for a Supreme trial at Cheltenham in November he seemed to want to drop himself out going to the third-last (hit 85 in running) before finishing with a rattle to get up on the line. He again looked a bit lazy when upped 2m4f in the Winter Novice Hurdle at Sandown but put his head on the line at the right time for a short-head victory over Shantou Bob before falling a neck short behind Parlour Games in the Grade 1 Challow. There doesn't seem to be any mistaking his willingness at the business end, but it's hard to know whether he really wants 3m or cheekpieces or both and even Henderson says "he's not as slow as he tries to make out". Form is as good if not better than most in the field.

Beast Of Burden

6 ch g; Trainer Rebecca Curtis
Hurdles form (left-handed) 211, best RPR 143

Started his career only in October with a bumper win but is clearly a very useful son of a sister to Voy Por Ustedes. Broke the ice with a 27-length 2m win on his second start over hurdles and was then upped to 3m at Bangor in early February. Again scored pretty much as he liked, making all to beat useful chaser Mendip Express by 11 lengths, after which Rebecca Curtis said she might drop him down to 2m5 for the Neptune. However, he does look a strong stayer in the making and he's considerably shorter in the betting for this than either of the other novice races. Untested on good ground but won bumper on good to soft.

OTHERS TO CONSIDER

Second-guessing the final line-up of any of the novice races is never easy, not least because of the strength in depth and multiple entries from the Willie Mullins yard. Of those he could send here, **Arbre De Vie** was impressive in winning a 2m5f contest at Warwick in February, although his main market rival Kingscourt Native didn't seem to run his race. **Tell Us More**, a stayer with speed according to Mullins, is probably more likely to go for the Neptune and so, you would imagine, is **Outlander**, although nothing is set in stone. Nicky Henderson's **Out Sam,** who beat Thomas Brown on his debut in November and has won again since, is more likely to wait for Aintree according to his trainer. **Tea For Two**, top-rated on RPRs following his Lanzarote Hurdle romp, was mentioned as a possible for the World Hurdle but equally could go to France, where he will get the soft ground he reportedly needs. **Fletchers Flyer** could be a useful second string for Harry Fry but is another who might be ground dependent and he was outbattled by **Definitly Red** in the Grade 2 trial at Haydock in February. Brian Ellison's winner has the potential to go well at a price, having finished seventh in the Champion Bumper last season.

Albert Bartlett Hurdle results and trends

	FORM	WINNER	AGE & WGT	Adj RPR	SP	TRAINER	H.Runs	BEST RPR LAST 12 MONTHS (RUNS SINCE)
14	-1253	**Very Wood**	5 11-7	143^{-18}	33-1	N Meade (IRE)	4$^{(18G)}$	3rd Naas Gd2 nov hdl (2m4f) (0)
13	-1111	**At Fishers Cross** CD	6 11-7	161^{T}	11-8f	R Curtis	6$^{(13S)}$	won Cheltenham Gd2 nov hdl (2m5f) (0)
12	2111	**Brindisi Breeze** D	6 11-7	157^{-6}	7-1	L Russell	3$^{(20G)}$	won Haydock Gd2 nov hdl (3m) (0)
11	1-111	**Bobs Worth** C	6 11-7	160^{T}	15-8f	N Henderson	3$^{(18G)}$	won Cheltenham Gd2 nov hdl (2m4½f) (0)
10	12F34	**Berties Dream**	7 11-7	155^{-3}	33-1	P Gilligan (IRE)	14$^{(19G)}$	3rd Cheltenham Gd2 nov hdl (2m5f) (1)
09	-5112	**Weapon's Amnesty** D, BF	6 11-7	150^{-12}	8-1	C Byrnes (IRE)	4$^{(17GS)}$	2nd Leopardstown Gd2 nov hdl (2m4f) (0)
08	1-212	**Nenuphar Collonges** CD	7 11-7	146^{-12}	9-1	A King	4$^{(18GS)}$	2nd Warwick Gd2 nov hdl (2m5f) (0)
07	-1211	**Wichita Lineman** C	6 11-7	161^{T}	11-8f	J O'Neill	4$^{(20GS)}$	won Gd1 Challow Hurdle (2m5f) (1)
06	1-111	**Black Jack Ketchum** CD	7 11-7	161^{T}	EvensF	J O'Neill	3$^{(19G)}$	won Cheltenham Gd2 nov hdl (3m) (0)
05	62162	**Moulin Riche**	5 11-7	149^{-8}	9-1	F Doumen (FR)	8$^{(18G)}$	2nd Haydock Gd2 nov hdl (2m7½f) (0)

WINS-RUNS: 5yo 2-36, 6yo 5-78, 7yo 3-45, 8yo 0-19, 9yo 0-2 **FAVOURITES:** -£0.38

TRAINERS IN THIS RACE (w-pl-r): Jonjo O'Neill 2-0-2, Alan King 1-1-9, Charles Byrnes 1-2-5, Lucinda Russell 1-0-1, Nicky Henderson 1-1-7, Noel Meade 1-0-7, Rebecca Curtis 1-0-5, Colin Tizzard 0-1-5, David Pipe 0-0-5, Emma Lavelle 0-1-5, Evan Williams 0-0-2, Gordon Elliott 0-0-1, John Ferguson 0-0-1, Mouse Morris 0-0-2, Mark Bradstock 0-0-3, Margaret Mullins 0-1-1, Nicky Richards 0-0-1, Nigel Twiston-Davies 0-1-9, Paul Nolan 0-0-2, Sue Smith 0-0-3, Willie Mullins 0-3-13, Warren Greatrex 0-0-2

FATE OF FAVOURITES: 31132P121F **POSITION OF WINNER IN MARKET:** 5115401219

Key trends

🐎 At least three runs over hurdles, 10/10

🐎 Adjusted RPR of at least 146, 9/10

🐎 Top-three finish in a Graded hurdle last time out, 9/10 (five won)

🐎 Won over at least 2m5f, 8/10

🐎 Aged six or seven, 8/10

Other factors

🐎 Seven of the British and Irish-trained winners had won a Graded hurdle, while the French-trained victor had won a Listed handicap hurdle

🐎 Six winners had raced at least twice around Cheltenham (five had previously won at the course)

Notes

Third time lucky for Silviniaco Conti? Surely there will never be a better opportunity for the dual King George winner, who fell three out on his first attempt in 2013 and was fourth last year – on both occasions leaving the feeling that he could, and should, have done better. The belief in the Paul Nicholls camp is stronger than ever after Silviniaco Conti came back brighter from treatment last spring for gastric ulcers, but now he has to deliver. The three who finished in front of him in last year's race – Lord Windermere, On His Own and The Giant Bolster – are all set to return as well, although none of the trio has won this season. More serious rivals on this term's form are three newcomers to the Gold Cup scene – Lexus Chase winner Road To Riches, Hennessy hero Many Clouds and Carlingford Lough, who landed the Irish Hennessy.

Silviniaco Conti

9 ch g; Trainer Paul Nicholls
Chase form 31241111F33141511, best RPR 178
Left-handed 31111F334151, best RPR 178
Right-handed 12411, best RPR 178
Cheltenham form (all) 3F4, best RPR 169
At the festival 15 Mar 2013: tracked leaders, mistake 9th, 1½-length 3rd and travelling well when fell 3 out in Gold Cup won by Bobs Worth
14 Mar 2014: towards rear but in touch, steady headway 18th, challenged 4 out and soon led, ridden approaching 2 out, went left and then wandered right under pressure run-in, headed final 110yds, not recover, finished fourth, beaten one and three-quarter lengths by Lord Windermere in Gold Cup

Highest-rated chaser in training who, after a rather tame opening effort in this season's Charlie Hall at Wetherby (beaten eight lengths into fifth), has proved better than ever. Bounced right back to form to land his second Betfair Chase at Haydock, overturning Wetherby form with Menorah with a battling display, and turned in his most commanding performance as a chaser to double up in the King George at Kempton, making all the running and winning by an easy four and a half lengths from Dynaste. That gives him far and away the best form going into this year's Gold Cup and the only reason he is not shorter than his current odds of around 11-4 is that not everyone is convinced he is a Cheltenham horse. Admittedly the critics have reason to doubt as his two previous Gold Cup efforts have ended in failure. In 2013 he was seemingly travelling well only to fall three out, while last year he led over the last but then wandered all around the track and threw it away, allowing three outsiders to overtake him in the final half-furlong. That form is not far short of 10lb below what he has shown on flatter tracks, so he does have it to prove. However, trainer Paul Nicholls maintains that he wasn't right last season, with a bad bout of ulcers to blame for his wayward antics at both Cheltenham and Aintree, where he won despite also wandering around approaching the last. He has had a pair of cheekpieces for his latest two runs and he has run straight as a gun barrel in them. The one to beat.

Road To Riches (right)

8 b g; Trainer Noel Meade
Chase form 13P4121211, best RPR 172
Left-handed 1P41, best RPR 172
Right-handed 312121, best RPR 170

One of the coming forces in Ireland and has had a terrific run in the past 12 months. A winner over 2m1f at Fairyhouse in April, he really started to blossom in the summer and, upped to 2m6f for the Galway Plate, he took his field apart to win by 11 lengths under 7lb claimer Shane Shortall off a mark of 149. That left him still some way short of Gold Cup class, as did a head defeat to the veteran Sizing Europe over 2m4f at Gowran in October, but the step up to 3m has resulted in his two best efforts. It was easy enough to question the form of his 11-length success from the disappointing Rocky Creek in the JNwine.com Champion Chase at Down Royal, especially as plenty

of others didn't run their race, but his Lexus Chase victory at Leopardstown in December is much harder to crab as it featured most of the top Irish chasers. He set out to make the running, as he had at Down Royal, but was happy enough to take a lead from halfway and, despite dropping to third five out, stayed on well in the straight and was going away at the finish to beat last year's Gold Cup runner-up On His Own by a length and a half. That's not standout form by any means, but only because we've been spoiled in recent seasons and an RPR of 172 is 2lb higher than Lord Windermere achieved when winning the Gold Cup last season, so it certainly puts him in the right ballpark. He acts on good ground as well as soft and there doesn't seem to be any reason why he won't stay the Gold Cup trip, so there's plenty to like, although Noel Meade's spring strike-rate is often a cause for worry and he's yet to train a chase winner at the festival.

Many Clouds (below, right)

8 b g; Trainer Oliver Sherwood
Chase form 1212B4111, best RPR 169
Left-handed 21B411, best RPR 169

Right-handed 121, best RPR 158
Cheltenham form (all) 9B1, best RPR 169
At the festival 14 Mar 2012: towards rear, headway 6f out, chased leaders 5f out, ridden over 2f out, one pace over 1f out, finished ninth, beaten 15 lengths by Champagne Fever in Champion Bumper
12 Mar 2014: in rear, still behind but going okay when mistake, hampered and brought down 14th in RSA Chase won by O'Faolains Boy

Useful novice last season and was still going well enough without looking totally happy on the ground when brought down four out in the RSA Chase, but closed his campaign with a heavy defeat at Aintree behind Holywell, again on good ground. However, presented with soft ground this season he has done nothing but progress, warming up for the Hennessy with victory in a traditionally decent intermediate chase over 2m4f at Carlisle and then turning in a strong staying performance to win at Newbury from Houblon Dex Obeaux. Took the step up to Grade 2 company in fine style, too, disputing the lead most of the way and battling all the way to the line to give 8lb and a length-and-a-quarter beating to Smad Place in the BetBright Cup on Trials a Day at Cheltenham in January, with Dynaste a neck back in third. That confirmed the track holds no fears for him and he is a likeable chaser who jumps really well and gives willingly. There remains a suspicion that soft ground is very important to him, though, and good-ground form figures of 902PB4 against 12121212111 on soft or worse seem to confirm that.

Carlingford Lough

9 b g; Trainer John Kiely
Chase form 33574PP21221U6151, best RPR 169
Left-handed 74221U651, best RPR 169
Right-handed 335PP121, best RPR 158
Cheltenham form 6, best RPR 154
At the festival 12 Mar 2014: blundered 1st, in rear, not fluent 3rd, hit 5th, hampered 14th, headway 4 out, chased leaders 3 out, one pace from 2 out, finished sixth, beaten nine and three-quarter lengths by O'Faolains Boy in RSA Chase

Late maturer who took nine tries before finally getting off the mark over fences and did so in the 2013 running of the Galway Plate from a mark of 133. Progress since has been pretty astounding as he won the Grade 1 Topaz Novice Chase at Leopardstown that December and completed his novice season with victory in the Champion Novice Chase at Punchestown, beating a non-staying Ballycasey. Before that he had been no more than a creditable sixth in the RSA Chase, making quite a few errors and getting hampered along the way. He has been much more lightly raced this term, possibly because he was lame when set to take on Don Cossack at Down Royal in November, and his fifth to Road To Riches in the Lexus was a much-needed first run of the s e a s o n . He showed the benefit of that run in the Irish Hennessy, coming through with a late run to deny the improving F o x r o c k by three- quarters of a length with Gold Cup winner Lord Windermere back in third. That represented a clear career-best and showed he is still improving at the age of nine – arguably he would have won a shade more easily if hadn't clouted the second-last. Jumping can be an issue, but he has a terrific attitude and if he gets it right he has the form to be a major player as he has won three of his five Grade 1 races at 3m-plus. Will certainly raise the roof if he can give retiring champion jockey Tony McCoy a third Gold Cup success in his final season.

Holywell

8 b g; Trainer Jonjo O'Neill
Chase form 32U11113U1, best RPR 170
Left-handed 21111U1, best RPR 170
Right-handed 3U3, best RPR 152
Cheltenham form (all) 11, best RPR 162
At the festival 14 Mar 2013: tracked leaders, went 2nd after 3 out, challenged after 2 out, led travelling comfortably well before last when 4 lengths clear, driven out run-in, won Pertemps Final by one and a half lengths from Captain Sunshine
11 Mar 2014: tracked leaders, not fluent 12th, going well upsides after 3 out, ridden after last, led final 110yds, ran on well and in command towards finish, won Baylis & Harding Affordable Luxury Handicap Chase by one and three-quarter lengths from Ma Filleule

Has been brilliantly produced to win in handicap company over hurdles and fences at the last two festivals and went into summer quarters as ante-post favourite for the Gold Cup following a ten-length success from Don

Cossack in a Grade 1 at Aintree. Has run only three times this season, though, and while not too much was expected of him at Carlisle over 2m4f on his return, he did not jump particularly well in the soft ground and was well beaten by Many Clouds. He should have done much better next time at Aintree, though, when the ground was in his favour, but he unseated at the eighth in a Listed chase won by Sam Winner, having jumped poorly throughout. He subsequently lost his position in the market but, having been pulled out of a couple of engagements due to the ground, connections managed to get a run into him at Kelso, where he won by 25 lengths. He didn't have much to beat and his jumping wasn't always fluent, but it will have been good for his confidence. He has won on soft ground, but a better surface suits him ideally and, more importantly, the blinkers he has sported for all three of his major successes will be on again, having gone on for the first time this season at Kelso.

Foxrock

7 b g; Trainer Ted Walsh
Chase form 2131193212, best RPR 168
Left-handed 23119212, best RPR 168
Right-handed 13, best RPR 146
Cheltenham form 9, best RPR 129
At the festival 11 Mar 2014: mid-division, headway and not fluent 14th, headway to chase leaders 3 out, blundered and weakened 2 out, finished ninth, beaten 13 and a half lengths by Midnight Prayer in National Hunt Chase

Dual Grade 2 winner over 3m as a novice and was sent off a well-backed favourite for the four-miler at last year's festival, although might not have stayed the extreme trip. Following an eyecatching first start of this campaign at Punchestown, he was again a well-supported favourite in the Paddy Power

Chase off a mark of 142 at Leopardstown, but was headed near the finish of that 26-runner handicap by outsider Living Next Door. He soon made amends dropping back to 2m5f in the valuable Boylesports Handicap Chase at the same track next time, powering home by five lengths, and was yet again well supported on his following start, this time when upped to Grade 1 level for the Irish Hennessy. The fact he was sent off at just 7-2 gives an indication of the regard in which he is held and he looked the likely winner heading to the last, but once again couldn't contain a finisher on the run-in, this time going down by three-quarters of a length to Carlingford Lough. That must sew some seeds of doubt about his stamina for 3m2½f at Cheltenham, but he has run a clear career-best on each of his last three chase starts, so it might not be wise to crab him. Was not entered for the Gold Cup but no surprise if he is supplemented.

Bobs Worth (below, right)

10 b g; Trainer Nicky Henderson
Chase form 1321116158, best RPR 181
Left-handed 11116158, best RPR 181
Right-handed 32, best RPR 162
Cheltenham form (all) 111115, best RPR 181
At the festival 18 Mar 2011: midfield, headway approaching 7th, led between last 2, jumped left and tried to assert last, edged right towards finish, driven out and stayed on well, won Albert Bartlett Novices' Hurdle by two and a quarter lengths from Mossley 14 Mar 2012: held up in midfield, headway to go prominent 8th, led narrowly when stretched for 4 out, headed on bend approaching 2 out, regained lead just before last, ridden run-in, stayed on well and drew away towards finish, won RSA Chase by two and a half lengths from First Lieutenant

15 Mar 2013: in touch, headway 16th, pushed along 18th, one pace 4 out, driven and hampered 3 out and 8 lengths down, strong run approaching 2 out, led well before last, gamely forged clear final 120yds, won Gold Cup by seven lengths from Sir Des Champs

14 Mar 2014: in rear, not fluent 4th and 9th, improved 16th, chased leaders from 4 out, not fluent 3 out, stayed on under pressure approaching next to chase leader last, pushed left soon after, wandered flat, no extra final 110yds, finished fifth, beaten four lengths by Lord Windermere in Gold Cup

....

Three-time festival winner and top-class chaser in his prime, winning the 2013 Gold Cup by seven lengths from Sir Des Champs. That race, run on a day when it rained persistently, turned into a really gruelling battle, though, and he has not run to within a stone of that form since. After a dreadful reappearance last season he did manage to win a below-par running of the Lexus, after which he was sent off at just 6-4 for a Gold Cup repeat. However, while he put up a brave display and was in there pitching at the last, his trademark finish up the Cheltenham hill, where he had never been beaten before, deserted him and he could manage only a one-paced fifth. This season connections were making the right noises about him being back to himself before his return in the Lexus and he was sent off 5-2 favourite, but he never jumped or travelled well and trailed in last of the eight finishers, albeit beaten only 12 and a half lengths. It does seem as though age and, more importantly, the legacy of several really hard races has caught up with him, and it would be some feat if Nicky Henderson could bring him back to win another Gold Cup.

Lord Windermere

9 b g; Trainer Jim Culloty
Chase form 2212318761373, best RPR 170
Left-handed 21231876173, best RPR 170
Right-handed 23, best RPR 159
Cheltenham form 11, best RPR 170
At the festival 13 Mar 2013: waited with in rear, steady progress from 15th going well, close up in 6th when stumbled after 3 out, pulled out and driven to renew effort 2 out, left 2nd last, led final 150yds, stayed on well, won RSA Chase by one and three-quarter lengths from Lyreen Legend

14 Mar 2014: in rear and detached 10th, driven 4 out, still plenty to do next, headway under pressure approaching 2 out, chased leaders last, led and hung badly right final 110yds, held on all out, won Gold Cup by a short head from On His Own

....

Tough staying chaser who seems uniquely suited by the test Cheltenham provides in the spring, with a strongly run race on good ground bringing out the best in him. Indeed, he has won only three chases in his life but the last two have been the RSA and Gold Cup. There was plenty expected of him following his RSA success as trainer Jim Culloty was adamant it was no fluke, but he didn't manage to finish in the first five on his first three starts of last season, first of all in the Hennessy at Newbury (eighth) and then in the Lexus (seventh of nine) and the Irish Hennessy (sixth of seven, beaten 26 lengths). Then he went to the Gold Cup and, having been a 50-1 shot in the morning, was a fairly well supported 20-1 shot by race time. Held well off a strong pace, he was still way behind the leaders three out, but they began to crumble and he was suddenly one of several with a chance heading to the last. He was also one of a few to wander around on the run-in and many thought he was lucky to survive a stewards' inquiry after he carried short-head runner-up On His Own with him, but the connections of the runner-up sportingly didn't object and the Gold Cup was his. If anything this season's warm-up has been a bit better as he was an eyecatching third to Don Cossack over a woefully inadequate 2m4f and, following a disappointing seventh in the Lexus, was a highly encouraing third in the Irish Hennessy, in which he led over the second-last before being left behind by the front two. He is clearly being primed for just one race again and with Culloty proving himself such an adept target trainer (he has three festival victories to his name despite not having run more than 20 horses in each of the last two years) he is clearly not one to rule out lightly.

....

Djakadam

6 b g; Trainer Willie Mullins
Chase form 11F81, best RPR 160
Left-handed 11F8, best RPR 146
Right-handed 1, best RPR 160
Cheltenham form F
At the festival 13 Mar 2014: chased leaders, not fluent 3rd, hit 9th, disputing 3 lengths 2nd and going okay when fell 4 out in JLT Novices' Chase won by Taquin Du Seuil

Youngster who won his first two chases last season but was discarded by Ruby Walsh when sent to Cheltenham for the JLT Novices' Chase and was noted going well when falling four out. He was a talking horse after that and at one point he was as short as 7-2 in the ante-post betting for the Hennessy at Newbury despite never having tackled further than 2m5f and being only five years old. He was sent off market leader at 5-1 and travelled powerfully for a long way before ultimately being a well-beaten eighth. That was not an awful effort for a horse whose reputation had so far outshone his achievements, but he proved stable confidence wasn't far wrong, when dropped slightly in grade for the Thyestes Chase at Gowran Park and winning as he liked by eight lengths under 11st 10lb. An RPR of 160 puts him some way off the main contenders, but as a six-year-old he clearly has any amount of improvement in him and it is easy enough to see him shortening further on the day if, as seems likely, Ruby Walsh chooses him over stablemates with better form (On His Own, Boston Bob) but many more miles on the clock.

....

Coneygree

8 b g; Trainer Mark Bradstock
Chase form 111, best RPR 169
Left-handed 11, best RPR 169
Right-handed 1, best RPR 159
Cheltenham form (hurdles) 113, best RPR 148

....

Returned from nearly two years off to make

Lord Windermere (left) on his way to victory in last year's Gold Cup as Silviniaco Conti (second left) and Bobs Worth (second right) fade

remarkable progress as a chaser in just three starts, the form of his Denman Chase victory putting him within hailing distance of the best staying chasers around. Is also entered for the RSA Chase and is understandably much shorter for that, but connections are seriosuly considering going for Gold. Dealt with in more detail in Wednesday's RSA section.

The Giant Bolster

10 b g; Trainer David Bridgwater
Chase form 1F1UFU721423P2477U13754, best RPR 170
Left-handed 1F1UFU7214232477U13754, best RPR 170
Right-handed P
Cheltenham form (chase only) F1UU124134, best RPR 170
At the festival 17 Mar 2010: hampered 2nd, towards rear, ridden and hit 3 out, stayed on from 2 out and kept on run-in but never in contention, finished sixth, beaten seven lengths by Peddlers Cross in Neptune
16 Mar 2011: last when mistake 5th and eventually unseated rider in RSA Chase won by Bostons Angel
16 Mar 2012: tracked leaders, not fluent 15th, outpaced 17th, jumped slowly 4 out, good progress to chase leader after 3 out, led approaching 2 out, hard driven, joined last, soon headed and dropped to 3rd, rallied for 2nd close home in Gold Cup, beaten two and a quarter lengths by Synchronised
15 Mar 2013: tracked leader to 11th, stayed chasing leaders, hit 17th, driven and one pace 4 out, rallied after next and chased leaders approaching 2 out, weakened soon after, finished fourth, beaten 16 lengths by Bobs Worth in Gold Cup
14 Mar 2014: in rear, tended to run in snatches, jumped slowly 8th, 11th and 12th, ridden 13th, hit 15th, headway 3 out, bumped 2 out, stayed on well to chase leaders, carried right final 110yds, kept on well close home, finished third, beaten three-quarters of a length by Lord Windermere in Gold Cup

Has a few more ahead of him in the betting than those already mentioned, but deserves his own section more than most, having been a brilliant servant to David Bridgwater and a Gold Cup stalwart for the last three years, finishing second in 2012, fourth in 2013 and a close third last year. Indeed, he is one of a couple who could be considered unlucky 12 months ago as he took a fair old bump two out and was also carried across the track but was beaten less than a length. He tends to come alive at Cheltenham and his last two runs this season have been of a reasonable enough standard (fifth in the Betfair Chase, fourth in the BetBright Cup carrying 10lb more than when winning it a year earlier) to suggest he is going to do connections proud again. At the age of ten he has probably missed his chance, but no great surprise if he upstages a few more fancied runners once again.

OTHERS TO CONSIDER

Willie Mullins' pair **Boston Bob** and **On His Own** have every right to turn up again, although they have probably missed the boast at their age, while **Sam Winner** and **Houblon Des Obeaux** are strong stayers whose form is not a million miles off what will be needed. If the ground is deep the latter would be well capable of outrunning current odds of around 50-1.

Gold Cup results and trends

	FORM	WINNER	AGE & WGT	Adj RPR	SP	TRAINER	C.Runs	BEST RPR LAST 12 MONTHS (RUNS SINCE)
14	1-876	**Lord Windermere** C	8 11-10	161^{-24}	20-1	J Culloty (IRE)	9$^{(13G)}$	7th Gd1 Lexus Chase (3m) **(1)**
13	321-1	**Bobs Worth** C, D	8 11-10	178^{-6}	11-4f	N Henderson	5$^{(9S)}$	won Gd3 Hennessy Gold Cup (3m2½f) **(0)**
12	-P731	**Synchronised**	9 11-10	175^{-12}	8-1	J O'Neill	8$^{(14G)}$	won Gd1 Lexus Chase (3m) **(0)**
11	13-31	**Long Run**	6 11-10	184^{-2}	7-2f	N Henderson	9$^{(13G)}$	won Gd1 King George VI Chase (3m) **(0)**
10	1-P25	**Imperial Commander** C	9 11-10	181^{-15}	7-1	N Twiston-Davies	9$^{(11G)}$	2nd Gd1 Betfair Chase (3m) **(1)**
09	2-1U1	**Kauto Star** CD	9 11-10	188^{-1}	7-4f	P Nicholls	20$^{(16GS)}$	won Gd1 King George VI Chase (3m) **(0)**
08	1-111	**Denman** C, D	8 11-10	184^{-5}	9-4	P Nicholls	8$^{(12GS)}$	won Gd3 Hennessy Gold Cup (3m2½f) **(2)**
07	11111	**Kauto Star**	7 11-10	188^{T}	5-4f	P Nicholls	10$^{(18GS)}$	won Gd1 Betfair Chase (3m) **(3)**
06	11152	**War Of Attrition**	7 11-10	168^{-7}	15-2	M Morris (IRE)	9$^{(22G)}$	2nd Gd1 Lexus Chase (3m) **(0)**
05	B1211	**Kicking King**	7 11-10	181^{T}	4-1f	T Taaffe (IRE)	11$^{(15G)}$	won Gd1 King George VI Chase (3m) **(0)**

WINS-RUNS: 6yo 1-3, 7yo 3-24, 8yo 3-40, 9yo 3-36, 10yo 0-27, 11yo 0-10, 12yo 0-3 **FAVOURITES:** £8.25

TRAINERS IN THIS RACE (w-pl-r): Paul Nicholls 3-6-27, Nicky Henderson 2-2-8, Jim Culloty 1-0-1, Jonjo O'Neill 1-2-6, Mouse Morris 1-0-3, Nigel Twiston-Davies 1-0-5, Alan King 0-0-3, Colin Tizzard 0-0-1, David Bridgwater 0-2-3, David Pipe 0-0-2, Mark Bradstock 0-0-3, Noel Meade 0-0-2, Philip Hobbs 0-0-4, R Chotard 0-0-3, Venetia Williams 0-1-4, Willie Mullins 0-3-6

FATE OF FAVOURITES: 10121F1315 **POSITION OF WINNER IN MARKET:** 1312131317

Key trends

- Grade 1 chase winner, 10/10
- Aged between seven and nine, 9/10
- Two to five runs that season, 9/10
- Ran between five and 11 times over fences, 9/10
- Won Graded chase that season, 8/10
- Achieved pre-race chase RPR of at least 171, 8/10
- Won or placed previously at the festival, 8/10
- Won over at least 3m, 8/10
- Within 7lb of RPR top-rated, 7/10

Other factors

- Three-time victor Best Mate was the last to win back-to-back Gold Cups and the only one to do so since L'Escargot (1970-71). Kauto Star is the only horse ever to regain the crown

- Five winners had previously won or made the frame in championship novice hurdles at the festival (Bobs Worth, Denman, War Of Attrition, Kicking King and Best Mate)

- Three winners had contested the Arkle the previous season, finishing 27F, while four had contested the RSA, finishing 1311

- The last winner not to have run at a previous festival was Imperial Call in 1996

- The most popular reappearance run among the last ten winners was the Hennessy, with three victors making their seasonal debut in the Newbury handicap. Two won (Denman and Bobs Worth) and the other finished eighth (Lord Windermere)

- Bobs Worth in 2013 is the only one of the last ten winners not to have run in the King George or Lexus that season

Notes

4.00 Foxhunter Chase C4/RUK
3m2½f · Amateur riders · £40,000

With almost two-thirds of the winners coming from pointing yards, this is not the strongest race for trends.

Eighteen of the past 24 winners have been aged nine or below – that age bracket provided four of last year's first six from less than half the runners.

The five biggest shocks of recent years (20-1 or bigger) have been since 2002 and, despite that, 12 of the past 21 winners were sent off at single-figure odds (seven were favourite).

Since the first Irish-trained victory in 1983 there have been eight subsequent wins, including in each of the last four years.

The Raymond Smith Memorial Hunters Chase at Leopardstown in early February is the best Irish trial. The last three winners have gone on to do the double here, but this year's winner (Prince De Beauchene) is ineligible for hunter chases in Britain. Runner-up On The Fringe, who now has Raymond Smith placings of 1322, has been fourth and third in his two previous attempts at Cheltenham.

The leading British hope is Teaforthree (trained by Rebecca Curtis), already a festival winner in the 2012 National Hunt Chase, and another from a leading jumps yard is Paint The Clouds (Warren Greatrex). A younger contender to note is the eight-year-old Current Event, trained by Rose Loxton.

Foxhunter Chase results and trends

	FORM	WINNER	AGE & WGT	Adj RPR	SP	TRAINER	C.Runs	BEST RPR LAST 12 MONTHS (RUNS SINCE)
14	-6213	**Tammys Hill** BF	9 12-0	139^{-9}	15-2	L Lennon (IRE)	14$^{(24G)}$	2nd Down Royal hunt ch (2m7f) (2)
13	-1221	**Salsify** CD	8 12-0	143^{-6}	2-1f	R Sweeney (IRE)	14$^{(23S)}$	won Foxhunter Chase (3m2½f) (5)
12	-11P1	**Salsify**	7 12-0	132^{-14}	7-1	R Sweeney (IRE)	8$^{(22G)}$	won Leopardstown hunt ch (3m) (0)
11	44-21	**Zemsky**	8 12-0	125^{-23}	33-1	I Ferguson (IRE)	6$^{(24G)}$	won Musselburgh cl 6 hunt ch (3m½f) (0)
10	2-121	**Baby Run**	10 12-0	144^{-7}	9-2jf	N Twiston-Davies	9$^{(24GS)}$	won Warwick class 6 hunt ch (3m½) (0)
09	11	**Cappa Bleu**	7 12-0	130^{-14}	11-2	S Crow	0$^{(24GS)}$	won Chaddesley Corbett open (3m) (0)
08	-P211	**Amicelli**	9 12-0	128^{-6}	33-1	C Coward	8$^{(23GS)}$	won Brocklesby Park open (3m) (1)
07	19F0-	**Drombeag**	9 12-0	119^{-17}	20-1	J O'Neill	8$^{(24GS)}$	9th Foxhunter Chase (3m2½f) (2)
06	1-34U	**Whyso Mayo**	9 12-0	120^{-30}	20-1	R Hurley (IRE)	5$^{(24G)}$	3rd Punchestown hunt ch (3m1f) (2)
05	5-1U1	**Sleeping Night**	9 12-0	150^{T}	7-2f	P Nicholls	12$^{(24G)}$	won Wetherby class 6 hunt ch (3m1f) (2)

WINS-RUNS: 6yo 0-2, 7yo 2-20, 8yo 2-40, 9yo 5-47, 10yo 1-40, 11yo 0-43, 12yo 0-31, 13yo 0-10, 14yo 0-3 **FAVOURITES:** £0.25

TRAINERS IN THIS RACE (w-pl-r): Rodger Sweeney 2-0-2, Jonjo O'Neill 1-0-5, Paul Nicholls 1-0-10, Alan Hill 0-2-6, Brian Hamilton 0-0-1, Colin McBratney 0-1-1, Enda Bolger 0-1-2, Gordon Elliott 0-0-2, James Joseph Mangan 0-2-4, Rebecca Curtis 0-0-3, Willie Mullins 0-0-2

FATE OF FAVOURITES: 1P2P014215 **POSITION OF WINNER IN MARKET:** 1980210314

Key trends

- Won over at least 3m, 10/10
- Aged seven to nine, 9/10
- Ran between 20 and 34 days ago, 9/10 (exception was having first start in nearly a year)
- Recorded a pre-race RPR of at least 130, 8/10
- Won last time out, 7/10

Other factors

Record of previous year's winner is 204U1.

- In 2013 Salsify was the first winner to follow up the previous year's success since Double Silk in 1993 and 1994
- Three winners had competed at the festival before and all had been in the first four
- Five winners were former handicap chasers and five had come from point-to-points
- Those aged 12 or older have produced no winner and just one third from 44 runners in the last ten years. The 13-year-old Earthmover (2004) is the only winner from this category since 1990

Big prices have been the norm in the six runnings, with winners at 12-1, 14-1, 16-1, 20-1 and 25-1 – a sequence interrupted only by 9-2 winning favourite Sir Des Champs in 2011. All the winners have been aged five or six (five were in their second season over hurdles and Don Poli, last year's winner, was a novice).

Nicky Henderson has been a threat in most renewals, with a winner, a second and two thirds (from a total of 17 runners). David Pipe has yet to win the race named in honour of his father, having had the beaten favourite three times and two unplaced second favourites.

Ireland has been a growing force in the County Hurdle and the same appears to be happening here – in the past four years they have had two winners, a second and a fourth from nine runners. Gigginstown House Stud's strength in depth means they are always likely to have runners and they have had several in the first four, including winners Sir Des Champs and Don Poli.

Martin Pipe Handicap Hurdle results

	FORM	WINNER	AGE & WGT	OR	SP	TRAINER	H.Runs	BEST RPR LAST 12 MONTHS (RUNS SINCE)
14	2-211	**Don Poli**	5 11-5	143^{-4}	12-1	W Mullins (IRE)	4$^{(24G)}$	won Clonmel Gd3 nov hdl (3m) **(0)**
13	-4251	**Salubrious** D	6 11-5	141^{-9}	16-1	P Nicholls	5$^{(23S)}$	won Musselburgh cl 3 hcap hdl (2m4f) **(0)**
12	135P1	**Attaglance**	6 11-3	139^{T}	20-1	M Jefferson	13$^{(24G)}$	won M Rasen class 3 hcap hdl (2m3f) **(0)**
11	1-1	**Sir Des Champs**	5 11-3	134^{T}	9-2f	W Mullins (IRE)	2$^{(23G)}$	won Navan hdl (2m) **(0)**
10	-445U	**Pause And Clause** D	6 11-10	137^{-3}	14-1	E Lavelle	8$^{(24S)}$	4th Haydock Listed hcap hdl (3m1f) **(2)**
09	-4134	**Andytown** C, D	6 11-2	133^{-6}	25-1	N Henderson	7$^{(23GS)}$	won Chelt class 3 cond hcap hdl (2m5f) **(1)**

WINS-RUNS: 4yo 0-1, 5yo 2-36, 6yo 4-44, 7yo 0-33, 8yo 0-16, 9yo 0-6, 10yo 0-4, 12yo 0-1 **FAVOURITES:** -£0.50

FATE OF FAVOURITES: 3010P0 **POSITION OF WINNER IN MARKET:** 061086

Notes

5.15 Johnny Henderson Grand Annual H'cap Chase   RUK
2m½f   *Grade 3*   *£90,000*

Bellenos: Dan Skelton's seven-year-old is prominent in the ante-post betting

This has become the 'getting out stakes' on the final day of the festival, but Alderwood in 2013 is the only winning favourite since 2004 and six of the last nine winners have been 12-1 or bigger.

A strong recent trend is that four of the last six winners were officially novices. This has been the best race for novices at the festival with 12 winners, rated from 129 to 140, since 1983.

The race's title has commemorated Nicky Henderson's father Johnny since 2005 and the trainer won the following year with Greenhope and again in 2012 with Bellvano (both 20-1 shots). He has also had four runner-ups and two thirds from a total of 34 runners.

Paul Nicholls has had the topweight in five of the past ten years and won twice, with runners carrying 10st 1lb and 10st 11lb, but he has also had four beaten favourites. His best prospect is likely to be getting a novice under the radar.

In the two decades up to 1998 the winners were almost evenly split between those carrying more than 11st and those carrying less, but there had been 14 consecutive winners carrying between 10st and 10st 13lb until Savello scored last year under 11st 5lb. Savello (off a mark of 147) was the highest-rated winner since My Young Man in 1992.

Victory went to runners rated 129-134 in nine out of ten runnings up to 2010 but, as with the other festival handicaps, the threshold is moving upwards (three of the last four winners have been in the 140s).

Just seven winners since 1973 had failed to make the first four last time out and 32 of the winners were aged seven to nine.

Three of the six recent Irish-trained winners prepped over hurdles – two of the exceptions were the novices Fota Island and Alderwood. Seven of the last eight British-trained winners had won at Cheltenham before.

Grand Annual Handicap Chase results and trends

	FORM	WINNER	AGE & WGT	OR	SP	TRAINER	C.Runs	BEST RPR LAST 12 MONTHS (RUNS SINCE)
14	-3439	**Savello** D	8 11-5	147^{-2}	16-1	A Martin (IRE)	9$^{(23G)}$	3rd Leopardstown hcap ch (2m1f) **(1)**
13	-S312	**Alderwood** C, D	9 10-11	140^{T}	3-1f	T Mullins (IRE)	4$^{(23S)}$	2nd Punchestown hcap ch (2m) **(0)**
12	-1621	**Bellvano** D	8 10-2	138^{T}	20-1	N Henderson	5$^{(21G)}$	won Kelso class 2 nov ch (2m1f) **(0)**
11	U6483	**Oiseau De Nuit** CD	9 10-13	145^{-3}	40-1	C Tizzard	20$^{(23G)}$	3rd Newbury Gd2 ch (2m1f) **(0)**
10	222F5	**Pigeon Island** C, D	7 10-1	129^{T}	16-1	N Twiston-Davies	7$^{(19S)}$	2nd Cheltenham Gd2 nov ch (2m5f) **(2)**
09	423F2	**Oh Crick** (1oh) C, D	6 10-0	130^{-13}	7-1	A King	6$^{(18GS)}$	2nd Hereford class 3 nov ch (2m3f) **(0)**
08	4P-36	**Tiger Cry** D	10 10-6	134^{-1}	15-2	A Moore (IRE)	12$^{(17GS)}$	3rd Ascot class 2 hcap ch (2m1f) **(0)**
07	3-333	**Andreas** CD, BF	7 10-11	143^{-1}	12-1	P Nicholls	11$^{(23GS)}$	3rd Sandown Gd3 hcap ch (2m) **(0)**
06	163-5	**Greenhope** C, D	8 10-11	132^{-9}	20-1	N Henderson	5$^{(23G)}$	6th Grand Annual Hcap Ch (2m½f) **(1)**
05	33212	**Fota Island** (2oh) D, BF	9 10-0	130^{-6}	7-1	M Morris (IRE)	7$^{(24G)}$	2nd Navan ch (2m1f) **(2)**

WINS-RUNS: 5yo 0-6, 6yo 1-27, 7yo 2-41, 8yo 3-59, 9yo 3-39, 10yo 1-28, 11yo 0-13, 12yo 0-1 **FAVOURITES:** -£6.00

FATE OF FAVOURITES: 0F620P0012 **POSITION OF WINNER IN MARKET:** 3042280019

Key trends

🐎Distance winner, 10/10

🐎No more than 12 runs over fences, 9/10

🐎Aged nine or under, 9/10

🐎Top-three finish on at least one of last two starts, 9/10

🐎Carried no more than 10st 11lb, 8/10

🐎Officially rated 129 to 143, 8/10

🐎Yet to win that season, 7/10

🐎Course winner, 6/10 (two of the exceptions had finished second in this race)

🐎No more than four runs since August, 6/10

Other factors

🐎There have been five winning novices

🐎Seven winners had previous festival form, including three who had run in the race previously

🐎Two winners prepped for this race over hurdles

🐎Since 2005, when the race was renamed in honour of his father, Nicky Henderson's runners have finished 346, 180P, 800, 20, 3P, 20P, 60, 1240PF, 2589PF, 590

🐎The record of the previous year's winner is 045B

Notes